Grey Cup Edition

Rider Pride
On
The American Side

Grey Cup Edition

Rider Pride On The American Side

A Minnesota Family Discovers the Saskatchewan Roughriders

By Terry McEvoy

Northern Road Press

Copyright © 2006, 2008 Terrence J. McEvoy

Printed in Canada

All rights reserved. No part of this book may be reproduced by any means, electronic or mechanical, including photography, recording or any information and retrieval system, without permission in writing from the author.

Page 252 photo courtesy of Jonathan Carriere
Page 269 photo courtesy of Andrew Sedley
Page 299 photo courtesy of Joe McNeill
All other photos are property of Terry McEvoy

Taylor Field and Mosaic Stadium photos used with the permission of the Saskatchewan Roughrider Football Club

Sources:

    CFL.ca

    Riderville.com

    Saskatchewan Roughrider fact books

    2003 CFL Facts

    Dave Ridgway and David A. Poulsen, *Robokicker*

Cover photos and design by Terry McEvoy

First Printing

Northern Road Press
Roseville, Minnesota
www.northernroadpress.com

McEvoy, Terry 1949—
Rider Pride on the American Side
ISBN 978-0-615-19344-1

To our friends in Saskatchewan……

……who so deeply deserved the football events of 2007

Acknowledgments

Many of the names appearing in this text were instrumental in helping with its creation, and I thank them all for their support and encouragement.

Dave Ridgway was invaluable, sharing his insights, proofreading, making suggestions and kindly providing the Foreword.

Dustin Cherniawski is a great representative of the many good things about Canadian football and his Introduction was deeply appreciated.

Govind Achyuthan and his amazing Rider memory were, as always, inspirational.

Kelly Ramler, Jeff Banow and Troy Souster provided facts, great feedback and constantly renewed my passion.

Carson McEvoy passed on important comments that only a parent could deal with.

Will Chabun volunteered much time and effort in advising, revising and proofing the original edition. He saved the day.

Dr. Jack Bedell was a great sounding board for many ideas and freely shared extremely helpful and valuable information on the big picture.

Contents

Introduction
Author's Note
Foreword

1 The Road To Riderville/Page 17
2 Taylor Field Debut/Page 24
3 The Early Years/Page 31
4 Grey Cup Virgins/Page 42
5 Close Encounters of The Rendezvous Kind/Page 50
6 The Internet Intervenes/Page 59
7 "Got Everything You Need?"/Page 70
8 Calgrya/Page 79
9 Season Tickets/Page 92
10 The Luckiest Man on the Face of the Earth/Page 106
11 Edmonton, Buffalo, and The Pack/Page 125
12 A Hall of Fame Kind of Guy/Page 137
13 Flat Out With The Elk Man/Page 146
14 Saskatchewan Nice/Page 166
15 Vegetable Lasagna in The Nation's Capital/Page 178
16 Happy Birthday, Saskatchewan/Page 195
17 The Winds of Change/Page 218
18 Eric Who?/Page 231
19 Kerry On/Page 245
20 West Division All-Stars/Page 262
21 One Fine Day/Page 270
22 "Is It Irish Day?"/Page 279
23 The Joy of Troy/Page 289
24 The Cup Runneth Around/Page 301

Introduction

I am an Eskimos fan. It's true. Growing up in Edmonton, I was a member of the Knot-Hole Gang - a special section of Commonwealth Stadium reserved for young fans who love football and hot dogs. I would go to all the games with my older brother Tyler and watch our favourite players compete while we tried desperately to catch the mini footballs being thrown into the stands. We'd watch the games and daydream about what it would be like to stand on the field and see thousands of die-hard fans rooting for their team.

Well, those dreams became a reality for me at 1:07pm on Saturday October 15th, 2005 in front of 53,216 fans in a classic rematch after a previous 1-point Rider victory.

There I stood, on the 45-yard line at Commonwealth Stadium, waiting for the opening kick-off. I took a moment to look around and let it all sink in. Everything was just like I had imagined it. The atmosphere was electric and the air was crisp – a great day for football. The smell of popcorn and draft beer was eminent and I could barely hear blow-horns over the noise of the crowd.

Even Tyler was there.

It was exactly like my daydreams from the Knot-Hole Gang section except that, today, I was wearing green & white - and the thousands of die-hard fans were dressed exactly the same.

It was perfect.

I guess that was the very moment when I first understood why the Saskatchewan Roughriders are such a special team. The Roughriders are more than just a collection of players and coaches. Games are more than just an afternoon out of the house. And donning the green and white is more than just a fashion statement.

Rider Nation is an institution and Terry McEvoy embodies its true spirit. He teaches us that it's not about where you came from or where you are now. It's not about your age or how much money you make. It's about road trips and game-day BBQ's. Rivalries and re-matches. Trash talk and praise. Heart-ache and triumph.

It's going to the game with old friends as much as it is making new ones while you're there. It's deciding what you want to wear a much as it is dressing for the weather.

I've known Terry for as long as I've been a Roughrider. He showed up to practice one day and made an effort to introduce himself to the new guy. Since then I've always looked forward to seeing him and hearing commentary and insights on all things Roughrider. His loyalty for the team can only be rivaled by his loyalty for family and friends.

So, I hope you enjoy reading this book because it's about you. Whether you're actually in it or can simply identify with the characters who are, I'm sure you'll find his collection of stories both memorable and sincere.

Terry, you have done a wonderful job of capturing the true essence of Roughrider culture and I hope your passion continues to inspire.

Dustin Cherniawski

Saskatchewan Roughrider

2005 - Present

Author's Note

Some things in life are easier to explain than others. Here in Minnesota, it would be a simple task to state the many reasons why one might be, for example, a Minnesota Twins fan. There might be a bit more difficulty in explaining a Minnesotan's attraction to an American pro sports team in another part of the country, but this allegiance could still be documented to the satisfaction of any listener.

It's now been fifteen football seasons, however, and I still find it nearly impossible to explain how an American family became fans and season ticket holders of a far off team in something called the Canadian Football League. Some variant of "How did you become a Saskatchewan Roughriders fan?" is a question I have been asked literally hundreds of times and I am still searching for that perfect answer, since the journey leading the McEvoy family to where we are today is mysterious even to me. This book, thus, is my attempt to sort things out both for myself and for others.

Our first football trip to Regina, Saskatchewan was in 1994, when our son Carson was five and his brother Connor was three. As I look at them today, both taller than their dad and certainly just about adults, I am struck by two things. The first, as you might imagine, is how quickly time goes past us. That first game at Taylor Field seems like just yesterday rather than part of a lifetime ago. My second observation is just a bit more subtle and actually expands somewhat past the Saskatchewan Roughriders.

Illogically, almost accidentally, and really without major impetus from me, my life has changed dramatically since that 1994 trip. Fifteen seasons ago, my long term goals were quite hopeful but lacked much specificity. I had a good job, two older children successfully entrenched in college and looked forward to continuing to work hard, raise the two youngsters and retire eventually. Good fortune jumped into the way of those dreams with impacts that I did not possibly imagine and can only sit back, appreciate, and be thankful for.

Some part of this good fortune involved the evolution of our Saskatchewan experiences. As casual fans, present in Regina just once per year, we gradually discovered an attraction to the city, the province and the football team. Trips to Saskatchewan began to be planned for their own merit, not just as a stopover on another larger holiday. Very importantly, new good friends jumped into our lives, many in unexpected and nearly unbelievable ways. We traveled globally, meeting unlikely acquaintances in Australia who are now essentially part of our family. Early retirement, a seemingly impossible circumstance with two young children, grabbed hold and held on due to a series of nearly accidental but extremely favourable financial decisions.

But the key ingredient to the recipe resulting in this life changing experience certainly has been people. Not just any people, but people in Saskatchewan who became friends despite the limits of both geography and age. Beginning in about 1998, we somehow expanded our horizons significantly and suddenly, a few years later, had clearly found reasons beyond football to keep returning to Regina.

I've even been able to introduce a few Minnesota friends to the culture of the CFL and they now make it possible for me to enjoy Rider football several times per season. Since that almost accidental 1994 beginning, I have managed to fit in over forty Regina trips, eight Grey Cups and a memorable trip to see one of these new friends be inducted into the Canadian Football Hall of Fame. The experience has constantly been an unexpected thrill and has filled my life with companionship and fine memories that I never dreamed possible.

Our family slice of Rider Pride is clearly just a small one, especially when compared with the passion of those thousands in Saskatchewan whose team allegiance predates ours by a significant numbers of football seasons. However, the size of that slice is not important. The importance to our family is the slice itself, since it has opened an entire world of experiences to us that the average family in this world of ours will never have the opportunity to imagine. We've become part of the culture of another land, one similar to ours, but also different in so many ways. I've developed a passion that is personally important since it is one of the many things that make every day a journey to be excited about. This passion is easy to share and an interesting way for me to do that is through this book.

Since my Saskatchewan and CFL adventures have been overwhelmingly — in fact — nearly exclusively, positive ones, the tone of this book will follow that lead. Nothing in life is perfect, but I see no purpose in any negative remarks about any particular person, since those types are not representative of my many Canadian experiences. Thus, those persons will be largely ignored in print here just as they have been by me in person. I've also included a number of photos, and must explain my own image appearing in some of them. Your hobby may be fishing or hunting or perhaps stamp collecting — mine is having a photo of myself with people who have shared good times with me and, fortunately, I have a huge collection.

Please also note I have attempted to honour my Canadian friends by spelling certain words in their favourite way, a real labour of love.

The fraternity of Saskatchewan Roughriders fans is large, loud, and most certainly loyal. As I have become somewhat more increasingly exposed to that fraternity, if forced to name a single emotion I have felt in its presence, I believe the first word I would choose would be *appreciation*. As frequent visitors to Canada, my family, friends, and I have without exception enjoyed the fine hospitality and companionship offered by virtually everyone we have met. Some have become friends, but many remain strangers, though clearly tied by the bond of Rider Pride.

It's been a privilege and a pleasure to become just a small part of that bond and we deeply appreciate it.

Terry McEvoy

Roseville, Minnesota, USA – Spring, 2008

Foreword

It doesn't happen with alarming frequency, but when it does, it sneaks up on you with unexpected speed and with really no expectations as to the eventual outcome. I am talking about the Grey Cup, and in particular, the appearance of the Saskatchewan Roughriders in Canada's Holy Grail of football.

I don't want you to get the impression that it never happens, because the Roughriders have been there before. In  fact there was a time during the Ronnie and George era when it was almost expected that they would be there, or at least battling until the very end of the Western Final before it was decided who would be the Canadian Football League's representative from the Western Conference. But even during those long win-filled years of success the Riders came away from their Grey Cup appearances victorious only once, in 1966.

Then the drought happened, not just a Grey Cup appearance drought, but a playoff appearance drought that lasted...oh...oh so long, especially if you played through a bunch of it, like I did.

Eventually, and thankfully, that playoff drought ended in 1988, and I was there! But the enthusiasm of play-off fever and the possibility of a Grey Cup berth didn't last very long for either me or the long-suffering fans of the Riders, as we were bounced rather quickly by the B.C. Lions. The Lions, from the balmy coast of western Canada, a team that we were sure wouldn't be able compete not only in Taylor Field (it was still called that back then you know) but, more importantly, in the weather. Oh well, so much for that thought!

But we were back the following year, most unexpectedly after dropping four games in a row during the middle of the season. And not only did we make it to the play-offs again, but we also made it to the Grey Cup after beating the invincible

Eskimos (at 16 and 2 and after being unbeaten at home!) at Commonwealth Stadium, in Edmonton.

Then what seemed like a miracle happened; we actually went to Toronto and won the Grey Cup. It was 1989 and 23 long years after George Reed and Ronnie Lancaster and their supporting cast beat the Ottawa Rough Riders. Now can you appreciate why I would say that a miracle happened a few lines back! Twenty three years had passed since the fans of the green and white had experienced a Grey Cup Championship.

But, the fans had stuck with their team throughout the good and bad, not that there was a lot of good mind you. They enjoyed and reveled and partied because, well, their team had the makings of a dynasty. It had a great pair of QB's in Austin and Burgess, two of the best slots the league had ever seen on one team in Elgaard and Fairholm, a sound veteran offensive line, a decent kicker and defense that teams hated to play against. Oh, life was going to be good for the fans of the guys in green and white.

Cut to 2007....it has now been 18 years since the team last won a Grey Cup. They had been to the Cup back in 1997 but they had the misfortune of being paired against a team led by Doug Flutie and well, that brings us quickly back to 2007.

Some years after our win back in 1989 I met a fellow from Minnesota. He was just about to become a life-long fan of Saskatchewan's football team. In fall of 1996, I received a letter postmarked "Minneapolis, Minnesota." I opened it and read an extremely polite request for an autograph from a Terry McEvoy of Roseville, Minnesota, a suburb of St. Paul. Instead of just signing a picture and firing it off in the return mail, I took it home and wrote Terry a letter saying how nice it was to hear from a CFL fan based in the U.S. I managed to find a copy of our Grey Cup program from 1989, autographed it across the front and sent it back to Roseville with my letter.

The rest, as they say, is history! We corresponded several more times that year and eventually got to meet in, of all places, the Rendezvous Regina room at Grey Cup 1998, in Winnipeg, Manitoba. I was attending Grey Cup as a guest of a business client and had just walked off stage after welcoming the fans when some guy walked up to me and said, "Hi, I'm Terry from Minnesota." I knew who it was immediately. We chatted at length that night and eventually exchanged numbers and e-mail addresses. Over the next few years Terry and I would get together periodically, either Terry on his own, or Terry with Maura, or Terry with Maura and his two sons Carson and Connor. We always enjoyed each others' company and managed to find a lot of common ground when it came to the topic of football.

Terry has become one of the most dedicated Rider fans with whom I have ever had the chance to interact. He continues to hold season tickets to Mosaic Stadium and, yes, he actually shows up at the home games. Sometimes he's in attendance at more games in a year than the average fan who has season tickets *and* resides in Regina. He buys Rider lottery tickets, he spends *mucho* dollars on souvenirs in the Rider Store and he even traveled all the way to Calgary to see my induction in to the Canadian Football Hall of Fame. In addition, like many devout fans of this often-maligned game he tries to make the annual sojourn to the Grey Cup game. To put it bluntly, he loves our game and our/your team.

Last year he made it to Toronto and finally it was his turn to be in attendance when the Green Guys not only got to a Grey Cup game but also left town with it tucked under their arms. So he witnessed personally his team winning the big one. It doesn't happen very often as you may have summarized from this writing and I am so very happy for him that he was able to be there.

In chatting with him upon his return it sounded like he had himself a little fun while in southern Ontario. He was able to run in to more than a few people that are mentioned in this book. He likely quaffed a few brews at some point and he got to see a fairly decent football game, ironically at the same venue that holds more than a few nice memories for me also.

Even amidst all of the fun and events and things he had to do he still found time to remember to get his old friend (me) a copy of a program and a ticket stub from the big game. Now that's a good friend. If I had been there I probably wouldn't have even recalled where I was staying during the euphoria of the final minutes, let alone remember to get someone a program.

Plenty of lore surrounds the actual Grey Cup — it's been stolen, left in a cab, showered with players, sat on and crushed, and visited just about every corner of most of the provinces in Canada. Maybe someday Terry can talk someone from this winning Rider team into bringing it down to

Minnesota for a visit.

There are many more stories I could tell you about Terry McEvoy and what an absolutely outstanding person he truly is, but I would rather let Terry regale you with some of his own versions. Therefore, to the loyal fans of the Saskatchewan Roughriders who pick up this book, I invite you to enjoy the anecdotes and stories that follow. They really are from a man who is much enamored with your football team and your province.

He is a wonderful guy to get to know, with a very understanding wife and children, and he is truly passionate about the CFL. But to me, he is much more than just a fan — he is a friend. Better yet, he is one of those friends who sadly you may not see for a year or two, but when you do get the chance to get together again, it's just like old times and you carry on as if you have never been apart.

To all who pick this book up and give it a chance.....you will be rewarded with some great stories......

Dave Ridgway

Saskatchewan Roughrider

1982 – 1995

Canadian Football Hall of Fame 2003

Chapter 1

The Road to Riderville

Flight 2883 from Minneapolis to Toronto has a listed travel time of just over two hours. After I boarded on November 23, 2007, this interval gave ample time to reflect on the people and events leading up to my long-awaited journey to see the Saskatchewan Roughriders finally play in a game where the prize was nothing less than the Grey Cup itself. The upcoming weekend would be the third of the preceding four where I had traveled from my home in Roseville, Minnesota to see Canada's Team in action. The Grey Cup game, a contest many Rider fans had only dreamed about, would be played in just two days. It was an easy time to think back about the many circumstances in my recent life contributing to my presence on this airplane on this day

Many Americans, sadly, know very little about their Canadian neighbours. It's easy for me to hope I do not fit exactly into that mold. Since my mother had three aunts who moved to Saskatchewan in the expansion era around 1905, I grew up in Minnesota in the 1950's with a bit more than the average household mention of the Prairie Province.

One aunt, Emma Orth, moved to the Flaxcombe, Saskatchewan, area in 1905, and two of Emma's sisters soon followed. Eleanor married Cecil Down and settled in Flaxcombe, and Marie married Dr. Stone and lived in Arcola.

In 1928, my maternal grandfather died at a young age, and my mother, Eliene Kuschel, was sent to live for the 1928 – 1929 school year with Eleanor in Flaxcombe. Despite the opinions of my younger Saskatchewan friends regarding my age, even I know of these events only by family oral history, having not made my mark in the world until 1949.

Mother's memories of that year in Saskatchewan were mixed, since I believe she resented being sent away, but actually enjoyed the memories more in later years. At any rate, the presence of the Saskatchewan relatives, combined with my mother's stories and my own interest in history and geography, gave me a small, but real, connection to the Prairie Province. Little did I ever realize my later reconnection with these basically unknown Saskatchewan relatives would be the direct result of my eventual interest in the Saskatchewan Roughrider Football Club.

Growing up in St. Paul, Minnesota in the 1950s and '60s, reading the sports pages and watching sports on TV gave me some small amount of exposure to the Canadian Football League. I did see the 1962 Grey Cup game, dubbed The Fog Bowl, and viewed games that were, if memory serves, on ABC's Wide World of Sports. When Bud Grant headed south from Winnipeg to assume command of the Minnesota Vikings, I'm sure the term "Blue Bombers," the name of the team he left in Winnipeg, was one I knew. When a tough, excellent quarterback named Joe Kapp later followed Grant to Minnesota, his Canadian Football League experience was well documented in the local media.

The history of the Canadian Football League is long and rich with the tradition of rugby, the sport from which the current game evolved. Beginning as amateur federations, the Eastern and Western rugby leagues had transformed by the 1950's into professional football organizations. In 1958, the name "Canadian Football League" became the identifier.

In 1993, the CFL made the decision to expand into the United States, choosing cities of significant size that were without NFL teams. At various times in the next three years, teams in Las Vegas, Sacramento, Birmingham, Memphis, Shreveport and San Antonio would try unsuccessfully, both on the field and at the gate, to bring the Canadian product south. A team in Baltimore, first called the CFL Colts and then the Stallions, did much better, actually winning the Grey Cup in 1995. However, the inability of most of the expansion teams to succeed doomed the effort, and the league returned to an all-Canadian grouping in 1996.

Beginning with the addition of the Ottawa Renegades in 2002, the CFL consisted of nine teams, in two divisions. The Eastern Division was comprised of the Hamilton Tiger Cats, the Montreal Alouettes, the Ottawa Renegades and the Toronto Argonauts. Western teams included the British Columbia Lions (who play in Vancouver), Calgary Stampeders, Edmonton

Eskimos, Saskatchewan Roughriders (competing in Regina), and the Winnipeg Blue Bombers.

Regular-season scheduling included a home-and-away series against teams from the opposing division. The rest of the games are played with divisional opponents. To fill the 18 games, some teams played each other three times in a single season. The top three teams in each division qualify for the playoffs, with the divisional leader earning a bye in the first week while the second and third-place finishers square off. Divisional champions then play in the Grey Cup game, which moves around the league cities in an irregular rotation. Purists will note I have omitted a playoff exception called the crossover, but we can return later to explain that oddity.

Events in early 2006 culminated in April with the suspension of the Ottawa franchise for the entire 2006 season. Financial difficulties caused the abdication of the existing ownership, and the league searched for new investors. Failing to immediately identify an appropriate group, the decision was made to continue seeking a new owner, but to suspend the club's operations for the season. A new schedule was developed, with Winnipeg moving to the Eastern Division, and a player dispersal draft of the Ottawa squad was held in mid-April. Since the 2006 season, each team plays their own divisional opponents three times and has a home-and-away series with each team in the opposing division. To fill the 18 game schedule, a fourth interdivisional contest is also held, with the opponent chosen in a seemingly secret manner.

Well before I even remotely understood the nuances of a Canadian Football League schedule, I made my first foray into Saskatchewan. In the fall of 1970, friends and I were entering our final year at the University of Minnesota and decided to head out on a camping trip prior to the start of the school year. Our planning skills were woefully inadequate and we left St. Paul on Labour Day weekend, 1970, without enough preparation for the Canadian fall weather. After a stop at Glacier Park in Montana, we headed for the pristine beauty of the Banff area. Greeted by night-time temperatures well below zero degrees centigrade, we were forced into motels to survive.

Although chilled, we did manage to see the sights in both Banff and Jasper, and set the stage for me to make a number of visits to those areas in the future. Since my friends and I were limited in outside activities by the weather, we did watch some CFL action on television and I recall one of my companions wondered aloud if a fellow named Rick Shaw, who then played in the league, was possibly of Asian descent.

The weather finally became more conducive to camping, and we headed east across the Trans-Canada Highway toward home, camping at nice sites in Maple Creek and McLean, Saskatchewan. We even discovered during a stop in Moose Jaw that parking meters were free on Wednesday afternoons, helped by a zealous resident who kept us from wasting our coins. Although I wondered a bit about my Saskatchewan relatives, the thought of trying to discover them never struck me. I also have no recollection of going through Regina, although surely we must have done so.

This trip, however, ignited a desire to see the world that still burns in me to this day. I was eager to return to the beauty of the Rockies, and after Maura and I were married in 1972, we set out in our Volkswagen Bug for Banff and Jasper.

Our first real memory of Regina came at the end of the vacation, as we drove from Jasper to the Queen City, stayed overnight, and then made the first of what would be many single-day voyages back to Minnesota from Saskatchewan.

In the next decade I would really move no closer to becoming a fan of Canadian football. Our son Chris was born in 1973, and was followed in 1974 by his sister, Meredith. We returned to the Rockies in 1979, 1982, 1984 and 1987 on vacations and stopped on more than one of those trips to try to find a Saskatchewan Roughrider shirt for Dad. I have no idea if the Rider Store existed back then, but if it did, we never thought of trying to find it, and I believe we finally found a shirt in Moose Jaw.

Jasper National Park, 1972

The Road to Riderville

In the year of one of these family trips an afternoon of television watching tossed the first smoldering spark onto my personal Saskatchewan Roughrider fire. The National Football League was on strike for a time during the 1982 season, and the American networks filled the football time slots with CFL games. One Sunday, a game was televised in Minnesota direct from Taylor Field in Regina. We had driven through the Saskatchewan capitol just shortly prior to this, and as I watched the game and saw the stadium's unique profile, I was a bit amazed that we had very recently been nearly right there. In this game, the Riders manhandled the Stamps 53 – 8, and I saw a very good performance by a young Saskatchewan kicker named Dave Ridgway.

On our way home during our 1987 trip, we drove along the Yellowhead Highway into Saskatchewan from Alberta. We had made this same drive before, and enjoyed listening to the radio and hearing the messages for back home read on behalf of patients from the northern communities who were in hospital. It was a good indication that life everywhere was not just what we were used to, since we had not ever heard this type of programming at home.

As we slid around Saskatoon toward Regina, the radio sent out another interesting message, tuning us in to a fund-raising program to save the Saskatchewan Roughrider Football Club from financial extinction. With no real knowledge of daily happenings in Canada, it was certainly our first realization that times were tough for the team. As players and other supporters made their pleas, it was impossible to avoid feeling a small connection with the team's plight. After all, we not only had Saskatchewan relatives, but also were even driving through the province at the time!

Reaching Regina, we intended to stay overnight and go to the horse races but found we had not arrived on a scheduled racing day. We did drive close enough to see Taylor Field for the first time, and I remember thinking, in my sometimes too simplistic manner, that it looked very much like it had on television in 1982. I suppose it should have, now that I think about it.

Any thoughts I might have had about returning to Regina for a game found the backburner in 1988. Maura had returned to work, beginning a teaching career, and Chris and Meredith were 15 and 14, respectively. I had an excellent job as a manager in the technology department of a major financial services firm, and life was good. Life can also be surprising, and was just that when Carson was born in October of 1988. His brother Connor followed him in 1991, and suddenly we had two children in college and two in day care at the same time.

These were exciting and challenging times, and clearly something meant to be for us. I would guess a number of my Saskatchewan friends, some of whom have met the younger boys multiple times, are not aware of their older siblings. Some who are aware have assumed that a second marriage is involved and never seem to know how to ask. It is usually good for a laugh, and I am convinced that Carson and Connor have kept us young and much more open to a lot of things, including trying new adventures.

Today, Chris is a pediatrician in Honolulu, Hawaii and he and his wife Julie Chang, who is also a physician, have a lovely little daughter, Leah Megan McEvoy. Meredith is married to Bill Beardslee and lives in Frankfurt, Germany, where both work for the U.S. Department of State. They have a great little girl named Fiona and our newest grandchild Nathan, who was born in 2006. Mere is the other real football fan in the family, and I'd love someday to bring her to Mosaic Stadium.

Sometimes a single event can lead to some interesting changes in life. On November 26, 1989, I had watched the Green Bay Packers thump the Vikings early in the day. Turning on the Grey Cup, which at that time was always shown in Minnesota, I was really only hoping to see a better game than I had just viewed. No Rider fan needs me to go into the details of Saskatchewan's last second 43 – 40 victory, culminated by Dave Ridgway's "Kick," but we all know it would get a number of votes in an objective poll to determine the greatest football game ever played. As the ball went through the uprights, I could sense that the next phase of my Rider fan life was beginning to simmer.

I became somewhat obsessed with the need for a sweatshirt commemorating this Grey Cup victory. In the days before the internet, and with no real knowledge of Regina, this was a more daunting task than it would be today. It took a while, but my sister-in-law, Mary Dee McEvoy, somehow came up with one through a Canadian professional acquaintance. I have it to this day, and now wear it only on special occasions.

Eventually, I discovered the Saskatchewan Roughrider Store. We had once visited a place in Calgary called Jersey City, and I actually wrote an unanswered letter hoping to locate Rider items. Finally, proving how slow I can be at times, I contacted the Riders to ask if they happened to know of any place selling Rider apparel. I've probably been called a Dumb American once or twice, but I would guess that phrase was used about me for the first time when the Store received my query. A team selling its own merchandise – what a novel concept! Be that as it may, I placed a large order and a great, although costly (for me), relationship was born.

When Carson and Connor got a bit older, we began to travel again. Actually, we didn't wait long, for in the summer of 1992 all six of us flew to Edmonton, rented a car, and stayed in Jasper for a week. We then returned to Edmonton and enjoyed the West Edmonton Mall, especially the water park, for a few days. On this trip, I happened to find a sporting goods store with a wonderful sale on CFL apparel, and purchased a number of items, including a stylized Saskatchewan number five jersey. Ten years later, this item would make for a great story, but you will need to read on for that.

The momentum to make the pilgrimage to Taylor Field was building. However, 1993 was a strange year for us, since we decided to move, found the perfect house, and purchased it. Our housing purchase was an ideal buyer's situation, as the sellers were building a new place and wanted to move three months later. Although we had ample time, we weren't able to sell our house, and ended up owning two places for several months. This series of unfortunate events served to raise my stress level, and also prevented any type of trip that year.

We weren't about to let that happen again in 1994.

Chapter 2

Taylor Field Debut

Vacations in our family are a sacred rite, and our failure to take one in 1993 felt like a logistical failure in my responsibilities as family patriarch. My own parents did not enjoy long driving vacations, preferring the Minnesota staple of "going to the lake," although our cabin destinations were usually in western Wisconsin, just a short drive from the Twin Cities. I personally wasn't ever much of a fisherman, and when we owned our own lake place, I came to think that people had lake homes just so they could do yard work in two locales. Maura and I had traveled fairly extensively, budget permitting, when Chris and Mere were young and had no intention of discontinuing those noble journeys as we raised the second litter.

We finally became owners of only one house in December of 1993, and it did not take long for the vacation plotting to commence. My mother had her 80th birthday in early 1994, and I got back into the traveling swing by treating her to a few days in Las Vegas, joined by (and equally financed by) my brother Bob. We happened to wander into a gift shop at a hotel on the Strip, where I noticed and purchased a Las Vegas Posse shirt. I was aware of the CFL expansion into the U.S. and thought it was a nice item to have, plus it sported a decent logo.

The people working in the shop had no idea what the Posse was, and I was not very surprised later when the team failed to stay afloat. Much later, having worn the shirt only once, I sold it on eBay for a very nice profit, and certainly wished I'd purchased the entire inventory.

My brother Bob and his wife Mary Dee had moved to Seattle in 1992, and we decided to head to the state of Washington in June to visit them. A favourite aunt and uncle also lived in Seattle and the trip would also be a good

Taylor Field Debut

opportunity to catch up with them. I greatly prefer circular routes while on a driving vacation, so as to avoid traversing the exact roadways both ways. It was for me just a natural, and very logical, decision to plan a stop off in Regina, Saskatchewan, on the way home.

The availability of a football game to attend during that stopover was certainly pretty critical to the grand scheme. I also wanted to be certain to have tickets purchased in advance, to avoid any excess drama about waiting to buy them when we arrived. Although I had not been clever enough to realize a team might sell its own merchandise, I did have a good idea that they might sell tickets for their own games. Armed with this astute deduction, I called the team in late winter to jump-start the process.

You might imagine the result — I was introduced to an important CFL tradition, The Late Schedule, for the first time. The Rider ticket office folks were great, as they are today, but were not yet able to help. We worked through this, and subsequent calls eventually resulted in the identification of a preseason game against the Sacramento Gold Miners as the perfect placeholder at the end of our trip.

I asked for help on the choice of seats, since I obviously had little familiarity with the seating grid at Taylor Field. The person from whom I ordered the tickets personally preferred the west side, and I certainly had no reason to reject a suggestion made in obvious sincerity. As the years have passed, we have remained "west siders" even to this day. I often wonder how long our Rider journey would have lasted had we sat, for example, close to the sometimes boisterous Section 28 on that first trip!

Curious also about parking, we were told it was sometimes difficult, but that the Agribition grounds were a good bet and a safe, short walk from Taylor Field. To this day, although we sometimes walk if we are staying downtown, we nearly always park just west of Elphinstone Street and stroll east on 10th Avenue to the field.

In this June of 1994, Carson was about 5½, and Connor had turned 3 in mid-April. They have always been wonderful travelers, and even then we were able to drive more miles per day than most wayfarers.

When we arrived in Washington, we went first to the Olympic Peninsula and had a great time staying right on the ocean at a wonderful place called Kalaloch Lodge. For reasons I do not ever understand, I often associate an event with a place, and remember that we missed the infamous O.J. Simpson car chase because we did not have a television in our cabin.

We had a great family visit, and then headed north from Seattle to cross into British Columbia. The area we drove through was new to us and we had a very enjoyable initial day's drive, seeing a few sights and staying overnight in Golden, B.C. The next day, we made touristy stops in Banff and then Calgary. Maura and I both noted how much each had changed since our last trip in 1987. Our stops enabled us to make progress that day only to Medicine Hat, Alberta, but certainly within easy reach of Regina.

Having traveled the route several times previously, we knew of a restaurant in Swift Current, Saskatchewan, where we had stopped for breakfast on prior trips. It was on the east side of the city, in a small motel on the south side of the Trans-Canada Highway. On our previous two visits, in 1984 and 1987, the same group of ladies had occupied the same table in the restaurant. It actually doesn't take much for me to find humour in everyday events, but I had trouble keeping myself from laughing aloud when we entered the building in 1994, and found the same group at the same table — again. When I related this story much later to my Saskatchewan friend Darwin Gooding of Swift Current, he was surprised that I found this unusual. As I think about it, what seemed to me like incredible coincidence was likely just a daily gathering that we would have observed regardless of our arrival date. It's much more fun to view it as an amazing bit of happenstance.

We had planned a couple of extra days in Regina before the football game, and spent that time exploring the city and visiting the usual places that a family in a new place would enjoy. We toured the RCMP Museum, Wascana Park and most of the museums. My first impressions of Regina were positive; it was a city easy to get around in and the people we interacted with all seemed very friendly. A family tradition began when we attended the Disney film *The Lion King* at the Cornwall Theatres, the first of several annual Disney screenings at that venue.

Regina is the capitol of the province of Saskatchewan, and has a population of approximately 190,000. Situated on the Trans-Canada Highway about halfway between Winnipeg

Taylor Field Debut

and Calgary, Regina is, interestingly, one of only a very few major North American cities not located on a significant river. Named in honour of Queen Victoria in 1882, Regina now is sometimes referred to as "The Queen City." It boasts the headquarters of the Royal Canadian Mounted Police and is an important regional agricultural and commercial centre.

RCMP recruits, 1994

Not everyone is necessarily familiar with the Saskatchewan Roughriders, professional football's occupant of Mosaic Stadium in Regina. Before the 2007 season, I sometimes compared the team to the Chicago Cubs of professional baseball, since both teams had seemingly endless streaks of futility. In 2007, the Canadian Football League played its 94th Grey Cup, and the Saskatchewan Roughriders had taken the top prize but twice, in 1966 and 1989. They actually reached the final an additional dozen times, including an interesting streak beginning in 1928 when the then-Regina Roughriders lost the Grey Cup game six times in seven years. "Saskatchewan" replaced "Regina" in the late 1940s as the nickname's identifying locale, but the new name took a few years to catch on. I can still recall references to the Regina Roughriders in my youth, in the mid and late 1950s.

The mathematical illusion of a team becoming the league champion only twice in 94 attempts in a league currently populated by eight teams is interesting. The team's inability since for nearly 20 years dating from 1988 to gain a

Rider Pride on the American Side

home playoff game by finishing either first or second in a four- or-five team division was equally as improbable. When that streak ended, on November 11, 2007, one could literally feel the sign of provincial relief.

The team enjoys a following that is legendary in CFL lore. Many natives of the province of Saskatchewan now live elsewhere in Canada, but their football allegiance remains in Regina. Tales abound of green-and-white seas of bodies in opposing stadiums, and the phrase "Rider fans are everywhere" has a distinct ring of truth to it. In Saskatchewan, the community-owned team is the dominant sports story daily through the football season, and often even in the off-season. Every Labour Day weekends and for many other contests in 2007, the team drew capacity crowds, with the equivalent of one in every 6 ½ Reginans in attendance. By contrast, when the Minnesota Vikings fill the Metrodome for a game, about 1 in 45 Twin Citians are present. Rider fans are well-known for a fierce loyalty to the Green and White, and we were eager to see it in person.

Mosaic Stadium, formerly Taylor Field, is the team's home and is located slightly north and west of downtown Regina. The original stadium name is in honour of Neil "Piffles" Taylor, a player, coach and administrator of the Regina Roughriders who died in 1946 at age 48. In 2006, naming rights were awarded to the Mosaic Company and the official name became Mosaic Stadium at Taylor Field. Mosaic is a world leader in crop nutrients and has a strong presence in Saskatchewan. Interestingly, the corporate headquarters is in suburban Minneapolis, giving me the eventual ambition of riding the corporate jet to a Rider game!

A long-range program to improve the stadium is currently under way, with a video scoreboard and new sound system coming during the 2005 season as the first tangible changes. Mosaic Stadium's current seating capacity is 28,800.

Back in 1994, the game day of our first visit arrived with warm temperatures but also with the threat of weather havoc. The game was in the evening and we were a bit concerned about Carson and Connor's staying power, but hoped they could just sleep it off on the trip home the next day. At the time, Scotia Centre downtown was a decently thriving retail area. We shopped, wandered, had a bite to eat, and headed to Taylor Field.

Taylor Field Debut

      It really did not take a meteorological genius to determine that the weather would be interesting that night. Hoping it would spare the poor Americans on their maiden voyage, we parked the car and walked to the stadium. We picked up our tickets, and went right inside to our seats. Our seats were in the middle of Section 43, fairly close to the field, and on the north end of the west side stands. Decent seats, a warm night and professional football outdoors were a great combination.

      My first impression of Taylor Field was a bit of surprise. It seemed older than I had imagined it would be, most particularly in the interior areas and ramps. Not a problem, mind you, but just different than I was expecting. I was amazed by the size of the field since we had never seen the longer, wider Canadian layout in person before. The width seemed gigantic and the end zones seemed to be, well, endless.

      One of my favourite players from seeing the Riders occasionally on TV in Minnesota was Jeff Fairholm. I remembered his long TD reception in the 1989 Grey Cup, and admired his smoothness when he had the ball. In fact, shortly after I first discovered the Rider Store, I had purchased two Rider jerseys for Carson and myself, and had Jeff's number 18 applied here in Minnesota. This was very likely in about 1990, before Connor was born. I was disappointed that Jeff was no longer a Rider, but much later, in 2005, my Fairholm story would have a happier ending.

      Something happened in the second quarter that made an incredible impression on me and I still tell the story occasionally. One of the boys needed a bathroom break and we left our seats to take care of it. You need to understand, if you have not experienced it, that professional sporting events in the Twin Cities have a much different level of crowd movement than does Mosaic Stadium. Midway through this second quarter in Regina, we were the only souls save the concessionaires in the entire interior area. Any game locally has a large number of fans milling around in the concourses, waiting in concession lines and ignoring the contest. I've never seen that in Regina and it was, and still is, very refreshing.

      In the fourth quarter, with the Riders leading 19 – 4, the weather potential became reality. Storms were visible all around Mosaic and the lightning put on a show unseen at that stadium until a memorable night in August of 2007. We were debating whether we should leave, being just a bit concerned for the young boys and a walk of decent length to the car. The decision to stay or leave was suddenly taken out of our hands, however, when a Big One hit close by and the lights went out in Saskatchewan, or at least the part we were in.

It was very easy to follow the crowd's lead, and we moved rapidly out of the stadium, found our bearings, and tried to move toward the car as quickly as we could. Although the weather looked and sounded terrible, as we started westward on 10th Avenue, the rain had not really done more than have an occasional spit. Mother Nature was not to be denied on this night, however, and we had gone only half the distance needed to get back to Elphinstone when she arrived in earnest. Just as we reached the corner of 10th and Athol, the skies opened up and the rain came down in the proverbial buckets. We shifted into overdrive, with Connor in my arms, and Maura and Carson hurrying along.

Unfortunately, Carson tripped on the curb as we passed Athol and went down in a heap. The combination of the frightening weather and a scraped knee caused some distress, but we managed to keep moving after only a short delay. We reached our car finally, safe but drenched, and tumbled in. It took several minutes to get calmed down, dried off as best we could, and finally we were on our way.

Our motel was on Victoria, east of the Ring Road, about as far away from Taylor Field as civilization then existed in Regina. Of course, I hadn't considered that any landmarks that I might have noted on the incoming trip would be virtually invisible, due to the darkness combined with a tremendously driving rain. We just followed the line of cars in front of us, and actually ended up going south on Albert in a direction that was not helping us, but eventually corrected our course. Certainly in times of stress and discomfort, everything seems to take forever, but I'm quite positive it was an hour or more from when the rain began until we reached the motel.

We can always recall, now with a laugh, as we walk down 10th either to or from the stadium, the first time we made that dash after a game. However, on this night in 1994, I wondered if our first trip to Taylor Field might not also be our last.

Chapter 3

The Early Years

Often I tend to make assumptions that are later shown to be incorrect. Since it's difficult to have a deep conversation with children who are five and three, my logical and occasionally feeble mind just assumed the boys would have no interest in returning to the land of scary thunderstorms and scraped knees. As preliminary conversations about our 1995 vacations began to surface, any reference to returning to Saskatchewan was for a time a subject avoided. However, sans the storm, I had really enjoyed Regina and the game. The long, cold Minnesota winter has a tendency to make one think of summer, warm weather and good road trips, so I began to think of the best way to introduce the Green Guys into the family planning process.

As noted, the Canadian Rockies are a favourite vacation destination for our family. I was a bit fascinated by the obvious changes we observed in Banff while driving through in 1994, and was very interested in returning to some of the places we had visited on previous trips to see those improvements on a wider scale.

Lest anyone become concerned that I might be obsessed with Canada, a reminder of the economics of the situation is in order. In the summer of 1995, the Canadian exchange for U.S. dollars was .72, essentially meaning we received a 28% discount on any money spent. At least perceptually, many goods and services were priced about the same in the two countries, with of course certain exceptions, so vacationing in Canada appeared to be a great deal, both financially and esthetically. In the past few years, significant changes to the movement of the rate have occurred, culminating in September of 2007 when the Canadian dollar surpassed that of the U.S. for the first time in more than 30 years. What was once a marked financial advantage is now gone, but my Canadian friends have had remarkably little sympathy for our position in this turnaround.

With this needed rationalization of Canadian vacationing in place, my winter thoughts in early 1995 turned to the initial planning of the annual family trip. Chris had just graduated from Bradley University, in Peoria, Illinois. Meredith was beginning her final year at the University of Minnesota-Morris, in central Minnesota. Neither had any desire to be part of our traveling circus and Maura and I certainly understood. I devised a clever plan to plot out a wonderfully designed vacation and slip in a Rider game on the sly.

When I broached the subject, the response was surprising and I was even a bit ashamed of my attempted cunning. The drama of 1994 seemed to be erased from memory, and the idea to see the Green Guys play once more was received with enthusiasm by all in the household. Having learned from 1994 that the CFL schedule was a moving target, and armed with the probability that seats would be available for most games, we planned a jaunt for August in order to complete the boys' summer activity schedules and hope for some decent weather in Banff.

Saskatchewan's 1994 season had been decent, as the team finished with a record of 11 – 7, but lost 36 – 3 to the Calgary Stampeders in the Western Division semi-final. For 1995, though, the CFL had split into North and South divisions. The eight Canadian teams were in the North, with the five U.S. teams forming the smaller Southern group.

Since we were now seasoned vets in the ticket-purchasing realm of the Riders, I boldly explored new worlds by getting seats in section 39, the west side southern equivalent of our 1994 seats. Some of events from the Regina leg of this trip remain very clear but I would argue it's harder to recall a single day from a two-week multiple-stop journey than it is to remember the events of more recent weekend trips exclusively devoted to Saskatchewan football.

Disney was at it again, and we extended our string of Cornwall viewings to two with attendance at a screening of *Pocahontas*, one of my clear recollections.

The game itself was on a Wednesday evening, a bit unusual even for the CFL. The Riders played the British Columbia Lions, and it was our first exposure to a Taylor Field football mainstay: a very strong wind blowing through the stadium. Since the playing surface is roughly north/south, a wind of the typical Saskatchewan velocity could be game-changing. A breeze such as this directly impacts field position, and on this night much of the contest was played on our end. I understandably felt like a genius for my seat selection.

The identity of Saskatchewan's punter that day is not any longer retrievable from my memory chips and certainly more than one person could have handled the duties. However, another distinct memory was a punt by the Riders with the line of scrimmage directly in front of us. The wind was in the midst of a huge gust, but the kicker seemed to make solid contact. The arc of the football in the flight seemed to resemble a banana, as it appeared to do a right turn when it hit the plane of the scrimmage line. The game was close through three quarters, but BC had the wind in the fourth quarter and won going away, 43 – 25.

Football game in hand, we headed to Calgary, saw the sights, and spent several pleasurable days in Banff. Our return trip took us through Montana, to cities like Great Falls and Helena, where we had not been before. All in all, a good trip, with no traumatizing Saskatchewan weather incidents.

Don Narcisse, Number 80, warming up in 1995

Back in the CFL world of 1995, the Riders slumped to a 6 – 12 mark on the season, missing the playoffs and watching at home as the Baltimore Stallions defeated Calgary in Regina for the only Grey Cup win ever by an American team.

Rider Pride on the American Side

Because I don't particularly care for the Minnesota winter, especially its length, the New Year usually marks the beginning of the incubation of the plot for our annual trip. Since Maura is a teacher, she is off from early June until the last week in August. Back in 1996, the boys were not yet involved in organized summer sports and thus our window to choose for a trip was quite large. Since we have always thought of Banff and Jasper as similarly desirable destinations, the decision to go to Jasper in the summer of 1996 was reached. Wanting to avoid the certainty of July crowds, we decided to leave Minnesota at the very end of that month, stay a week in Jasper, and stop off at the West Edmonton Mall before watching the Riders play the 1995 Grey Cup champions, the newly arrived squad from Baltimore, renamed as the Montreal Alouettes.

A brief stop in Caroline, Alberta, allowed us to visit with my cousin, Allan Down, and his wife Esther. Allan is from Rosetown, Saskatchewan, and was a toddler when my mother lived with the Down family.

After a fine week in Jasper and a stop at the West Edmonton Mall, we arrived in Regina with a full day to spare before the Sunday afternoon game. Saturday was spent museum-hopping, and seeing the latest Disney offering, *The Hunchback of Notre Dame*, of course at the Cornwall complex.

In the evening, we were a bit undecided about an activity, but I noticed in the city's newspaper, the Regina *Leader-Post*, that there was a Prairie League baseball game being played that evening. The Prairie League was an independent league, not affiliated with Major League Baseball, with Canadian teams in places like Moose Jaw, Saskatoon, Brandon, Manitoba, and the well-remembered Regina Cyclones. American teams came from cities like Minot, Green Bay, Grand Forks and the like. The Cyclones' opponent that August evening would provide the first of a long, very entertaining, string of Saskatchewan coincidences for me.

For the coincidence to take place, we would need to locate the baseball field. The newspaper listed Currie Field as the venue, a location we were woefully unfamiliar with. We were not alone, however, as I hesitantly asked around at our restaurant, and had surveyed most of the clientele before finding a young man who gave us mostly accurate directions. Keep me near Albert or Victoria and I now have a good

The Early Years

directional sense in Regina, but the location of Currie Field east of Albert off the Ring Road was then the McEvoy equivalent of trying to find the Northwest Passage.

Find it we did, eventually, arriving just as the teams were warming up. The Cyclones' opponent that evening served as the ingredient for that first Saskatchewan coincidence. A team called the Minneapolis Loons in 1995 had moved to Austin, Minnesota for 1996, renamed as the Southern Minny Stars. Austin is south of the Twin Cities, near the Iowa border, and is fairly renowned as the home of Hormel Meats and now the Spam Museum

Players in the Prairie League included a few Major League castoffs and players past their prime, such as former Minnesota Twins relief pitcher Juan Berenguer for the Stars and Daryl Boston, the Cyclones' manager that season. The rosters were filled with players released from the farm systems of major league teams, and also a few local players of strong talent. When I realized that the Southern Minny stars were playing that night in Regina, I had a good chuckle, since a friend of a friend actually was on the Stars' roster.

Back in 1996, I was still really waiting to come out of my shell. Today, with lots of CFL-induced practice, it's pretty easy for me to go up to a complete stranger, especially a person who may be well known, introduce myself, and have a brief, or sometimes extended, conversation. We'll visit a bit later with some of the events leading to my age-induced boldness, but in 1996, walking up to a stranger and having a conversation, even asking a question, was for me a painful experience.

As we walked down the third-base line toward the seats, I realized that it was now or never – I needed to take a deep breath and meet this friend of a friend, since it was amazing to me that he and I had both been deposited on this baseball field in Regina, Saskatchewan, at this precise moment. This player's name was Bobby Kneefe; he was a left-handed outfielder with a strong arm and a smooth stride. I had no idea what number he wore or even what he looked like. Juan Berenguer was alone by the left field-line fence, and easily recognizable to any Twins' fan. I tentatively approached him, explained I was from the Twin Cities, and that I remembered fondly his contribution to the Minnesota Twins' 1987 World Series win.

I then explained nervously that I'd like to meet Bobby Kneefe. Juan yelled out the outfielder's name and motioned for him to come over. A bemused and confused player interrupted his ball-shagging activities and came over to the waving motions of a person he had never before seen. At the mention of the name of our mutual friend, he slowly understood, but his amazement was equal to mine in terms of the unlikelihood of our meeting. Bobby was particularly surprised that we were not just passing through, but in fact had a Rider-driven purpose for our stay in Regina.

The game was actually fun to watch, although pretty average baseball, and I also was able to meet former Minnesota Gopher and Atlanta Brave Greg Olson, the Stars' manager, as we exchanged pleasantries while accomplishing our men's room business.

But we were in Regina for a football game, and Sunday was Game Day. This was not just an ordinary contest in the season of a squad that would end its schedule with a 6 – 12 record. We had picked this game due to its logical spot in our travels, and had no idea that the Riders had decided, as part of the festivities, to retire the jersey Number 36, mostly recently worn by place-kicker and 1989 Grey Cup Most Outstanding Canadian Dave Ridgway.

Like any Saskatchewan Roughrider fans, lifelong or fledgling, we knew the story of "The Kick." At that time, my status at work allowed me a private office, and a framed poster of that Nov. 26, 1989 dramatic moment hung proudly on the wall. The poster was actually a great office conversation item, and became even more so in later years.

If memory serves, the jersey retirement took place right before the game. We were again in the south part of the West side, in section 101. A reenactment of "The Kick" began the ceremony, with original broadcast adding to the moment. The crowd, including us, loved it. Dave then gave a brief speech, one I felt good about and still remember parts of today. As I would hear him do again seven years later, he showed appreciation for family, teammates, and, most particularly, the wonderful fans of the Saskatchewan Roughriders. I have to be honest – I had never met the man, but was moved by what I viewed as an exceedingly nice gesture towards very appreciative football fans.

The game was very average, won by Montreal 32 – 20. Heath Rylance played most of the way at the pivot position, and Robert Mimbs gained 108 yards on the ground for

Saskatchewan. Wondering if we would ever see a full-length Rider victory, we left immediately after the end of the afternoon game, driving about 250 miles to Minot, North Dakota. This was not the sharpest idea we ever had, and we have since succumbed to the foolish notion of a long drive begun late in the day only very occasionally. On the drive home, I admit to thinking a bit about the jersey retirement. An idea that would expand beyond my wildest dreams began to form.

A Taylor Field ornament

Our game tickets had been salvaged, although we do not generally hold on to such things. Since it was beginning to appear that the CFL and Saskatchewan attraction might be more than a passing fancy, the thought of starting a collection of autographed items seemed like a fine idea. I was not much of a collector; in fact I remember my only set of collectibles as a child was a never-finished booklet of Canadian pennies.

Thinking it would be great to get these tickets autographed by the game day celebrity, I decided to send them with a note to the Roughriders in hopes they would find their way to Dave. This was before internet access in our household, and I went to the library to get the mailing address for the team. I wrote a short note to Dave, explaining where we lived and a bit about my family and its mild history of CFL travels. Enclosing the tickets and some money for return postage, I hoped for the best.

A month or so passed and I really didn't think much about the tickets or their return. One day, I opened the mailbox to find a large envelope with a Regina postmark. Truthfully, I was expecting a small envelope with just four tickets mailed from Regina, and was puzzled. Opening it, I found the tickets and a very nice note from Dave, telling me he was flattered I had "The Kick" poster in my office, and correctly supposing that its presence took a bit of explaining to the average American. He also noted that he drove through Minnesota quite often, going to Ohio to visit his sons.

Also enclosed in the envelope, and explaining its larger-than-expected size, was an autographed, personalized 1989 Grey Cup program. This remains a favourite CFL artifact, and Dave's generosity in sending it touched us all. (By the way, he also sent back the return postage money.)

There have probably been several turning points that transformed me into as real a Saskatchewan Roughrider fan as one not born in the province can be, if in fact I meet that description. The receipt of this program was one of them, since random acts of kindness by total strangers are great things, in my estimation. Maura remembers me saying at the time, "I hope I can meet this guy someday."

Santa, not surprisingly, is clearly a Rider fan, and Carson and Connor received, with just a bit of help from Dad, Dave Ridgway Number 36 green jerseys that year for Christmas. I called The Store to order them, and gave the person the information of sizes, colour, etc. She then asked, "Do you want them autographed? Dave comes down and autographs them if you'd like." Still not quite used to how nice things can be in Saskatchewan, I recovered quickly and also ordered one for myself. "Never in the NFL" is all I could think then and now.

The Saskatchewan team fared poorly again on the field, finishing 1996 with a dismal 5 – 13 record, and again missed the playoffs. The Doug Flutie-led Toronto Argonauts defeated the Edmonton Eskimos to win the Grey Cup.

Hercules was Disney's 1997 animated offering, and we decided to go to Regina and the Cornwall Centre to see it. The spring of 1997 brought terrible floods to the Red River Valley area on the Minnesota/North Dakota border, and the devastation was still very evident as we stopped for lunch in

Grand Forks. I can still visualize the furniture scattered on the sidewalks, water marks high on houses, and debris everywhere.

When we reached Regina, our Cornwall streak reached four, and the personal McEvoy Rider losing streak moved to three, as Edmonton beat Saskatchewan 24 – 18. We stopped for a day in Winnipeg on the way home, and were fascinated to see how high the floodwaters still stood. Winnipeg's decision to spend many dollars on flood diversion in past years had worked, however, and the city was spared the Dakota devastation.

Connor (left), Maura, Carson in 1998

In August, we vacationed eastward, spending 10 days touring Nova Scotia. There is a lot of talk about CFL expansion to the Maritimes and I am greatly in favour of it, since I would love to go back, and the Riders versus the Schooners would be the perfect reason.

Even in Nova Scotia, we had a small Saskatchewan experience, being in the hotel elevator in Dartmouth several times with the Saskatchewan provincial lawn bowling team, an interesting collection of lovely ladies. I also had my first encounter with Canadian medical care in the beautiful town of Lunenburg. In the course of just an hour or two, I went from feeling great to having pain in my lower back that doubled me over and sent us searching for a physician.

A great lady, Dr. Kelly, diagnosed probable kidney stone problems, gave me some wonder drugs for the pain, and apologized for charging me $10 for the office call. We were staying in a very nice bed and breakfast, so I took the drugs and went to bed. Maura and the boys, a bit terrified, walked around the town and saw the sights on their own.

In the morning, I was exhausted, but had apparently gotten rid of my problem. All of us, but the boys especially, were extremely relieved. They were happy to retrace their steps of the previous day, so I could share in the interesting shops and museums they had visited. One of them was a fine gift shop called Admiral Benbow's, a locale that would cross my CFL path again much later, as the determined reader will discover.

Shortly after we returned from Nova Scotia, I had my first Rider conversation at home with a stranger. In Minnesota, with no television coverage and extremely scant newspaper coverage, it is very unusual to have any incidental contact with other Rider fans or even find anyone having a passing fancy to the CFL. In the years I have followed the Riders, I have had only a half-dozen or so random exchanges in Minnesota regarding either the team or the province. The first of these caused very little thought at the time.

Making a quick run to the grocery store on a fall day, I was approached by a man I did not recognize. He said he had seen me in church wearing a Saskatchewan Roughriders jacket, and wondered if I knew of an acquaintance of his who had been a Rider, a man named Tim Roth. By this time, I had done a decent amount of catch-up on Rider history, and recognized, though somewhat vaguely, Tim's name. I correctly answered that he was a lineman, and I thought he had played in the 1970s. The man knew Tim, and indicated the former Rider lived in western Minnesota. The gentleman in the grocery store also filled me in a bit on Tim's very solid career. We parted ways, and I have never since recognized him in church. Tim Roth would of course jump back into the picture again but we'll get to that.

This happenstance was followed by another Rider contact, again both jacket and church related. We were attending Mass at a place other than our usual spot one Sunday and I was again wearing a Rider jacket. At the end of the service, a young couple hesitantly approached us, and asked if I knew anything about the Saskatchewan team. I replied in the affirmative, and he smilingly told me that his brother-in-law was Mike Saunders, then the featured Rider running back. Calling up memory reserves I did not know I

The Early Years

had, I blurted out, "Number 32, University of Iowa." We had a good talk, but I have also never seen them again.

There are also a few Rider names in and around the Minneapolis/St. Paul area. Possibly the best known is Ron Goetz, a former Minnesota Gopher and Rider linebacker, and a fellow still on my list to meet one day. Maura has a school acquaintance who knows Tuineau Alipate, a Rider in 1989 – 90, who now lives in Minneapolis. Another friend worked with the son of former Saskatchewan assistant coach Gary Hoffman, who kindly sent me several autographed items. After friend Tim Anderson made his first trip to Taylor Field in 2003, he met mid-90s linebacker Joe Toth at a seminar and evidently surprised the former Rider by mentioning our recent trip.

At the end of the 1997 CFL season, I was also able to follow the Riders' late season surge. Making the playoffs with an 8 – 10 regular season mark, they won two close playoff games, but were defeated by Toronto in the Grey Cup 47 – 23. It was Doug Flutie's last game in the CFL, and also the last CFL championship game televised in Minnesota.

In early 1996, I began working with two young men, Chris Melin and Corey Edmondson. When this working relationship began, it never occurred to me that Chris and Corey would each be a sailor on the next leg of my CFL voyage.

Chapter 4

Grey Cup Virgins

With the approach of the 1998 season, I realized something interesting about our travels to Saskatchewan. Trips to see the Riders play had been a part of our summers for the past four years, but they were more of an interesting lark than a fan-based activity. Our travels had deposited us annually at Taylor Field, but we still had no roots or real acquaintances in the city and had not developed a prairie native's appreciation for the fan friendly CFL. Regina had been a fun place to spend a few days each year, but we had not formed any permanent bond with either the city or the Saskatchewan Roughriders. Conversations with other fans at the games were essentially non-existent and we did not reveal our Minnesota heritage beyond the sign-in sheets at our motels. I know I had the thought that these trips were not likely to continue indefinitely, since we had yet to establish any deep reasons to warrant ongoing return journeys to the Queen City.

Try as we might, each game we attended was also a little mystery in some ways. The Canadian rules sometimes confused me and I was too embarrassed to ask anyone sitting near us for clarification. I had seen a number of games on TV, but the Canadian announcers logically assumed that viewers knew the basics, and rule explanation understandably was not a large part of their descriptions. This is likely true for any sport televised outside its native land with native announcers – I had watched Australian Rules Football many times, but really had no real inkling of how the game actually worked until I attended one.

There are actually quite a number of differences between the National Football League and the Canadian game. Most visible, certainly, is the size of the playing field, with the CFL field being 10 yards longer (at 110 yards) and having end zones

20 yards deep versus the 10 yards of the NFL. The width is significantly different also, with the CFL fields measuring 65 yards, 12 yards more than the American field. I found this to be the key to a play that is very strange to see until a fan is used to it —a pass the width of the field may need to travel 40 or 50 yards in the air for potentially a gain of only one or two yards. A public address announcer barking "Saskatchewan's ball on their own 53-yard line" also has to grow on a person to sound normal.

In the NFL, teams gain a first down by gaining 10 yards in four plays; this must be accomplished in three in Canada. Goalposts on CFL fields are located on the goal line itself, not on the back end line as in the NFL.

On both sides of the ball, Canadian football uses twelve players. The additional man is a receiver on offence, and a defensive back on defence. Defensive players in the CFL must line up at least a yard off the ball. This rule often allows an offence to take a fairly safe calculated risk on third down and less than a yard, a play where a quarterback sneak is commonplace.

A couple of rule differences cause the Canadian game to flow at a much quicker pace than its American counterpart. Each team is allotted only one timeout per half, and, most importantly, the offence has only 20 seconds in which to put the ball in play, compared to 45 seconds in the NFL.

Scoring differs a bit also. In the CFL a single point (now generally called a single, but occasionally still referred to by the French "rouge") is awarded for missed field goals and end zone punts if the receiving team cannot run the ball back across the goal line – there are no touchbacks. The CFL also disdains the fair catch on punts, and punts cannot roll dead, but players on the punting team must give the receiver a 5-yard circle of freedom in which to catch or pick up the ball.

Gradually, though, I began to figure things out and now seldom have problems. The differences in the game strategy also took time to digest and, truthfully, I'm still working on that, but now have knowledgeable friends to ask if needed. I remain convinced, however, that there is a receiver offside on nearly every pass play when the whole world goes in motion before the snap, as the CFL allows.

The area in which the CFL has it all over its American nephew, in my opinion, is the pace of the game. The shorter time between plays combines with fewer timeouts to keep the game moving and much more enjoyable to me.

Carson had joined a baseball team in the summer of 1998 and I was helping as an assistant coach. We needed to figure out a way to head to Regina for a game during the baseball season, since our summer trip that year was planned for Colorado. Even I was having trouble finding a way to stop in Regina on the way to Colorado, so we found a window in the baseball season that enabled us to miss only one game while catching the Riders for the fifth time.

Although Maura and I had both been born and raised in Minnesota, we had not seen certain parts of the northern portion of our state. We decided to do a bit of home state exploring, met Paul Bunyan and Babe the Blue Ox in Bemidji and walked across the source of the Mississippi River at Lake Itasca.

We arrived in Regina for the 1998 home opener against the Toronto Argonauts, played on July 3. Many refer to this game as "The Bobby Jurasin Game." You might recall that Jurasin, long a leader on the Rider defensive front, had been released by Saskatchewan and signed with the Argos for what would be a short career in the Eastern Division. The Regina *Leader-Post* overflowed with stories about the ironic switch, and Jurasin was loudly and fondly welcomed to Taylor Field.

Both McEvoy Regina streaks ended that trip. The Riders, led by three sacks each from newcomer linemen R-Kal Truluck and DeWayne Patterson, defeated the Argos 19 – 10. Bobby Jurasin was not a factor, and Toronto released him on July 12. For a change, the newest Disney animated feature *Mulan* failed to generate sufficient family enthusiasm to send us to the Cornwall Cinema.

I had forgotten the camera at the motel, and this is the only game from which we have not even a sliver of photographic memories. We sat again on the West Side, this time in Section 102, a place that would enter our lives again later. At the time, I really wasn't much into photography but have since been captured by the Digital Age and now take some sort of photo nearly every day. Our collection of Taylor Field, Mosaic Stadium and Grey Cup pictures is now huge, but the majority of these photos begin later this pivotal year of 1998.

With the taste of autograph quest success still present

from 1996, I was determined to try again in 1998. Although I felt bad about Bobby Jurasin's fate, I found it interesting that the players kept in his spot had played so well. A name such as R-Kal Truluck has some instant appeal, and the *Leader-Post* published a great photo of him clowning around at practice with Patterson.

When we returned to Minnesota, I sent this photo and our tickets to R-Kal, again at the team's address, told him we had been at the game, and asked him to sign the items. Amazingly, another larger-than-expected envelope soon arrived in the mail, bringing the photo and our tickets, plus the next game's program with R-Kal on the cover. All had been autographed by Truluck and DeWayne Patterson. I am betting that getting the autograph request meant as much to them as receiving the finished goods meant to me.

The timing of this trip was interesting, since we entered Canada on July 1, Canada Day, and returned to the States on July 4, American Independence Day. Upon entering Canada, we were warmly greeted, welcomed to Canada, and given a Canadian flag pin and car decal. When we re-entered the U.S. on July 4th, we were greeted with just grunts and questions. A bit ironic, we thought, but as time has passed, I've found the Customs officers on both sides of the border to be very friendly, and easy to get along with, with an interesting exception we'll discuss later.

Another discovery on this trip was that the 1998 Grey Cup was being played in Winnipeg in November. Although by this time, in mid-1998, we finally had home internet access, I had not yet become a frequent surfer, and didn't follow CFL happenings online. Many people I meet, when they find I am from Minnesota and a Rider fan, naturally assume that I must have attended the 1995 Grey Cup game in Regina. Actually, at the time, it never really crossed my mind. I have mentioned that we had no real connections then in Regina and 1995 was only our second season of attending games there.

It became perfectly normal that I would talk about the CFL a little at work. The poster of "The Kick" had always been a good icebreaker, and the fact that I had actually managed some contact with the poster's subject gave even more mileage to the story. Chris Melin and Corey Edmondson, the two young fellows who recently began working in the same general vicinity in the building as my office, were both very interested in sports. Because of that common interest, a partnership was formed. It was an unlikely one, possibly, since my older children were just slightly younger than Chris and Corey, but I've certainly been pleased to find on many subsequent occasions that my age is actually not a handicap in my CFL travels and even provides ample opportunity for some good jokes.

In some manner, this new trio decided to attend the Grey Cup game, to be held in Winnipeg on November 22, 1998. We would certainly not see Saskatchewan in the game, as they slumped back to a 5 – 13 record and failed to qualify for the playoffs. Obtaining game tickets was not an issue, but the $183 cost was a surprise. As head of logistics, I arranged for a motel. Word spread through the office grapevine and the most common question asked on our floor soon became, "You're going WHERE?" Undaunted, the new adventurers held their ground, and on the Friday before the game, Chris picked me up, and we drove to Corey's house a bit northwest of Minneapolis, since he was driving his Jeep to Winnipeg.

Any tale of Minnesotans attending football games in Canada would be incomplete without some conversation about the drive itself. I have met a few people in Regina over the years who have made this trek regularly but, like Americans, some Canadians are pretty geographically challenged also. Many people assume we arrive in Regina by driving to Winnipeg, and then heading west on the Trans-Canada Highway. This route is actually the longest, at about 815 miles, and requires either driving around Winnipeg, a time-consuming endeavor, or cutting cross-country on two-lane roads. We have used this passage only when we have had reason to spend time in Winnipeg. Nothing personal to my Canadian friends, but gasoline purchased in Canada is a good 25% higher than in the U.S., even after the exchange rate, and this route adds some to the fuel cost.

A jaunt from Roseville to Fargo, North Dakota is always the opening scene in our driving drama. One option from there is to drive north to Grand Forks, and from there head west on U.S. 2 to Minot. In Minot, U.S. 52 jumps in and goes to the Canadian border at Portal, North Dakota/North Portal, Saskatchewan. We have tried this jog two or three times, but have failed to make good time on the Grand Forks to Minot portion. This method is about 775 miles.

Another option from Fargo is to continue on Interstate 94 to Bismarck, North Dakota, and head north past the Space Aliens Café to Minot, and then on to Regina. This allows for four-lane travel until Minot but measures in at about 800 miles. I find this route attractive because the North Dakota interstate speed limit is 75 miles per hour.

The most direct route is Roseville to Jamestown, North Dakota, then a northwest jog on U.S. 52 to Minot, and on to Regina. It's the shortest trip at about 760 miles but most of the distance between Jamestown and Minot is only two lanes.

It's hard to make a long drive on exactly the same route twice in four days, so we will often take the Jamestown route on the way north, and the Bismarck leg coming home. The time commitment is essentially equal most trips.

We have also experimented with different routes once we pass into Saskatchewan at North Portal. There are other border crossings too, but we are used to this one and it is almost always very quick. It's fun once in a while also; on occasion, we have had the same Canadian crossing official on successive trips. When I am asked the purpose of the trip, I usually say, "To see the beloved Saskatchewan Roughriders" or some such nonsense, and generally get a laugh. I was extremely impressed one trip when the official said back, "Yeah, but you're in a different car than you were last time." How's that for an impressive memory?

Grand Forks or Jamestown, Bismarck or Minot, it's still a long trip. Our average time is usually in the neighbourhood of 12 ½ hours, giving a pretty respectable full-day average of 62 miles, or basically 100 kilometers, per hour. Unless very late in the season, we do gain an hour due to the Daylight Savings Time maneuvering, but lose it on the way home, obviously. We always pretend it's an hour later when we go to bed the night before the trip home, a tactic that causes very early Regina departures on occasion.

But back in this November of 1998, the weather north of us had not been good in the preceding days, and we experienced rough going on Interstate 25 north of Fargo. I was glad Corey was driving, and happy we had 4-wheel drive, since small patches of freeway were still covered with snow and ice. The driving seemed awful at the time, but would prove mild when compared to a later trip.

We stopped in Grand Forks for lunch at the somewhat

famous Red Pepper, home of the unusual Grinder sandwich. Chris' mind is a collector of unusual things, and he recalled the restaurant from his college days, when he occasionally went to Grand Forks for partying and University of North Dakota hockey. Seven years later, one of his acquaintances from these days past would briefly jump back into his life in an unlikely, but CFL-related, way.

Surviving the Grinders, we had an easy trip to Winnipeg, and headed to our motel. Our standing in life as Grey Cup Virgins was probably best expressed in our lodging choice. Ever the thrifty consumer, I had snagged a very inexpensive spot, but it was well west of the stadium, and a long ways from downtown. The room was small, and we had not been able to get a rollaway. The Older Person volunteered for the floor, since we had all brought sleeping bags. I don't always sleep well in motels anyway, and figured I'd do the youngsters a favour.

Our virgin ears had not yet heard important Grey Cup terms like Spirit of Edmonton, The Tiger's Lair, Riderville and the like. It was late afternoon, and we knew that the Grey Cup celebrations included a parade, scheduled that day for early evening and having a route in downtown Winnipeg. We headed toward that part of the city and wandered into a large convention centre-type building. The Touchdown Manitoba party was just breaking up, and we were surprised, but in a very positive way, with the level of celebration.

Seeing a room marked "Saskatchewan Roughriders Hospitality," we slid in, had a beverage or two, and found out exactly where the parade would be. Stopping at a table in the back of the room, I purchased three tickets for an event called "Rendezvous Regina," to be held the next afternoon. Chris and Corey were not fully on board with this decision, but the fact of me popping for the tickets helped their mindset a bit. Although Corey has since moved to North Carolina, Chris is still part of my Grey Cup travels and we discuss the wisdom of this purchase nearly every year, since it ended up being a good one.

We had some time until the parade, and walked around the complex. A smaller room had a sign welcoming the 1958 Grey Cup Champion Winnipeg Blue Bombers to a 40th reunion, and we stopped at the door. Certain we would be able to meet the legendary Bud Grant, we entered the room. However, even I didn't look old enough to be a '58 Bomber, and we were politely, but firmly, told to disappear.

Grey Cup Virgins

It was parade time anyway, and we found a spot on the street. Downtown Winnipeg reminds me some of downtown Minneapolis, with a river on the eastern border, and a slightly angled street (Portage in Winnipeg, Hennepin in Minneapolis) leading toward the river. It was bitterly cold, with a brisk wind, but we had come reasonably prepared. I was wearing a Rider parka and was pleasantly surprised by friendly shouts of "Hey, Saskatchewan!" directed my way. The parade was enjoyable, and a much bigger event than we were expecting. When we were sufficiently chilled, we went inside, found a nice restaurant and had dinner. Our virgin status caused us to return to the motel earlier than I now care to admit.

The evening ended on a sad note, when we watched the news and heard a Blue Bomber player from the '58 team had died of a heart attack during the parade. Feeling a bit reflective, we retired to prepare for what would be a very interesting first Grey Cup Saturday.

Chapter 5

Close Encounters of the Rendezvous Kind

Grey Cup Saturday dawned with an improved weather forecast and we eventually tumbled out for some breakfast. The stadium was on the way to both downtown and Rendezvous Regina and seemed like a logical place to look for souvenirs from our first Grey Cup. A few small purchases were made at the Bomber store and a couple of other interesting looking storefronts were visited as we headed east.

Not knowing exactly what to expect, we arrived close to the very beginning of the gala event. Rendezvous Regina, now called Rendezvous Saskatchewan, is one of many annually scheduled events during the Grey Cup weekend. It usually includes a good band, many door prizes and celebrity appearances. Also available are lots of beverages, certainly a Grey Cup party staple.

We had barely entered the building when we all received pins, stickers and even a mini football or two. As we navigated the hallway to the large auditorium where the party was to be held, I encountered my very first CFL luminary. In our path was the very famous Saskatchewan Roughrider mascot, Gainer the Gopher. A photo opportunity awaited us and a new collection for the family room wall was begun. Gainer was happy to pose with the smiling Minnesotan and his huge paw on my shoulder is a nice touch. I now have somewhere in the vicinity of 75 such photos, enlarged to 8x10, with this grinning gray-haired guy posing with CFL players, coaches, broadcasters, friends and even CFL commissioner Tom Wright. I enjoyed getting Gainer's autograph and paw print on a Labour Day weekend a few years later. Skeptics among you may question whether a giant stuffed gopher can sign an autograph but we know rodent residents of Parkbeg, Saskatchewan are a special breed.

A Gopher get-together, Grey Cup 1998

A bit star-struck, we entered the Rendezvous area. People were beginning to filter in, and we soon realized it was far from just a Saskatchewan fan event. All of the CFL teams were represented and the excitement of a good Grey Cup party, with wonderful fans from all cities, was beginning to build. We decided to have a beer, and, while waiting in line, I saw for the first time a Saskatchewan end-of-season mainstay, a jersey with "Next Year" in the back name panel, and the following calendar year as the jersey number, in this case "99." This became my second photo of the party, and I chuckle now that I even asked permission before taking the picture.

We were fascinated and uncomfortable at the same time. Corey, Chris and I were captivated by the crowd and the happenings but uncertain of the best way to participate since we knew no one save ourselves. A second beer seemed like a good idea, but it was very clear we were close to a crossroads. I felt a bit like the dog that chases the car but has no idea what to do with it when he catches it. Unconsciously, but as one, the three of us decided we needed to make our own fun and thus had to initiate some human contact.

Walking past right then were three young men in Rider

apparel, all with quasi-musical instruments. The apparent leader was a tall, pony-tailed lad with the name "Spanky" on his jersey. We stopped them to talk, and had a nice chat, not yet breaking, but certainly cracking, the ice of our Minnesota shyness. Having a mild hope of meeting Dave Ridgway, but having no idea at all if he was even in Winnipeg, I asked them to let me know if they happened to spot him. Gladly agreeing, the three were soon on their way. When they left our company, Chris, who is inspirational with nicknames, immediately christened them The Three-Man Band.

The legendary Three-Man Band, 1998

Exhausted by this supreme effort to socialize, we again began to wonder what to do with ourselves. My recollection is we discussed departing but decided to wait a bit and hope for divine intervention. We were standing in the back of the large room and suddenly spotted a crew coming towards us wearing the very identifiable Green Bay Packer Styrofoam cheeseheads. Corey is originally from Wisconsin; he and Chris are both Packer fans and this vision was like a Sign from Above. Of course, these were not Packer fans, but followers of the like-uniformed Edmonton Eskimos. Corey blocked their approach and we discovered a very agreeable bunch whose future impact on our Grey Cup travels would become very important to us

Introductions were in order; we had the pleasure to meet Arnie Fearon, Bambi Gerard (now Bambi Fearon), Rob

Close Encounters of the Rendezvous Kind

and Sheila Gaudreau, and Audrey Kent. They welcomed us warmly and we knew immediately that this would be a great party. It was great fun to get to know them, explain how three Minnesotans had happened to be in Winnipeg, and find a nice sense of companionship. Corey happened to have his Packer cheesehead in his car and quickly retrieved it. By the end of the afternoon, all of the cheeseheads were plastered with stickers, stuffed with wheat stalks, and no longer on the heads of their rightful owner.

I made certain to get Bambi's address and we later exchanged photos and corresponded occasionally. E-mail now makes it easier, and we have been able to get together with this group and several more of their friends each year we all make it to Grey Cup. It is very clear to me that their friendly attitude toward us enabled us to make the very important discovery of the amount of good times that can be had at Grey Cup, and we are forever grateful to them for that. All of them, with Bambi and Arnie leading the way for us, embody the true spirit of the Canadian Football League fan.

With our new friends – from left – Chris Melin, Rob Gaudreau, Arnie Fearon, Sheila Gaudreau, Corey Edmondson and Audrey Kent

The Minnesotans were finally on a roll. I wandered a bit and managed pictures with fans of nearly every other CFL team. One of these was with a gentleman from Calgary named Walter Jarrett, who would briefly re-enter my Grey Cup life when I recognized him on the street in Ottawa in 2004. I also met, for the first time, Baltimore fan Joe Short and have touched base with him on multiple later occasions. I even, though shyly, joined in on the "Oskee Wee Wee" proclamation of some Hamilton Ti-Cats fans. Fortunately, the words were not too complex for me.

To be honest, the festivities were great, and I had totally forgotten about the Three-Man Band and my earlier request of them. Suddenly, one of the three was at my side, indicating they had indeed spotted Dave Ridgway. Right then, Dave was going up on stage to make a few remarks and I could see him from across the room. The unexpected opportunity, however, made me nervous and I debated whether to approach him. I hesitated briefly, but as my almost-same-surnamed movie hero, Roy "Tin Cup" McAvoy once said, "When a defining moment comes along, you define the moment or it defines you." With these thoughts stumbling through my head, I approached the stage and waited for Dave to finish his business.

The stage was actually a platform, in the middle of the room. Dave came down the stairs and signed an autograph or two. I extended my hand, leaning toward his ear to be heard above the roar of the crowd, and said, "Terry McEvoy. Roseville, Minnesota." He smiled immediately in recognition, and said, "I was just thinking about you." I asked why and he explained he had just visited his sons, Chris and Drew, in Ohio, and had, of course, driven through Minnesota. Dave then mentioned that he had kept my '96 letter in his car, with the intent of getting in touch sometime while passing through the Twin Cities, but had just never had the time.

Dave Ridgway at Grey Cup 1998

Close Encounters of the Rendezvous Kind

My expectations of ever meeting Dave were rightfully pretty small and it was exciting not only to meet him, but also to have him know who I was. We talked for a time more and I introduced Dave to Chris, Corey and our new Edmonton friends and was able to get a decent picture of Dave and I. Knowing I would be back in Regina the next season, Dave took my e-mail address, which I wrote on a U.S. dollar bill. We talked for a while longer and he was on his way. Of course, as soon as Dave left the Edmonton fans, I heard a comment or two about Dave's unfortunate fall in the 1992 Western Division semi-final in Edmonton, when the icy turf cost the Riders the game, but at least they politely waited until he was out of earshot.

Rendezvous began to wind down, and we decided to head back to the motel for a bit. Bidding good-bye to our new friends from Alberta, we pledged to keep in touch and see them at another Grey Cup. I was certain that this would not be our only Grey Cup, and the double dose of good fortune at this party went a long way toward cementing my association with the CFL. I believe I even realized it right at the time.

After a brief nap, we ventured forth for a good steak and then visited a casino for our expected donation. We still weren't aware of all of the Grey Cup party happenings but at least this night we showed a bit more staying power than the previous evening. It had been a good day and even the sleeping bag on the floor was nearly bearable.

Sunday, Game Day, arrived with an unexpected bonus. The weather forecast for the day had significantly improved and a forecast high of 10 degrees was expected. It's a good time to mention that I am not completely lost on the Fahrenheit/Celsius conversion, although I do struggle at high and low temperature ranges. The simple equation of multiplying Celsius by two and adding 30 works wonderfully at 10 degrees Celsius, and I knew we were to be treated to an unseasonable high of 50 degrees Fahrenheit. We came prepared for much worse and were pleased at our good fortune.

There was a shopping centre close to the stadium and we headed there well before game time. A mall kiosk was selling Grey Cup merchandise, and prices were already cut in half, so we all pulled out our plastic. Because I like traditions, I started one by buying myself a cap, and T-shirts for Carson and Connor, and have made those purchases at all eight of the Grey Cups I have attended. I am still surprised that the items were on sale before the game since we have not seen that in subsequent Canadian November visits. The enthusiasm for the game seemed below average that year and perhaps is why prices had been reduced. As I look at my photos from the game, there are a large number of empty seats. Apparently others in addition to the three Americans were just a little staggered by the ticket prices.

With time to spare, we found a sports bar and settled in to watch the Green Bay Packers disappoint Corey and Chris by losing to the Vikings in a 28 – 14 game. We sat, the three of us, at a table for four, and were introduced to a bit of Saskatchewan culture when a young guy from Saskatoon pulled out the fourth chair and pleasantly joined us. It may be just my perception, but the friendliness of this action of just sitting down with strangers is something I've experienced many times since in Canada and it is a welcome relief to our American hesitation. He was fun to talk to and added more than just a bit to our weekend experience. He asked what types of things we had done and we told him we had been able to meet Dave Ridgway the previous day. I swear his eyes widened, as he exclaimed, with real astonishment, "You met Robokicker?!" I never got the fellow's name and often wonder if somehow our paths have crossed again without either of us realizing it.

We had parked between the shopping center and the stadium and walked to the car to dress for the game. The vehicle was packed with boots, coats, mittens and other cold weather attire since we knew that the climate of Winnipeg and Siberia were not far apart. The balmy temperatures allowed us to be comfortable with fewer layers and we were able to be very snug during the game even though the car was still half-full of winter wear.

Our seats were decent, on the west side at about the 30-yard line. Some parachutists were to bring in the game ball, and one of them sailed out of the back of the end zone. Laughingly, we wondered aloud if that misfortune counted as the game's first single. I actually chatted a bit with the gentleman next to me, in a departure from my usual shyness. He was friendly, and very interested to hear we were from Minnesota, remarking he assumed I was Canadian because I knew the words and sang along to *Oh, Canada*. Well, I happen to think it's a great song and am always in my seat when the anthem is sung before a game.

Having been introduced the previous day to the Hamilton fight song, we were quite thrilled to have a Ti-Cat fan just a few rows behind us who enthusiastically slurred it loudly for most of the game. The shouts of "Oskee Wee Wee, Oskee Wa Wa" kept on until he was exhausted, or asked to be calm by his friends — or both.

Corey Edmondson and Chris Melin at GC 1998

Like most Grey Cups games, this one did not disappoint as the Hamilton Tiger Cats and the Calgary Stampeders battled to the wire. Calgary's Mark McLoughlin kicked a 35-yard field goal as time ran out for the Stamps' dramatic 26 – 24 victory. It was a solid game and a great ending for our first Canadian championship visit. Corey, Chris and I left on Monday morning satisfied that we had made a good choice for November recreation.

Our return home was uneventful, but the three of us were captivating storytellers upon our return to our workplace. The chance meeting with the player pictured on my office poster was a tale worth telling to many and I tried to fulfill my responsibility in that regard as best I could. Dave had sent me an e-mail when he returned to Regina and thus the beginnings of a good friendship took root.

I decided a Mark McLoughlin autograph on my Grey Cup program would be a nice item to have. A letter to the

Rider Pride on the American Side

Stampeders found him and he very gracefully obliged my request. So gracefully, in fact, that he was added to my new list of people I had hopes, although unlikely of meeting someday. I would guess I am one of only a few CFL fans who saw Mark kick in college, at a game in Vermillion, South Dakota, in 1987, when he was a South Dakota Coyote.

Attendance at the 1999 Grey Cup game was an impossible task since my daughter Meredith was being married that weekend but I moved on to the upcoming CFL season with an increased appreciation for how interesting this new hobby could be.

Chapter 6

The Internet Intervenes

Since my major field of study at the University of Minnesota was history, I tend to spend time mentally trying to relate current events to their potential historical context. I think a person can realize as they unfold that certain specific events, such as the Kennedy Assassination or the September 11 tragedy, will have a spot in future history books. Other less specific happenings may not be quite as obvious, however. As I think about the numerous technology changes in my lifetime, one in particular jumps out as, at least to me, the most significant in the context of how it impacted my personal history.

As a person in his sixth decade, I have seen a lot of technological improvements. From cordless phones to cell phones, from Pong games to Guitar Hero, from the first colour TV's to the first HD screens, we now have all sorts of everyday items that would have seemed impossible just a few years before their introduction. But for my money, the one single happening that has really changed my life is the widespread usage of the internet.

Despite my career in the technology field, our family was not exactly on the leading edge of learning to use this new tool. My experience was with large mainframe computing languages and the company I worked for was not a leader in any movement to PC usage. We purchased our first home computer in late 1997, and it was then that I discovered the potential wonders of the 'Net.

Almost immediately, an event related to this discovery would come to have a very large and favourable impact on the lives of multiple McEvoys. While stumbling around attempting to create an e-mail account, I happened across a user ID with a name similar to mine.

This was pure circumstance since I had no idea what I

was doing. Blindly moving from screen to screen, I saw some form of TMcEvoy flash quickly past. A listing of user names showed one Terry McEvoy, located in Adelaide, in South Australia. Now, although not completely uncommon, McEvoy is a fairly unique surname, and Terry a mildly rare given name. One of the first e-mails I ever sent was to this newly found, wonderfully named, person.

Imagine an e-mail from Terry McEvoy, addressed to Terry McEvoy, with the subject of the note also Terry McEvoy and perhaps you can realize the surprise this note generated when received halfway around the world. I had no inkling of anything about this person save the name, and eagerly awaited a response, knowing neither age nor gender of the person I was contacting.

A day later, I received a reply from a man living in Henley Beach, South Australia, and a suburb of that state's capital city of Adelaide. Aussie Terry was very responsive to my questions, and we spent the next few months, both still quite shocked, getting to know each other much better. In the days before either of us had digital photography equipment, we traded photos through the mail of ourselves and families. Terry is eight years my junior and it was evident immediately that we shared many common interests, including football, traveling, and early retirement. He and his wife Kerry and their son Aaron had been to the U.S. several times on holiday and had attended more than one NFL game.

As I would come to discover, having the Australian Terry McEvoy as a friend would be the source of some great adventures, many of them football-related, and even the opening of a new world for myself and my family. An immediate benefit in early 1998 was the rapid advancement of my web surfing skills as a result of our new correspondence. It was also easy to put these new skills to use to become a more knowledgeable fan of the Saskatchewan Roughriders.

Discovery of sites devoted to the CFL and its member teams, including the Riders, was not a difficult task. I was able to easily "study up" on the Saskatchewan team and learned many new things about team history and players of years past. Although I will never have even a fraction of the knowledge of my Saskatchewan-born friends, the volumes of information readily available on the internet allow me to have as close to an intelligent conversation about the CFL and the Riders as an

American-born fan is able to.

As 1998 moved toward 1999, work and family obligations, a lot of baseball coaching and other kid activities, (plus a slow dialup connection) limited the time I was able to spend on the internet. My CFL knowledge had certainly increased, but I had not advanced to using the internet, as noted in the previous chapter, to research happenings at an event like Grey Cup. Likewise, I had not discovered, except in passing, any of the numerous "fan" websites.

In early 1999, we decided to accept Terry and Kerry's invitation and travel to Australia to meet them in person. This was a huge decision for us, both financially and emotionally. Airfare for four to Australia is expensive, and we had decided that nothing shorter than a three-week trip made any real sense. Other than trips to Canada, we had not traveled internationally, and felt a certain amount of nervousness in that area also. Finally, only a family with extreme self-confidence would have no worries about meeting literally total strangers halfway around the world, and spending a week with them.

Qualms were cast aside, and we made plans to leave Minnesota on July 29 for our three-week journey. Fitting in our annual Rider game was a concern, since I had graduated to head coach of Carson's baseball team, and could not find a gap in our game schedule allowing for even a long weekend off. It might have been easy to skip the 1999 CFL season, but my renewed CFL interest resulting from the Winnipeg trip, plus an invitation to get together with Dave Ridgway and his family while in Regina, made it important to try to find an alternative. In Minnesota, school is out for a four-day weekend in late October, and we identified an October 24 game against Hamilton as a great compromise.

The trip to Australia was as if a dream had come true. The flight of 16 hours from Los Angeles was ugly, but also a necessary evil. The other difficulty was driving on the "wrong" side but I finally mastered that after a few major scares. We landed in Sydney, and drove all the way to far north Queensland, where we stayed for several days on the beach near Cairns. It was then back to Brisbane, and then a flight to Adelaide to meet the Aussie namesake.

Our hosts were wonderful and it was as if we had known this family all of our lives. To be honest, it was a feeling I have felt only a few other times in life and some of those later involved Saskatchewan football. The bond we felt with Terry and Kerry, through just the commonality of a name, is not unlike the bond I have felt on occasion with strangers linked only by the commonality of being Riders fans. Many of you can undoubtedly relate.

An interesting afternoon was spent attending an Australian Football League match between the hometown Port Adelaide Power and the visiting Sydney Swans. Like my first CFL game, it was an enlightening experience, since the game was completely different in person from what I had seen so many times on television. The field was nearly 200 yards in length and the 18 players on each side seemed intent on maiming one another while trying to get the ball. It's a game where quickness, endurance and athleticism make the difference, and I enjoyed it immensely.

The Adelaide fans were as close to Saskatchewan fans as I have ever seen. Loud, a bit boisterous and fiercely loyal, these people follow the game extremely closely. That evening, we were at a family party at Terry and Kerry's and everyone present knew the winners of each match in the sixteen-team league.

The time in Adelaide passed much too quickly, and after a day in Sydney, we headed home. Terry had mentioned a desire to visit us in Minnesota and wanted very much to visit the Pro Football Hall of Fame in Canton, Ohio. Shortly after we returned, we found he would be coming in March of 2000, but never realized then the adventures he would manufacture once he arrived.

I especially looked forward to our late fall trip to Saskatchewan, since we had not been in the province at that time of year. We left home in the early afternoon on the Thursday preceding the game and drove only about half of the distance, again a departure from our usual. Dave Ridgway had invited us to his home on Friday evening and even came to our downtown hotel to pick us up. It was a good visit, and especially enjoyable for me to see the vast collection of memorabilia from his long career. Another random act of kindness, but we were moving along the path to being friends rather than strangers.

In Saskatchewan, the Roughriders were having a dismal year, the last in then-general manager Al Ford's era. They had a 3 – 6 record after defeating Winnipeg in the Labour Day Classic, but failed to win another game and ended the season at 3 – 15. Any nine-game losing streak has some ugly moments, but I doubt that many that year were much uglier than the Hamilton game we saw on October 24. The Ti-Cats won 42 – 12, in a game actually not nearly as close as even the lopsided score made it appear. The Riders' statistical highlights were a 58-yard Paul McCallum field goal, and a late, meaningless touchdown scored in front of a lot of empty seats. The announced crowd was only a bit more than 18,000, and a number of those faithful found reason to depart the premises prior to the final whistle.

To be honest, this was a painful game to view. I do not claim to know the intricacies of the game of football, but it was easy for even the casual fan to see that the Saskatchewan team was outclassed and overpowered. Like any fan, my hopes for the Roy Shivers/Danny Barrett era were never completely realized, but thinking back to this game always makes me remember the progress the previous Rider regime did make. The true game highlight for me, in fact, was Hamilton linebacker Calvin Tiggle commandeering Gainer's bicycle for a short ride during a timeout. I hoped changes would be made for the 2000 season because this was a game I had not enjoyed viewing at all.

Our drive home on the next day was a bit eerie, as we followed on the radio the unfortunate plight of the airplane carrying golfer Payne Stewart. An apparent loss of cabin pressure killed all aboard, and the pilotless craft veered off course, crashing in South Dakota when its fuel was exhausted. For a time, as we drove from Minot, North Dakota to Bismarck, the reported route of the plane was right in our path.

By late 1999, my Rider-related internet activity had increased and I had discovered a CFL fan site called Total-CFL.com. The webmaster and creator of this site was a man named Brad Lawryk, originally from Regina, who now lives in Williams Lake, British Columbia. I enjoyed the site immensely, and found it an excellent source of CFL news and good-natured fan discussion. Brad clearly was extremely devoted to it, and poured a lot of time into design and extra features such as contests and even a column called "Ask the Pro," where Dave Ridgway answered questions that the rest of us dreamed up.

Rider Pride on the American Side

    Not all of you are likely familiar with internet discussion forums, so a quick primer may be in order. These forums exist for literally any subject matter imaginable, from sports, to arts, to furniture and everything in between. Discussion items, called threads, are initiated by anyone, and other members of the forum can comment on the thread, add information, or seek clarification. In the latter stages of the 1999 CFL season, many of the Rider-themed discussions revolved around the probable and anticipated changing of the guard in the Rider hierarchy.

    On many discussion forums, members can choose to create a nickname, or handle, when they join the group. Since Total-CFL.com was a forum for all teams in the Canadian Football League, the handles were many and varied, often times with a team reference. Brad's, for example, was Legendary Rider Fan, and I became Minnesota Gopher, since both the Riders and the University of Minnesota have furry rodent mascots. As time progressed, it was in a way fascinating to visualize the faces behind the nicknames and try to imagine what type of person really existed behind a given handle.

    In more recent years, I have spent some time on a Rider fan website called Riderfans.com, the proud creation of Shane Chapman of Regina, and also on Riderville.com, the official Saskatchewan Roughriders web site. For those of us without access to Saskatchewan sports reporting, the Riderville videos are in particular a very welcome dose of Saskatchewan football medicine. Both websites are a good way for an out-of-towner to try to keep up with CFL and Saskatchewan Roughrider happenings. The official league website, CFL.ca, is also an excellent source of information and news.

    Despite the wealth of great information on these sites, some at times have a huge downside. Although I believe the internet is by and large a great tool, the anonymity it allows is a frightening enabler for certain types of individuals. Many people do not use or ever refer to their own name and a few use any opportunity to make public display of their prejudices, grudges, and personal agendas and, after Rider losses, frustration to unhealthy extremes. Hiding behind this faceless and nameless existence, a small number of people unfortunately show what sad individuals they really are. Unfortunately, this group seems to get a bit larger with each passing year and I find my time spent reading their deranged

The Internet Intervenes

thoughts decreases proportionally.

It's beyond my comprehension to imagine anonymously blasting a player, coach, or official who will never read the nasty missive anyway. It is impossible to have any respect for people who feel the need to write things they would never be bold enough to say in person. Rest assured that these forums are well moderated by some great people, and the worst of the trash is usually quickly removed.

In person, I've met well over 100 people from these websites, and many have become very good friends. Various Grey Cup web-site functions over the years, both organized and informal, have also helped me to put names with faces. As you might expect, the worst offenders of decency on the discussion forums never appear at any of these gatherings, but I'm guessing their parents do not often let them out of the basement.

Right about the time we went to the Hamilton game, I saw a Rider jersey for sale on the internet and was extremely interested in it. It was advertised as a mint condition, game-worn Saskatchewan road jersey from the early 1980s, having the older-style Saskatchewan "S" logo. Attractive on its own with just that description, but the inclusion of jersey number 36 and the player name panel with "Ridgway" made it for me pretty close to a must-have item. Being a bit slow sometimes, it took me a bit of time to realize that the seller was, in fact, Brad Lawryk, but we were soon able to work out a deal and I "met" Brad for the first time in this business transaction. Dave was very helpful, indicating this very jersey has been worn when he kicked eight field goals in a game for the first time in Ottawa during the 1984 season. It remains my proudest Rider possession and the source of a good story a bit later on.

Our family increased by one on November 27, 1999 when our daughter Meredith married Bill Beardslee. Meredith and Bill had met in Washington, D.C. while attending training as new Foreign Service officers for the State Department. At the time of the wedding, Meredith was assigned to the U.S. Embassy in Haiti and we were not extremely sad to see her leave there to join Bill in Frankfurt, Germany. Since I had missed the 1999 championship game, our new Edmonton friends, Arnie and Bambi, even sent a stack of photos from Grey Cup weekend in Vancouver. Quarterback Danny McManus and his Hamilton Tiger Cats celebrated Meredith's wedding by defeating Calgary in the Grey Cup game that very weekend.

As 1999 came to an end, the Saskatchewan Roughriders announced the hiring of Roy Shivers as the club's new general manager. The man's name rang no bells in my ears, but the cyberspace conversations about him seemed all very positive, and it was a sign of optimism for this fan. In early 2000, Roy announced Danny Barrett as the Riders' new coach and pieces for the new season, the next Next Year, were in place.

The Australian Mr. McEvoy, though, would cause some other football fun before the 2000 CFL season was to begin. He visited in late March, arriving at the end of a uniquely designed route that took him from Adelaide to Los Angeles, and then to North Carolina, where he rented a car and drove to Minnesota. A strange sense of geography or a desire to see the country, or some of both, it would appear.

Our game plan was to visit Canton, Ohio, a long day's drive from Minnesota, then tour the Pro Football Hall of Fame. We set off on a Friday, and reached Canton easily in late afternoon, since Aussie Terry and speed limits had not made acquaintance. The Hall of Fame was interesting, but smaller than we expected, and a full stay lasted only until about noon on Saturday. Terry then expressed a strong desire to see the adjacent field, Fawcett Stadium, from the inside. I thought at first he was joking, but soon realized his determination.

The stadium is south of the Hall of Fame, and, while used for the NFC – AFC Hall of Fame Game each year, is actually a Canton high school field. A school was across from the stadium, opposite the Hall. After determining that the stadium gates were locked, we proceeded into the school. Even though it was Saturday, some type of Girl Scout event was taking place, and we actually rounded up a custodian who had the proper keys we needed.

I didn't know Terry well then, but saw immediately a new side of my Australian friend. His Crocodile Dundee accent became just a bit thicker as the custodian was convinced to open the field and let us stroll around. This naïve American, however, did not realize that this was just the first of several jaunts into locked areas, and was, in fact, only a good warm-up.

Leaving Canton, we drove north to hook up to Interstate 80 in order to return to Minnesota. Terry's mind was working overtime and as we approached our intersection, he informed me that a quick detour to Cleveland would be in order. In rapid succession on the ride home, the two Terrys found themselves inside Jacobs Field, home of the Cleveland Indians, the Cleveland Browns' stadium, Comiskey Park (now U.S. Cellular) in Chicago, and historic Wrigley Field. Remember this was in March, with neither football nor baseball in their season, and I would have to submit these as impressive feats of verbal maneuvering. Great photos were taken in all locales, but the Aussie was just hitting his stride.

At the time, in the spring of 2000, Dennis Green was the coach of the Minnesota Vikings and had groomed a physically imposing, high-potential player from the University of Central Florida as the quarterback heir apparent for the Purple squad. Daunte Culpepper was not yet a local celebrity or really even a household name, but would soon play a role in our next caper, one that even had a CFL connection.

Aussie Terry at Fawcett Stadium, March 2000

Terry decided it would be a great time to meet Coach Green. I tried to explain that such meetings do not happen in the world of the NFL due just to a fan's desire, but he would have no part of it. Again sharpening his accent, he called the Vikings' office and eventually reached, after several false starts, the secretary of the coach. Explaining he was a huge NFL fan direct from Down Under, he requested a meeting with Coach Green, since he, the Aussie, happened to be in the Twin Cities. The poor lady would initially have no part of it, but perseverance prevailed in the end and we were given an appointment to see Coach Green on the following Thursday, three days away. Terry was actually scheduled to leave on Wednesday, but changed his flight for this important audience.

As fate would have it, we decided to attend a Minnesota Timberwolves basketball game on Tuesday, and ran into none other than Daunte Culpepper. The Aussie had never heard of the new quarterback before that day, but certainly approached Daunte as if his biggest fan. Daunte was very friendly, and was amused, as are many, by two guys with the same name and completely different speech patterns. Terry excitedly told our new friend about our appointment with Coach Green, and received a highly raised eyebrow for his troubles.

Thursday arrived, and we drove to the Vikings facility in Eden Prairie, about 20 miles from my home. Presenting ourselves to the receptionist, we mentioned our appointment and were asked to have a seat. Amazingly, she had the same doubting eyebrow flip we had seen from Daunte Culpepper. I really thought the jig was up since her phone call to the inner offices to announce us did not seem to be going well. However, a few minutes later, Dennis Green popped out, introduced himself, and said, "Hey guys, let me show you around!"

The Aussie and former Vikings coach Dennis Green

Many Canadians who follow the CFL would not necessarily think this meeting to be unusual, since the access in the Canadian league to players, coaches and the like is so refreshing available. Rider fans know they can attend nearly any practice and, if they care to, approach their favourite player for an autograph. Not the case in the American world, where I believe it is an accurate statement to say that the average Vikings fan has never seen Vikings players except on television. Our ability to meet Coach Green spoke volumes for Terry's skills of persuasion, but also gave me a new, much better, feeling about the Head Viking.

The facility included a full-size indoor practice field, and Coach Green led us to a small balcony overlooking this. He said he would be back, but needed to watch some free agent tryouts. We watched also from our vantage point, as a receiver or two and a defensive back were put through their paces. Throwing practice balls was none other than Mr. Culpepper, and soon finished, he was walking toward a door right beneath us. Calling loudly, "Daunte, remember us?" Aussie Terry waved at the quarterback. I may be overstating, but in my mind Daunte's look was one of close to sheer disbelief. When he stopped laughing, he came up to see us, and was a great person to talk to.

Coach Green returned, showed us the rest of the facilities and sent us on our way. Yet another random act of kindness from a total stranger, although I'd say this one was a bit Aussie-goaded. By the way, I noted in the newspaper the next day that the Vikings had signed, as a result of the tryout we witnessed, BC Lion defensive back Carl Kidd. Carl would later have the dubious pleasure of hearing the Daunte tale in person.

Terry headed back home, and I was left to marvel at our adventures, gain from the experiences, and get ready for the start of the Roy Shivers era in Saskatchewan Roughrider football.

Chapter 7

"Got Everything You Need?"

The name of Roy Shivers really rang no bells with me when I heard it for the first time. I didn't really know much, relatively speaking, about the Saskatchewan team and knew even less about the CFL's other teams. Somehow, his name associated with the NFL's St. Louis Cardinals did sound vaguely familiar, but I could not mentally establish exactly where this distant association initiated. But a person doesn't need to attend too many games like the 1999 Hamilton nightmare to realize that changes are both overdue and readily accepted. It was thus very easy to look forward to our summer trip in 2000.

Early in that year, I had another rare Saskatchewan contact locally. I was having some medical tests, and was sent to a large hospital in Minneapolis for an MRI. When the technician entered the room to explain the procedure, some small talk ensued.

At the time, the Riders sometimes sent injured players to Edmonton for MRI exams due to the wait time in Regina. I mentioned this in passing to the technician, and he told me, with an incredulous laugh, that he in fact was from Regina. The lack of job opportunities in his field at home had sent him to Minnesota. He recounted a story of when "Mr. Ridgway" had spoken at his high school, and told me the name of his uncle, who worked at SaskTel, as Dave did at the time. I later emailed Dave with the name of the uncle, and he knew the man well. We shared a good cyberspace laugh about the coincidence.

The Shivers/Barrett regime had a rough and rocky start in the 2000 season. The team lost its first three contests, before tying Calgary in a 52 – 52 overtime shootout on July 28. Any potential momentum from that game disappeared when the Riders were thumped 62 – 7 the next week in Montreal. We were hoping to see some forward progress in the game we

"Got Everything You Need?"

planned to attend, the Hamilton matchup on August 11.

Once again, we were swinging through Regina on our way to the Rockies. In 2000, we planned a camping vacation, a manner of leisure we had often chosen with Chris and Meredith but had somewhat abandoned with Carson and Connor. The plan was to attend the Hamilton game and then camp in the Canadian mountain parks while heading toward Seattle to visit my aunt and cousins.

We arrived in Regina on the evening of the 9th, and made plans to attend the Rider practice on the day before the game. It would be our first ever time at a Rider practice, simply because I just had never figured out that plain old fans can, and are even encouraged, to attend the team's workouts. Sometimes I just miss the obvious, and the ability to attend practice was something I just never realized we could do. In my defense, it's such a foreign concept in the States that it never crossed my mind.

The four of us walked out onto the Taylor Field sidelines just as the players were heading out of the locker room onto the field. I think the entire family was a bit nervous, hoping we had not misunderstood, but we quickly saw other fans present and felt better. Maura and I thought it would be fun to meet R-Kal Truluck, and thank him in person for the autographed items, but I couldn't spot his number. Needing some help, I wasn't sure just who to ask, but then I was suddenly saved by the internet.

Standing right near us was a jersey number and face whom I recognized from my Rider web surfing. I couldn't remember the player's first name, but knew he was a first round draft pick from the University of British Columbia, and hoped that would be sufficient to make acquaintance. Trembling just a bit, I walked up and introduced myself to a very pleasant fellow who identified himself as Tyson St. James.

He explained R-Kal was not in Regina that day, due to a family matter, but promised to pass on our thanks. We had a nice conversation for a few minutes, and he happily posed for a photo with me, the first of very many mementos from Taylor Field practices. I'm sure Tyson never realized that he was a giant icebreaker for us at Rider practices and we will always recall warmly his friendly manner. From that day forward, I always tried to make sure I touched base with him, even when he later played with Winnipeg and still hear from him occasionally today.

After Tyson left, I realized Roy Shivers had walked out onto the field and was standing just a few feet away. So, I gathered up the entire McEvoy group, and we walked over and introduced ourselves. Like most people we meet even to this day, Roy was more than a little surprised that a Minnesota family drove to Saskatchewan to attend football games, and he asked several questions about our CFL history. Right from the start he was easy to talk to, and stopped by a couple of additional times while we were still hanging around.

A good man, Tyson St. James

The last time he came over, he uttered a phrase I remember well because he's repeated it every time I've seen him since. He said, "Got everything you need?" I have come over the years to find that this is a sincere query from him, and occasionally I will even take him up on it. This first time was one of those times and I asked if I could send up the photos we had been taking to get them autographed. He indicated he would take care of it and I had Maura take my picture with the general manager also.

Actually, it became a photographic frenzy of sorts as kicker Paul McCallum and quarterback Henry Burris also joined in the fun. Paul commented on my NFL Europe shirt from the Frankfurt Galaxy, as he had played in that league, and I explained my daughter lived there and had sent it to me. Henry was a gentleman. He was great with Carson and Connor, and one of the players they always remember.

Given what happened, or didn't happen, with Burris in

the months before the 2005 season, as he spurned the Riders' offer and signed with Calgary, some Rider fans reading the preceding paragraph likely view me as a traitor. My response is that Rider football is important to me, but not at the expense of normal decency. It's important for me to judge people I come in contact with by their actions toward me and Henry Burris that day was a person who treated our family well.

My first impression of him stays with me to this day. I certainly wished the Riders had signed him back in 2005, but that didn't happen and for me it did not remove the impressions he had made on that day in 2000. It's not necessary to hate the other teams' players to be a Rider fan, I hope.

Connor with Henry Burris, August 2000

I had recently read Dave Ridgway's book, *Robokicker*, and really enjoyed the portrayals Dave did in it of a number of friends, teammates and the like. When we left Henry, I had the first of what would become several encounters with some of those characters — in this case, Norm Fong, the Riders' legendary equipment manager. Norm is a pleasant, but businesslike, guy and it helped the conversation when I mentioned I knew Dave. He was next in line for a photo opportunity and it's one of my favourites. I would venture to guess that few Rider fans have an autographed Norm Fong picture.

The Riders were about done for the day, and the TiCats from Hamilton were on the field. I had another autograph score to settle so we stayed around for a bit. During the Hamilton game we had attended in 1999, I had taken a photo of TiCat

Rider Pride on the American Side

kicker Paul Osbaldiston kicking a field goal. It was not a great picture, but I had it enlarged and sent it to the TiCat office, asking for an autograph. In Dave's retelling from *Robokicker,* Paul had returned at game's end the ball used for The Kick to Dave, and that gesture was very meaningful to the Rider kicker on that November day in 1989. I had also thought it was a neat thing for Osbaldiston to do, and that's possibly why I had chosen him as an autograph victim. He returned my photo with a couple of extra autographed items early in 2000, and I wanted to find him and say an appropriate Thank You.

Paul was not to be found, but I did meet a giant guy named Joe Montford in the process, and suddenly found myself right in the path of Danny McManus, the Hamilton quarterback. Again the internet action helped, for I recognized him immediately and introduced myself, saying I had been at the 1998 Grey Cup and felt it was unfortunate one team had to lose such a good football game. Danny was very friendly, amused by the Minnesota angle and happily posed for yet another soon-to-be autographed picture.

As he walked away, he said something that is still as fresh in my mind as Roy's earlier remark. He shook my hand and said, "Thank you for supporting the Canadian Football League." I've had the good fortune to cross paths with Danny at multiple Grey Cups since and, to tell the truth, have been just thrilled he has actually remembered me from that day in Regina in 2000. When I try to explain to Minnesotans why the McEvoys enjoy the CFL the way we do, the McManus encounter is usually a necessary ingredient.

By the way, I never have caught up to Paul Osbaldiston, also just missing him by a few minutes at a Grey Cup party. However, the way my CFL life tends to work makes me fairly sure we'll meet some day. I also foolishly failed to meet then-Hamilton coach Ron Lancaster, the greatest Rider quarterback of them all, but later was able to rectify that omission.

If forced to identify a single hour in the past 15 seasons of football trips to Regina that was the most significant to helping create permanent fan status, that hour on Aug. 10, 2000, was it. We saw in person the fan friendliness of the Saskatchewan Roughriders and the league itself. We met players on the field for the very first time and began what has become a good relationship with Roy Shivers. Like the

"Got Everything You Need?"

accidental meeting in Winnipeg with Dave Ridgway, it was another key event in our transformation to CFL fans, and seemed so even right at the time.

Dave Ridgway's sons Chris and Drew were in Regina visiting and Dave and I made arrangements to meet for pizza with the four boys, plus Dave's two stepsons, Bret and Derek. All six of the boys were within about three years of each other, and had a great time while Dave, Maura, and I had a good visit. My recently purchased game worn number 36 jersey was in the car and Dave obliged with a personalized autograph after dinner. We made plans with Dave to meet after the game the next day and went back to the motel, unaware there would be yet one more significant meeting on this trip.

Game Day was a Friday and we needed a way to keep busy before the evening kickoff. I think there are many things to do in Regina, but this was our seventh trip and the family fun well was getting a bit dry. We had seen somewhere that the Regina *Leader-Post*, the city's newspaper, offered tours and had called to set one up. It wasn't quite a desperation move to find something to do, but certainly came close.

Arriving at the newspaper's offices on Victoria and Park, we were greeted by one Will Chabun, writer and tour guide extraordinaire. Like many we meet, he was very interested in our Minnesota background and told stories of baseball in the Metrodome and listening to Minnesota Public Radio. It was actually a pretty interesting tour, but in meeting Will we found a kindred spirit, a man who is curious about nearly all things and passionate about more than a few, and a new Regina friend. He even gave us a suggestion to visit Ipsco Park, and we had a very pleasant afternoon there.

In the game that evening, Henry Burris passed for 458 yards in a losing effort, as Paul Osbaldiston's five field goals were more than the difference in a 29 – 23 TiCat win. The first half in particular was exciting to watch, but the Riders were outscored 16 – 3 in a listless second half.

We returned to our motel and a message from Dave indicating his boys were beat and were not good candidates for further socializing. Our boys were very tired too, and it was a good decision. I had bought some beer for the occasion and made a young hotel desk clerk very happy when we checked out the next morning by presenting a 12-pack to him.

We enjoyed our camping excursion immensely, had a

nice Seattle visit with the relatives and then spent a few days camping on the Pacific Ocean at the mouth of the Columbia River. Then it was back home to school and work, and at the time I was unaware a second trip to Regina that fall was in the making.

In the fall of 2000, the Saskatchewan Roughrider Plaza of Honour Banquet was welcoming three new members – Bruce Cowie, Dave Ridgway, and Cleveland Vann. Maura and I had decided to send Dave a small gift in honour of his induction, so she completed a stylized drawing of his field goal motion superimposed on the Regina skyline. Wanting to get it up there in plenty of time for the October 20 induction date, we mailed it about the 10th of that month. Thus began another learning experience, this one in a better understanding of the necessary lead-time in mailing items between Minnesota and Regina.

After a week or so had passed, I contacted Dave to let him know a package was on the way and wondering if it had possibly arrived. It had not; I mentioned I wished I was coming up for the induction and actually kicked myself for not deciding earlier to go. I was very busy at work right then and didn't want to take any more time off, but finally decided just a few days before to at least get up to Regina for the game.

This became the first of only three Regina trips I have made solo. The game was Sunday, so I drove up on Saturday, making very good time and arriving at Taylor Field in time to pick up the game tickets I had ordered. My new friend Will Chabun had agreed to go to the game with me and I looked forward to getting to know him a bit better.

Dave had invited me to a Saturday night party at his house; it was very interesting to meet several of his friends whom I would see in Calgary three years later, and even recognize a face or two from Dave's book. I also was able to meet Dave's brother Neil, the only person who has ever recognized my St. Kilda Football Club jacket as one from an Aussie Rules team

I was certain the package would have arrived by then, but it had not. It finally showed up many days later, 26 days after I had mailed it. Ironically, when I purchased a Rider share in 2005, the share itself also took exactly 26 days, via expedited mail, to get from Regina to Minnesota. That must be the delivery standard, I would have to speculate.

To give equal play to decent postal service, I had

"Got Everything You Need?"

actually taken Roy Shivers up on his August offer, and sent a packet of 8x10 photos up for autographs. I received them back very promptly and while in Regina for this second trip, penned a thank you note to Roy for this favour and mailed it from the hotel. A couple of weeks later, I received a neat letter from Roy, thanking me for thanking him and for being a long-distance fan. I was tempted to write back thanking him for thanking me to see if we could keep the chain going, but thought better of it.

Will picked me up on Sunday and we headed for Taylor Field. The previous season, the family had also attended the Plaza of Honour game, and then the game program had cover photos of the inductees. Life is very logical to me at times, and I just assumed the October 22, 2000 program would have Dave and the other two inductees on the cover. Since we were just a bit late, I hurriedly purchased three of them as we entered Taylor Field, figuring I could have Dave autograph them later. Somewhere around the house I have three programs with Eric Guliford on the cover, since my logical thought process is evidently not quite up to Rider standards.

Everyone loves the Riders, October 2000

Montreal would make the Grey Cup in 2000, and played like it that day. The final was 39 – 22 for the Alouettes, in a game where the Riders had only 37 rushing yards as they played catch up all afternoon. The team would win only once more in 2000, finishing 5 – 12 – 1 and out of the playoff hunt. However, in my judgment there had been improvements over the previous year and I began the thought process on the drive home that would allow me to continue attending more than a single game per season.

Chapter 8

Calgrya

After taking 1999 off, Chris and Corey had no hesitations about heading to Grey Cup weekend once again. The championship weekend at the end of the 2000 season was scheduled to be in Calgary, a much longer drive from our world than Winnipeg had been in 1998. After a very brief discussion, we decided to fly, since Calgary was two very long days of potentially hazardous early winter driving from here in the Twin Cities. As a group of three, we were not slow learners and resolved to improve our hotel locale from the blunder we had made by staying in extreme suburban Winnipeg. With a three-way split of the room and a favourable rate of exchange, we reserved a spot right in the thick of the downtown events and easily purchased game tickets right on the internet.

Exciting things were planned. The group from Total-CFL.com had organized a party for Friday night and attendance would afford the opportunity to meet literally dozens of people whose existence to that point was simply an internet handle. The event, called "Meet and Greet," was set up for the party room in the condo building where one of the regulars lived. Brad Lawryk and others had lined up sponsors, discounted beer and door prizes for a very reasonable admission fee. As I had done with Rendezvous in 1998, I popped for the tickets so Chris and Corey would feel like ingrates unless they attended.

As our departure date approached, the three travelers again became curiosity items in the workplace. I was by then in a different area of the company, but still interacted quite a bit with Chris and Corey's group, and a work-related social event right before we left almost turned into a game of Twenty Questions about our trip. Winnipeg was one thing, but the idea of going to far-off Calgary for a strange football game was nearly beyond the comprehension of the Minneapolis masses.

Rider Pride on the American Side

It remains a perception I have finally stopped trying to deal with. Americans on average know little about Canada, and even the staunchest sports fans know virtually nothing about the Canadian Football League. That's the way it is and my ability to influence change is limited. It is pretty disappointing, though, to discover that many people down here couldn't find Saskatchewan on a map even if I spotted them Alberta and Manitoba.

I also heard from Aussie Terry shortly before we left. He told an interesting story, with a Saskatchewan twist. Terry was on a business trip to Tatarestan, a former Soviet republic, and was in the airport in Frankfurt, Germany between planes. He wandered into the bar and took up a bit of conversation with the man on the adjacent stool. As they exchanged a bit of information about themselves, Terry was surprised to hear that this gentleman, one Bill Donison, was Canadian and in fact lived in Regina. Terry said his own mention of the Roughriders nearly made his new Canadian acquaintance fall off his seat.

Bill was also traveling on business, although not just some everyday type of occupation. He owned elk back in Saskatchewan and was traveling to sell elk semen in Eastern Europe. Australians seem to love to hang nicknames on everyone and Terry's new friend, when he called me to relate the story, had been dubbed "The Elk Semen Man." An interesting story, but little did I know what turns it would take in the following years. Terry mailed me a business card from Bill, and I pledged to try to contact the Reginan in the next football season.

Less than two weeks before Grey Cup, my world turned a bit upside down. My mother, who was 86 and lived about a mile from us, was diagnosed with throat cancer. Our initial instructions from the physician indicated it was reasonably advanced and he recommended she not be left alone for any length of time. With a job, two fairly young children and no siblings in town, I had my work cut out and a football trip to Calgary seemed pretty inappropriate.

At this time, my brother Bob was living in New York, having stayed in Seattle for just a few years in the early 1990's. He immediately headed home upon hearing the news, and we worked together plotting out a strategy. Since he is also a physician, he understood the situation much better than I, and was able to better explain it to our mother. They both agreed I should go to Calgary and Bob stayed for the long weekend to allow me to attend Grey Cup.

A direct flight is in place to Calgary from Minneapolis and it was an easy trip. We checked in to our hotel, went for a walk, and had a late lunch. I was really looking forward to the Total-CFL party, and Chris and Corey were both climbing on the bandwagon also. It looked like the light rail was our best bet to get there, so we hopped on and were impressed. Although we now have a similar transportation system from the Minneapolis – St. Paul International Airport, we did not in 2000, and enjoyed the comfort and relative convenience of Calgary's C-Train system.

We may have disembarked on the incorrect stop, for our destination was quite a long walk. Brad Lawryk was greeting people at the door; it was actually pretty exciting to meet him, and I found that same feeling a few dozen more times that evening. It was a good-sized room, but eventually was quite crowded as CFL fans from across Canada gathered to begin the Grey Cup weekend.

The beer was flowing, amid shouts of introduction and laughter. Unlike our Rendezvous experience in 1998, we blended in easily and mixed well. Corey and Chris were not much into the website, so it likely wasn't quite as exciting for them to meet total strangers, but I was having the time of my life. It's really hard to estimate, but I would guess I met at least 50 people that evening whom I still see, some in Regina, but many more just at Grey Cup. If there is such a malady, I may have been suffering from Introduction Overload.

The concept of internet "handles," or nicknames, is quite interesting to me. As I mentioned, mine is Minnesota Gopher and is arguably logical. Many of the people I met that night had equally logically and obvious ones, such as Born CFL, the lanky Ken Smith from Calgary, and Lady In Red, his always enthusiastic wife Jacky. Others in this category also included Eskinator, Brian Edwards from Edmonton and GITC (for Green Is the Colour), Rider fan Bill Wakefield.

A number of fans have chosen some variation of their own name. My good friend Jeff Banow is Mr. Jeph, a university carryover, and his buddy Marty Neumeier, also a great friend of mine, clearly spent days in deep thought to come up with the complicated Martyneu as his handle.

Some other handles were not quite as clear, but made a

bit more sense with just a little bit of additional information. Linda Edwards, Brian's wife, is True 42, a reference to her admiration of the playing days of former Eskimo great Dan Kepley. Linda's dad, I.H. (Woody) Wood, by the way, played for the Regina Roughriders in the 1930s, and was considered a giant of those times at 250 pounds. She is thus more of a Rider fan deep inside than Brian would care to admit.

A friend whom I met later, Jason Isaac, is Green Viking, a combo of his allegiance to both the Riders and my hometown Vikings. One that confused me for quite some time is The Hold, used by Gerard Stang of Calgary. I finally found out it is an attempt to give Glen Suitor, the holder for The Kick, a bit of well-deserved credit.

Still another category includes handles that must be explained in detail to understand. A fellow I met that evening in Calgary was Dale Kennedy from Prince George, B.C. His handle is Hambone and he is well known by it. I have no clue whatsoever what it means for Dale, but it doesn't matter anyway. I am just always happy to run into Dale at Grey Cup – he's been at about 25 consecutive games and I'm proud to say I'm seen him at nearly every one I've attended since we met.

Not everyone at the Calgary party, of course, was an internet junkie with a handle. Many of the folks I met were just good CFL fans, present to have a fun time, and usually connected in some way to someone with a Total-CFL association. A very nice lady was having a great time applying temporary CFL tattoos to anyone who would stand still, and she ended up being Rande Allison, Jacky Smith's sister. My friend Chris took a great shot of Rande giving Minnesota Gopher a big kiss on the cheek to go with his tattoo and I even had presence of mind to get her address. This picture became yet another of my autographed collection and Rande was just a great sport about it. Of course, as things happen, we'd meet again, and I would be able to at least partially repay the favour.

Although I think handles are OK, as I have noted, I dislike the anonymous nature of the internet. Handles are obviously a small part of that nature. I try always to introduce myself by name and believe as many people know me as Terry from Minnesota as know me as Minnesota Gopher. Even I have to admit, however, it is pretty hilarious to be involved in a conversation where handles are used exclusively. In addition, a few people have given names that don't easily lend themselves to simple pronunciation and, on occasion, a handle can be helpful. Far and away the league leader in this category is Govind Achyuthan, much more commonly known as CRF, for Calgary Rider Fan.

The gourmet item of the Total-CFL evening was Rattlesnake Chili. A picture of the main ingredient in better days had been posted on the website right before the party, and I was, amazingly, not at all attracted to chili that evening. Chris and Corey had some, though, and gave thumbs up to the dish.

Another Rider fan I met for the first time that evening was Dave Fulton, originally from Regina, but living and working in Toronto. Dave was with his dad, Tom, and his brother, Kevin – I've since met the third Fulton, oldest brother Warren, but don't believe he was with them that night. Tom Fulton, who lives in Regina, seemed to be about the same age as Aussie Terry's depiction of the Elk Semen Man, and I took the opportunity to tell the story to the Fulton group in hopes Tom might know of Bill Donison. I even had Bill's business card with me, and none of the Fulton clan could place the Albert Street address. I actually asked a few other Reginans about the Elk Man, but no one had any knowledge of him. I finally gave up.

Dave and Tom Fulton

In retrospect, that was one great party. If I still needed one more little nudge to go over the CFL edge, this was probably it. It certainly rates in the Top Five of any non-family celebrations I have ever attended and was the basis for some really fine friendships and a host of casual, but important, acquaintances. I was hoping it would last forever.

All good things come to an end, however, and Chris, Corey and I tumbled outside to attack the rest of the evening. I wanted to take a cab back to the centre of the city, but my friends convinced me that the walk would be good for all of us. Possibly I should have had some chili since I may have had a bit more beer than I am accustomed to consuming. The brisk walk revived me and we were ready to head for the legendary Spirit of Edmonton Party.

On occasion, I have tried to explain Grey Cup parties to various Minnesotans. Even though knowledge of the Canadian Football League is pretty limited hereabouts, the name of the championship game has much better name recognition. To say "We're going to Calgary for the Grey Cup game" will mystify more sport fans here about location than about the event itself. However, I'm usually lost for a meaningful description of the parties themselves, for a couple of reasons.

Total-CFL.com guys Brian Edwards, Martin Skrt, and Scott Oberg

First, similar parties may happen here, but if they do, I'm about thirty years removed from attending them and thus have no comparative event to associate my description with. But, more importantly, I think these parties are largely uniquely Canadian, and thus the average American may not exactly understand. There are several annual parties and hospitality rooms at Grey Cups and all are enjoyable. However,

I'd not be doing justice to the fine people of Edmonton if I failed to rank their party right at the top of the list.

On this night in 2000, we were fortunate and were admitted to the Spirit of Edmonton room after only a short wait. This party, typically held (at least in my experience) in the ballroom of the largest downtown hotel, can be very difficult to get into. There is even an unconfirmed rumour that Dave Fulton, along with brothers Warren and Kevin, once bypassed the admission line by posing as members of the Rider Pep Band. It's hard to exactly pinpoint the Spirit's extreme attraction, but good music, lots of people and free admission certainly all help. I particularly enjoy Spirit of Edmonton because it's the place where I am most likely to renew old acquaintances on Grey Cup weekend.

Corey, Chris and I learned immediately that the American social skills we had honed in drinking establishments at home did not exactly carry over at Grey Cup parties. In our experience, a large party in a hotel would mean a couple of things – first, the hotel sells all of the drinks and makes all the drink money. Secondly, a person goes up to the bar, or beckons a wait staff person, and orders a drink mixed by the bartender. Not the case at parties like the Spirit of Edmonton, where volunteers donate their time in shifts to help, the drinks themselves appear to be separate from the hotel and you are on your own for mixing your beverage.

It's actually a pretty simple process once we understood it – buy some drink tickets, stand in a usually long line, order the type of spirits you might prefer, take your glass after a shot is poured into it and move to a separate table where various types of mixes reside. It's a routine that is both efficient and orderly most times. We understood it even better once we figured out why everyone talked about Rye — it's much more commonly called bourbon or sometimes even just whiskey in our world. We thought everyone knew that Rye is a dark brown bread.

The three of us saw a number of people from the Total-CFL party and met a few new people also. People often post photos on internet sites, and I actually walked up to a few fans I recognized exclusively from seeing their photo on the 'Net. We were on the hunt for our 1998 friends from Edmonton, but in a loud, crowded, dimly lit room were not having much luck. Corey had a cell phone and we had Arnie's number; when

Arnie answered we realized they were all of about 20 feet away. Chris and I never found out what Corey's roaming charges were for the trip, but that call likely figured out to about 10 cents per foot. We were happy to reunite with our 1998 friends and met a few more of their group also.

Another interesting aspect of Grey Cup events is the fascinating collection, year after year, of regulars whom one sees, even though many of them might be described as slightly "irregular." I've observed the Booze Brothers, a group of Jake and Elwood clones, complete with baggy dark suits and the required shades. There's a Blue Bomber group wearing matching jerseys noting the various possible mixes that can combine with Rye. The Box J Boys, kilts and all, bring a little bit of Ivor Wynne Stadium in Hamilton with them each trip. The Baltimore Stallion fans are always around and I've met Sacramento Gold Miner followers also. Each Grey Cup I find myself wondering who is protecting Winnipeg, since the entire Police Department appears to be in their famous bagpipe group.

Dance teams from the various CFL cities and fun groups like the Saskatchewan Roughrider Pep Band are also constantly in demand and make multiple appearances each day at the various venues. These groups are enjoyable to see and hear and the dance teams always get a large dose of male attention. Once in a while, it can almost be too much of a good thing – in Ottawa in 2004, our schedule seemed to be just a few minutes ahead of the Rider Pep Band, and I believe we heard their gig seven times. I was nearly certain they were following us.

This night in Calgary we actually made it to last call, and headed back to our hotel, which was very close. This year, we had arranged for a rollaway, and the sleeping arrangements were much better than in Winnipeg two years before. On Saturday, the Grey Cup Parade went right by our hotel and we enjoyed the floats, marching bands, and celebrities. One convertible contained Michael Lysko, the new CFL commissioner, a man whose tenure would be short-lived and whose name I had completely forgotten. In another car rode Dave Dickenson, the Calgary quarterback, who had been named the league's Most Outstanding Player. I was a bit surprised when I saw him close-up, since I thought he looked smaller in person than the man I was expecting.

Calgrya

After the parade, we took the train out to the stadium for some shopping and to scout out our route for getting to the game the next day. A brief rest was then in order and, as evening approached, we decided to head to the Riders' hospitality room.

The Roughrider Pep Band with that Ryder Pride

On occasion, some CFL fans have been known to accuse the Edmonton Eskimos of being in violation of the league's salary cap. A parallel possibly also exists for the venues for Grey Cup parties – the Eskimos generally have the most elaborate. At times the Riders seem to stay within the Venue Cap, ending up with a location that provides a more unique experience. I felt this might was the case at the 2000 Grey Cup.

Riderville was well away from downtown, although still on the rail system. The evening was chilly and a bitter breeze accompanied us as we walked to the party from our stop. The establishment was a hall of some type and the décor could best be described as Spartan. Please don't misunderstand – it was fine, but a bit of a culture shock from the Edmonton opulence. We probably rushed our arrival time a bit also, since there were not yet many partygoers in attendance. I had no trouble staying, but Chris and Corey were more interested in heading back downtown, which we did after only a short visit.

Rider Pride on the American Side

Even then, we knew the Spirit of Edmonton Party could be very difficult to get into. Lineups and long waits are not uncommon even early in the evening as the demand for partying exceeds the supply of space. This night our position in the line was at least inside the building, but it took well over an hour to snake our way along with the queue and get inside the party itself. We had learned from the previous evening's Arnie and Bambi Search and were able to find them immediately. It was a pleasant evening with our new friends, and many people we had met the previous night came by also.

The three Minnesotans had discussed figuring out a way to go to Banff for a quick visit on Sunday before the game. We even tried to rent a car, but with the enormous influx of visitors that weekend, the Calgary car cupboard was bare. Arnie heard us discussing this, and offered to let us borrow his car the next day, a great gesture on his part. We finally decided not to attempt it since car trouble or other delays might interfere with the game. Now I wish we would have taken the leap, but hindsight is always pretty wonderful in that way.

Sunday morning and Game Day found us on the rail system, riding east in search of breakfast. We eventually found a shopping center, had breakfast and returned downtown to get prepared for the 4:00 PM game. Hopping on the C-Train, we arrived early and walked around the outside of the stadium before entering. The interior halls were jammed and progress to our seats was slow. We worked through the traffic and eventually settled in at our $177.70 seats, near the top at about the 10-yard line. It was to be an interesting next three hours, for multiple reasons.

We had immediate concern about the guy sitting directly behind me. He was already wobbly and on the path to potential obnoxiousness. However, as had happened with our Hamilton neighbour in Winnipeg, the fellow's companions intervened and eventually hauled him away for good. I was having a nice ongoing chat with the lady sitting next to me, since the first half was a bit of a snoozer, with BC leading Montreal 12 – 3 at the break.

About the end of the first quarter, we were in for a treat due to our Canadian TV famine status. Molson Beer had developed a great ad campaign based on a character named Joe Canadian, played by actor Jeff Douglas. "The Rant" as Joe's impassioned patriotic speech was called, was performed

Calgrya

live at McMahon Stadium and we loved it. It was the first time I had heard it in its entirety, and I still think it is in my Top 10 all-time of TV ads. It is still out on the internet, and much fun to listen to occasionally.

One handicap I always experience in Canada is my own cluelessness in various conversations involving Canadian television. It's not quite a mutual difficulty, since a decent amount of U.S. programming is shown in Canada and many of my Canadian friends know a lot more about American TV than I do. But since we have no Canadian broadcasts here in Minnesota, and do not even have CFL coverage, I'm constantly explaining I have just recently been able to see Saskatchewan-made sitcom program *Corner Gas* and would barely know CBC's Brian Williams from TSN's Dave Randorf.

It's thus been necessary to develop a Dumb American personification to be used to avoid the shame and embarrassment of my TV shortcomings. Most people are somewhat understanding. One day at Taylor Field I was standing on the sidelines when a gentleman who looked only vaguely familiar came up and stood beside me. We were making small talk and I had no real idea who he was. Finally, I decided if I introduced myself, I could find out, and was pleased to meet former player, former broadcaster, and recycled player Sean Millington.

Back in Calgary, halftime brought us the Guess Who, a band I can identify with. A song and dance show on the field displayed the wonders of the host city, and was well done, but did have a slight issue as shown in the photo below.

Nevertheless, a great halftime show in 2000

Rider Pride on the American Side

The family sitting beside us had rotated their seats; the lady I had been chatting with had switched seats with her husband for the second half. Being sometimes a bit paranoid, I hoped I hadn't done anything to offend her, but came to find the gentleman was possibly a bit curious about the gray-haired Minnesotan.

His name was Peter Lunde, a Calgary resident originally from Milestone, Saskatchewan. He seemed a bit pleased that I knew where Milestone was, and I even remembered Maura and I had stopped there for gas in 1972. It ends up that Peter is the cousin of Rod Pedersen, the Riders' fine radio voice, which was interesting, but is not the reason I remember Peter with a smile whenever I tell the tale of what he unconsciously did to help me along in my Saskatchewan journeys.

Peter, you see, explained to me that I did not correctly pronounce "Saskatchewan." Like every American, and a lot of Canadians, I tended to utter "SASK KATCH A WAN", pretty much like it would appear from the spelling. I received, however, a quick lesson from my new friend on a better method, roughly "SAS KATCH aWUN," with the final "a" a bit slurred and "WUN" or even "ONE" at the end. The cadence was as important as the sounds, with Peter's version spoken just a bit more quickly toward the end of the word.

Why is this significant? Well, it's probably a bit vain, but I really pride myself now in fitting in while I'm in Canada. It's important to me because I am aware that some Americans have left bad impressions in our northern neighbour, and I do not care to be one of those. To this day, I believe the lesson on pronunciation has helped me since many people I meet just assume I'm Canadian, or at least a native now living in the States. It's a subtle thing, and I may just be imagining it, but the story of Peter Lunde and pronunciation often leads to fun conversations about other words said differently in our two lands. A year or two later, it was great to meet Rod Pedersen for the first time and have him know vaguely who I was from Peter's description. Peter remains a guy who I will look up again some day.

Much like its 2005 counterpart, the 2000 Grey cup game heated up in the second half, especially in the final quarter. British Columbia held a slim 12 – 10 lead as the fourth quarter began, but the offences began to motor, and when Lui Passaglia, the 25-year BC vet playing in his last game, kicked a field goal with 1:25 left, BC led the Alouettes 28 – 20. Montreal was not done, as Anthony Calvillo drove his team to a score, completing a 59-yard TD to Ben Cahoon with 44 seconds to go. A two-point conversion attempt right in front of us barely missed, and the Lions held on for a 28 – 26 win. The remarkable Passaglia career ended on a high note, and he certainly deserved it.

After the Lions were awarded the Grey Cup, we joined the mad scramble for the train, and returned to our hotel. It was a great weekend, a welcome diversion from my Minnesota responsibilities, and perhaps the last step on my path to full conversion to the gospel of the Canadian Football League.

Chapter 9

Season Tickets

Charles Dickens wrote in the opening line of *Tale of Two Cities,* "It was the best of times, it was the worst of times," as he began a tale about the French Revolution. From my perspective, he might as well have been describing the Year of Our Lord 2001 for the McEvoy family.

Mother weakened gradually, having decided that the invasive treatment needed for her disease made no sense at her age. She was pretty calm about it and her only request, repeated throughout her life, was to avoid a nursing home at all costs. My brother Bob and I did our best, staying with her virtually every night for over four months. Bob took on the lion's share of the task, shuttling back and forth from New York a number of times. It was hard, but that's what sons are for. With a bit of hospice help, we were able to grant our mother's request and she stayed home nearly to the end before being hospitalized. She died on March 30, 2001.

Life slowly returned to some level of normalcy, as we worked on the tasks associated with estate settlement and vacating a condominium. There wasn't much time or reason to think about Canadian football, and I did not. In Saskatchewan, however, things were happening quickly. High-potential quarterback Henry Burris had signed with the NFL's Green Bay Packers, leaving a hole at the Rider pivot position. Marvin Graves, who had started two games in 2000, was the leading replacement candidate, backed up by rookies Kevin Glenn of Illinois State and Keith Smith of Arizona.

The Rider defense appeared improved, with new names like Eddie Davis and Shonte Peoples leading the way. Scott Schultz, a Canadian defensive lineman from the University of North Dakota, was Saskatchewan's first pick in the Canadian draft, but initially signed with the San Diego Chargers and did not make his Rider debut until halfway through the 2001 season. The team appeared improved, but the departure of Burris left a certain legitimate amount of uncertainty.

As things settled down in our household, a slightly radical idea began fermenting in my balding head. Things done out of the mainstream fascinate me and at work I was always judged to be better than the average bear at the overworked axiom of "Thinking Outside the Box." The Saskatchewan Roughriders, the Canadian Football League and the City of Regina had become important, and in my mind deserved a larger commitment. Thus, the idea of being a long-distance Rider season-ticket holder was born.

We certainly had no plans to dramatically increase our trips to Regina. Tickets were plentiful and we could easily have stayed on the pay as you go plan. But idealism can be a positive trait and, as a family, we saw the opportunity to give a bit back in return for the several years of good times we'd experienced in the Queen City. After ordering two adult and two teen tickets in Section 39, I started looking for an organization able to benefit from a donation of our unused tickets.

The Riders have a good ticket-donation program and it would have been very easy to just to use that avenue for our tickets. I hoped to make the donation a bit more personal and asked new Regina friend Will Chabun, who knows Regina as well as anyone, for some suggestions.

Helpful as always, Will put me in touch with a very interesting fellow named Russ Matthews, who had organized the Regina Outdoor Hockey League, an offshoot of Ehrlo Community Services. This league offered equipment and an organized setting enabling any youth in Regina, regardless of family income, to participate as a hockey player. I personally would have preferred baseball, but when Will sent me the full story, from the Canadian *Readers' Digest*, Russ and his work seemed like a wonderful fit. We got together on the phone, and made arrangements for the tickets, and I ended up donating eight games worth of tickets that first season.

Of course, there is some practicality in any donation, in terms of a tax deduction. It seemed like a solid plan, but I later found that U.S. residents are not allowed to deduct for tax-reduction purposes any donations made to organizations out of the U.S. I actually laughed when I discovered this, but it's a true statement the tax deduction was not the impetus for the

McEvoy decision. The good feeling for helping an excellent organization was enough reward, and when I finally met Russ, I could see immediately he was a special type of guy.

The purchase of season tickets also served a completely unexpected purpose. I enjoy being unique, but never realized how unique this transaction made us. I've been introduced many times with "Season-Ticket Holder from Minnesota" as literally part of my name, and still chuckle at the five seconds of fame awarded by a purchase we wanted to make anyway. We continued to donate our tickets to the OHL in 2002 and 2003, but Russ had moved on and I switched to turning them back to the Riders for their choice of distribution for a couple of seasons. A chance conversation with Regina mayor Pat Fiacco pointed me toward the Big Brothers of Regina and now we send some tickets their way each season.

Our family reached a season-ticket crossroads in 2007. As Carson and Connor get older, it's perfectly reasonable they may not choose to make the annual trip. I've been a parent for a lot of years, and one piece of advice I will stand by is this: it's not advisable to force your children, as they mature, to do something because YOU want to do it. We dropped to two tickets and you can likely guess the boys were still eager to make the trip. Good friend Jeff Banow came to the rescue and the boys sat with him for our summer trip.

To be honest, the cost is a bit of an issue – as you'll learn a bit later, our financial situation has changed since 2001, and the combination of rising ticket prices and an exchange rate unfavourable to the U.S. dollar have taken their toll. Our two seats in 2008 will cost us well over the 2001 cost for four tickets. By the way, I am gigantically in favour of the Taylor Field improvements and happy to pay my share for them – the viewing experience was fantastically improved in 2005, I felt, with the Maxtron addition. We actually started selling a few tickets in the past two years, but hope to be able to continue with a donation schedule as well.

We, of course, were eager to use our new season tickets, but scheduling again jumped in front of our plans. As in 1999, the summer sports calendars made trips in June and July very difficult, and we had again decided to travel Down Under, with another three-week trip in early August in the works. No late-season opening appeared as we'd found two years prior, so family plans were made to attend our first Labour Day Classic

Season Tickets

battle. But before that trip, some of Charles Dickens' "best of times" came into our lives. I was in my third season as head coach of Carson's baseball team, and was fortunate enough to have a decent amount of continuity in both players and other coaches.

It was a Miracle Season, one in which every player helped the team, every coach's decision was the right one, and, most importantly, all of the boys had a great time. The team finished the season undefeated, winning the league tournament game on two consecutive divine interventions. These kids are in college now and I see several of them occasionally. I'm still told it was an experience to last a lifetime and am very proud to have been part of it.

In the midst of all of this, I was trying to deal with another postal problem. Terry in Australia has a July birthday, and I had ordered a Rider jacket from The Store as a gift. Dave Ridgway had autographed it and it was shipped from Regina in plenty of time for the mid-July event. I had not told Terry it was coming, since even grown men like surprises.

His Big Day came and went, and I had not heard anything from him about the gift. Finally, he e-mailed me indicating Australian Customs had informed him that a package from South Korea containing valuable sport memorabilia had arrived, and a customs duty of $750 or some such was due before delivery. I was initially puzzled, but a few days later received another note with the news that the Rider jacket was the item in question. The autograph has been noted when the package was inspected, and the garment was deemed, obviously, to be incredibly valuable.

Terry from Australia is not a guy to mess with. He followed up immediately, and found that South Korean imports are subject to much attention, and the return address of "Regina SK" was interpreted as "South Korea", not the Prairie province. Of course, I thought this was pretty funny, having thought all my life that Aussies and Canadians belonged to the good old British Empire, and knew each other better. The situation was resolved when Dave helped us out by sending an e-mail indicating he had not charged for the autograph and that the jacket was a gift. I was able to tell this story in 2005 on the Rider pre-game radio show, the Touchdown Club. Dave happened to be listening via the internet at home in Indiana and got a good laugh out of it.

After the fact, it was funny, although very annoying at the time. I did have several conversations with Liz Measner at the Rider Store in the course of the investigation, and those helped pave the way for a good friendship in the years to come.

The baseball season ended with a party to rival any Grey Cup event and we headed for Australia on Aug. 2. This time, we reversed our itinerary once we arrived, and went straight through to Adelaide. The crossing of the International Date Line is a strange experience, as we left Minnesota Thursday at noon and arrived in Adelaide on Saturday morning. We're still wondering what happened to Friday, but got it back on the return trip when we saw the sun rise twice on the same day. Think back to the scene about programming a VCR in the movie *City Slickers* and you'll know what I feel like when I try to decipher time travel. It's small wonder Saskatchewan does not partake in Daylight Savings Time.

Aussie Terry had tickets for the biggest "Footie" game of the year. The Australian Football League match pitted the Port Adelaide Power against the Adelaide Crows in a hometown showdown. It's a bit of a unique situation, since the two teams share the same stadium and alternate their home dates. It's almost like a civil war, as some families have members feverishly backing each of the opposing teams. Adelaide is a large, diverse city, and I'm told the Crows fans are Chardonnay drinkers and the Power's group prefers beer, so that may explain some of the rivalry.

Two of Terry's friends accompanied us, and it was just a Naming Nightmare. Our group included Terry McEvoy, Andrew Andrews, another Terry McEvoy, and Spyro Spyropoulos. We tried to avoid meeting anyone where introductions might be necessary. The fans again showed their passion in ways new to me – in the Australian Football League, much attention is played to the number of league games a player has appeared in. Milestones such as 100 games are recognized, and that player runs through a large banner with his likeness on it during the introductions. A nice gesture, but would have been expensive if used in the CFL for the likes of 25-year veteran Lui Passaglia, I'd speculate.

The Port Power won the match, to the delight of its raucous fans, and I learned even more about the sport. Interestingly, fans can place legal bets right in the stadium on virtually unlimited items – things like the first team to score,

Season Tickets

the player scoring the most goals, and so on. Sounds like a great new fundraiser for the University of Regina Rams football team, I'd say.

We had decided to visit Australia's Northern Territory, a sizable drive from Adelaide. It's an enormous, flat, red-earthed area that normally is very desert-like, but this year was quite well watered by record rainfalls. There is no speed limit, making Aussie Terry's normal driving quite legal. The kilos fly past at a speed of 160 kph and we made excellent time, enjoying the opal mining town of Coober Pedy, where most houses are built underground, and then the splendor of Uluru, also known as Ayers' Rock.

As it had before, our Adelaide time passed too quickly. Bidding our generous hosts good-bye, we flew to Cairns, in Queensland, stayed for a week in a great apartment right on the beach, and spent a few days in Sydney before returning home.

In Minnesota, the school year begins on the Tuesday after Labour Day. Maura had teacher workshops beginning just three days after we returned from Australia, not really even enough time to shake the jet lag. After a hectic week, we left for Regina early Friday morning, August 31. The timing of this trip for us was not great, but we all agreed it was really our best shot.

We'd arranged to have dinner Friday with Dave and Michelle Ridgway and managed to arrive soon enough to meet them on their way home from work. It was a good visit, with lots of Rider and Australia stories, and compassion all around for the $225 speeding ticket I had received in Weyburn on the way up. It goes without saying that I was innocent, but I paid it anyway.

Saturday morning we stopped at The Store, told Liz the happy ending to the jacket story, and went to practice. Roy remembered our meeting from the previous year, and I made sure to say "Hi" to Tyson St. James again. I also met backup quarterback Keith Smith and mentioned to him that the airport in Adelaide, Australia, is named after Sir Keith Smith, an Australian aviation pioneer. As things go in the CFL, I would run into Keith again, and again, and even again.

The pool had a water slide, so Maura and the boys headed for it, while I wandered over to the casino. In a departure from the norm, I hit four aces on my very first hand of video poker, recouping my speeding fine, and took it as a sign from above that I was in fact guiltless. I left immediately, the only good choice in the particular situation.

Labour Day weekend, 2001

      For dinner, we hooked up with Bill and Cindy Wakefield, whom I had met at the Total-CFL.com party in Calgary. Again, the ease of communication afforded by the internet made setting up the meeting a very simple matter, and we enjoyed a good Italian meal and fine company. Bill is as avid a Rider fan as they come, and he and Cindy travel multiple times each season from Calgary to Taylor Field. He's a fortunate man to have a wife who does both understand him and keep him a bit in line! On Labour Day weekend, Bill and Cindy usually stay at the Hotel Saskatchewan and are renowned for arriving at tailgates via the hotel limo. Quite typically, they fly back to Calgary early on Labour Day to catch the Stampeders game also. They are good folks, and people we make certain to see.

      The day of our first Labour Day Classic arrived, and we headed to Taylor Field early. We enjoy wandering around the practice field and the crowd antics on Labour Day weekend usually are worth watching. The group this year was especially lively, and Carson and Connor watched in awe as a gentleman propelled by Pilsner shinnied up the practice field goalposts. We actually ran into a few other Total-CFL acquaintances and soon headed to our seats.

   The game itself was a disappointment, with Winnipeg defeating the Riders 20 – 18 on four Troy Westwood field goals and 167 yards rushing by a group of running backs. In addition, and unfortunately, the experience was somewhat distressing, marred by two vulgar drunks sitting in the row behind us.

   The presence of boorish fan behavior at Taylor Field was one we had avoided in our previous six trips to Regina. Another streak ended this day, as these two progressed to a higher level of indecency as the game went on and the empty beer cups multiplied. Please, don't misunderstand – I too think beer in moderation and Taylor Field can be a fun match, but these guys by half-time were straddling the line and threatening to cross over it.

   Various other fans in the vicinity addressed their behavior a few times, and they usually calmed down or went for another beer. When the third quarter began, I counted nine beer cups in one of their stacks and was getting increasing uncomfortable.

   Part of my dilemma was that a security person was in our immediate vicinity and also was certainly able to hear every crude remark we did, but took no action. I actually wondered if this was deemed acceptable behavior, and thus questioned whether a complaint would accomplish anything. These guys were paying no attention to the game itself, but were beginning to comment on virtually every female, especially the Rider cheerleaders.

   I actually wish now that I could relive this experience, because I would have handled it very differently. I did not want to risk a confrontation, but truthfully, one was appropriate. Finally, Maura, who was nearly directly in front of Buffoon #1, stood up, turned around, and subdued him with her very best elementary school teacher voice. The two dolts actually pointed to one another, as if to say, "It was him!" We heard not another peep, and they left shortly after. I was proud of her and glad it was over, but regretted everyone around the area had to sit through it. I'm eternally grateful this disturbance did not occur sooner in our Saskatchewan football career, because it might have caused us to give ourselves an unconditional release.

   Because of this experience, I personally really appreciate the visible efforts the Riders, with President/CEO Jim Hopson as the spokesperson, have made toward making Taylor Field an enjoyable atmosphere for all. It's interesting for me, because I have met some fans at tailgates who feel they are entitled to any behavior that in their mind helps THEM enjoy the game in their way and ignore the reality that their behavior may easily be spoiling the game for others. So in these minds, constant use of noisemakers, standing so as to block the view of those behind you and similar behavior is just fine, since it's what THEY want to do. It is clear the Riders' official position is right in my radar – behavior taking away from the enjoyment of others is not acceptable. Not only that, but the organization and those being bothered are the ones to judge what activities fit in this category, since a guy with nine beers in him always thinks his behavior is just wonderful.

Shortly after this game, our return to Minnesota and the start of another school year, the "Worst of Times" showed up in a particularly frightful way. I was at work on Sept. 11, 2001 getting ready to go to a meeting when the first news of a plane flying into the World Trade Center in New York began to drift around our floor. News of a second plane followed shortly, and thoughts of any cause short of the reality of a terrorist attack faded immediately.

Well before any real information was available, I was called into an emergency planning session that ended up lasting the entire day. The company for which I worked was New York-based and heavily tied to the New York Stock Exchange, and there was immediate concern both for the events of the day and their impact on the business. Most people left the office early and I returned late in the afternoon to a nearly empty office and rode home on an almost vacant bus. I may have been one of the last people in the U.S. to see the actual tragedy on television, viewing it only after I returned home well past dinnertime.

Like it was for most everyone, this was a tough day for me to take, and those following were a terrible grind at work. It was a few days before I returned to the internet, where I saw many strings of messages from Canadians friends who were just as upset as I. One of these was from Dave Ridgway, possibly his only message ever on Total-CFL.com, and was a poignant essay on his feelings; reading it actually sent a shudder down my back. These Canadian thoughts helped me deal with the whole mess of that awful week.

Season Tickets

At that time, Dave had a weekly radio show on Regina station CJME with Mitchell Blair and had asked me to be on it for a few minutes in mid-September. I'd never met Mitch, and he asked some good questions as we briefly discussed my history as a Rider fan. Dave and I then discussed September 11 for a bit, and that too had a part in helping me to move forward.

It wasn't too surprising that the Regina guest to follow me on the broadcast was none other than Keith Smith, who had almost no choice but to acknowledge he in fact did remember the idiot who talked to him about an Australian airport!

Regina sportscaster Mitchell Blair

In this 2001 season, I actually had a second trip planned, to make use of those new season tickets. My Grey Cup companion Chris Melin eagerly agreed to go along and we decided on the September 29 game against the Edmonton Eskimos. It would be the first of many trips together for the two of us since Corey was unable to come on this one, and soon would be moving to North Carolina. Despite the recent events, we decided to go ahead anyway.

The game was on a Saturday and we chose a travel schedule that has since become the norm. I enjoy the final practice before game day, a team walk-through without pads. The atmosphere is pretty loose, fan attendance is light and it is easy to renew acquaintances with players, media types and Rider administration.

Therefore, for Saturday games, we leave home on Thursday, and spend three nights in Regina, returning to Minnesota on Sunday. It's a bit more expensive than the minimum stay would be, but the drive is not a picnic and a couple days to recover before heading home is welcome.

Chris and I arrived in Regina in the late afternoon and found a now-favourite brewpub, Bushwakkers, for dinner. In honour of the occasion, he even ordered a dish called the Saskatchewan Plate. He had not been to Regina before, so I was tour master, and showed him around the parts I was familiar with. We arrived at Taylor Field in the morning, and he was able to view the Store's wares, and meet Liz. At that time, I really didn't know any of the media or Rider personnel except Roy, but I was glad to introduce the GM to my friend. The weather was fine, very unseasonably warm, and we were wearing shorts.

As the players walked off the field, I approached Keith Smith. Due to injuries to other players, he was that week's starting quarterback and was receiving a decent amount of media attention. No one from the Edmonton media really knew anything about Keith, and Chris and I had a good chuckle when a reporter approached us like we knew what we were doing, and asked about Keith. I think I just made something up about his strengths as a quarterback – after all, I'd never see him play either.

Rider pivot Keith Smith, September 2001

Keith was done with the media and the other players had long since left. Although he was in a hurry, we had a good laugh when I reintroduced myself, and a quick, but fun, little chat. I wished him well in the game and Chris took a quick

Season Tickets

photo, proving, as you see on the preceding page, I too am tall enough to play quarterback in the Canadian Football League.

    I found a phone and attempted to contact the mysterious Elk Semen Man of Frankfurt airport fame, but the number I dialed had been disconnected. Driving down Albert, we attempted to find the address we had, but could not, and forgot about him, telling Aussie Terry we had tried, but were unsuccessful. Often I am a bit obtuse, and often wonder why it never occurred to me that Regina probably had telephone books. We left Taylor Field and met Will Chabun and Dave Ridgway for lunch. While picking up Will at the *Leader-Post* office, we met Rob Vanstone, the newspaper's Sports Coordinator and fine columnist. My reputation, unbeknownst to me, had preceded me, and Rob even made note in the next day's edition of the Riders' poor record in games I had viewed.

    Michelle was curling that evening, so Dave invited Chris and I over for pizza, and we watched the Friday night football game. Armed with an invitation to watch curling the next morning, Chris and I headed back to the motel. More discussion on differences will come later, but a major contrast between life in Saskatchewan and in Minnesota is the virtual absence of curling in our state. There is a curling club in St. Paul and, I believe, one in Duluth, but I can say with all honesty I have lived here since the dinosaurs and have never met a curler. That's certainly not the case in Saskatchewan, and Chris and I thoroughly enjoyed viewing curling the next day. It was fun to attempt to understand the rules and scoring and we actually made some progress.

    We headed to the field, where just another strange adventure awaited us. At one or two previous Rider games we had attended in Regina, a familiar surname had been announced as one of the field officials. It sounded like our name, McEvoy, but seemed impossible. I ignored it the first time, but after hearing it again, I did some internet research and uncovered Art McAvoy, a CFL field official for many years.

    I had written to Art earlier in 2001, and like me, he seemed surprised at the coincidence. He had indicated he would be in Regina for this September game and it would be fun for both of us to meet. Art's branch of the family is likely a bit more forward thinking than mine, since its spelling is closer to the correct pronunciation of our surname. Both are pronounced identically as MAC-AVOY with a short letter "A" sound, but I'm betting his is a bit easier for the average wordsmith. The E in my name really raises havoc, and commonly, extra letters are mysteriously tossed in. I've been called "Mick Envoy" many, many times.

Art McAvoy

    Meeting Art would be great, but how does one find access to a field official on Game Day? Back then my contacts were limited, so I asked Liz Measner in the Rider Store if she had any idea how we might catch up to Art. It was really like asking a cat if it knew how to catch a mouse, and she led the two wide-eyed Minnesotans into the depths of Taylor Field to the officials' dressing room.

    Art was still getting dressed, but seemed really glad to meet us. We chatted briefly and he offered to meet us after the game, but we had decided to drive part way back home since the game would be over by 5 o'clock or so. It was thus a brief meeting, but an interesting one, and I chalked up one more that I owed Liz. Art retired as a field official in 2003 after 26 years with the league, and works with the league office. Although we've not met since, as you might expect by now, he would resurface a couple of more times into my CFL life and it was appropriate in 2006 to send him a copy of the first edition of this book.

    The 2001 version of the Saskatchewan Roughriders were struggling on the field. A promising 2 – 0 mark in preseason, and a 2 – 1 regular season start had given way to injuries and losses, and they were in last place that day with a 3 – 9 record. Although Keith Smith played decently, throwing for nearly 300 yards, the Eskimos' Jason Maas was too much in the 4th quarter. The Albertans came out on top, 35 – 19. Section 39 was much better than Labour Day, but some of the regulars were still somewhat livid. A few in our immediate vicinity had called the Riders to vent about the boorish behavior, and I was just thankful new occupants were in the seats behind us, and that I had a good-sized friend sitting with me.

Our few days of distancing ourselves from the recent terrorist events came to an end when we reached the U.S. border crossing at Portal, North Dakota. A high level of urgency was present, and, for the only time in many border crossings, we were firmly told to vacate the vehicle and it was thoroughly searched. To be honest, we certainly understood, but Chris and I were a bit uneasy – the new guard garb included automatic weapons, and they tend to make a person take notice.

Saskatchewan finally put together a little momentum late in the season, winning three of the last five games, but ended up out of the playoff hunt again. In a late October game in Hamilton, Keith Smith tore his Achilles tendon and broke his ankle on the same play, ending his Rider career. With a bit of searching, I found an address for him, and sent him some photos to autograph, plus a photo of his name on the Adelaide airport sign. Of course, he and I would live to meet another day.

Once again, I ended the season thinking there would not be any personal CFL-related contact until next season, and that the 2002 campaign would be more of the same for Family McEvoy. Of course, I was certainly incorrect.

Chapter 10

The Luckiest Man on the Face of the Earth

Maura and I would be celebrating our 30th wedding anniversary in 2002 and had talked a couple of times about having a slightly premature celebration by attending the 2001 Grey Cup game in Montreal. I was sure she would enjoy the game and the associated festivities and thought it would be great for her to finally meet some of the many fine folks I'd had the opportunity to get to know in my first two trips. Before our conversations even reached the preliminary planning stage, the events of September 11, 2001 reared their ugly head. Suddenly our hearts were not really into the idea and a half-hearted search for flights found them to be expensive, so it was a quick and easy decision to skip that year.

Calgary, despite finishing the regular season with an 8 – 10 record, won the Western Final over Edmonton, and continued its roll with a 27 – 19 victory over Winnipeg's Blue Bombers. Marcus Crandell was named the game's Most Valuable Player.

I had a new autograph idea – I had a program from the Plaza of Honour game in 1999 and decided to try to get Kent Austin and Ray Elgaard, two pretty special Rider players, to sign it. I also came up with an action shot of Elgaard, and remembered that, tucked away, I had a Saskatchewan number 5 jersey purchased on sale in Edmonton in 1992. Since Kent Austin had worn number five, I could possibly get two autographs for one attempt from each player.

Knowing Ray lived in Las Vegas, I found his address easily on the internet. I first sent him a note, asking if he would be willing to sign a couple of items. He replied in the affirmative, and I shipped off the picture and the program, with a postage-paid envelope, and received them back very quickly.

Kent Austin's address was tougher, but I soon had it, and sent him the permission note too. He also said he'd be glad to, and off went the jersey, a sort of "unofficial" white one, with glittery green lettering. I mailed it right around American Thanksgiving, in late November, and eagerly awaited its return.

As many Rider season-ticket holders know, the Early Bird renewal period is right before Christmas. We were renewing, but hoped to move our seats. Our location in section 39 was closer to the field than I really care to be, and we may have had a slight bad taste from our Labour Day experience. Calling the ticket office, I found out Section 102 is directly up from section 39, and the seats there were identically priced. Better yet, there were four seats available on the side of the section toward the 55-yard line. It was too good to be true when the person on the phone added that the seats were on the aisle. We became the proud owners of Section 102, Row 7, seats 1 – 4.

Dave Ridgway had contacted me in December and gave me the news that he and Michelle were divorcing. He had decided to explore his options outside of Saskatchewan, and indicated in a conversation later in the month that he had a job interview lined up in Colorado Springs, Colorado, in early January. Since Dave was going to Ohio and Michigan during the Christmas weeks, and then needed to be in Colorado, I had an idea that might help him.

I suggested he drive here from parts east, leave his car at our place, and fly to his interview. It made sense to him also, and we set it up.

Dave arrived about suppertime and it was good to see him. All four of us were home that night, and we had dinner together. He's great with kids – really keeps them engaged in conversations and asks lots of questions. After dinner, Dave and I settled into the family room for a good talk about life in general. Big life changes aren't easy and I hope I was of some help to him.

Of course, Dave's presence in our house was a golden opportunity for an autograph hound. My poster of "The Kick" had returned home due to office downsizing at work, and he gladly signed that, with a nice message. My daughter Meredith and her husband Bill had given me a black number 36 Saskatchewan jersey for Christmas, and it virtually begged to be signed. I don't think there any many black Ridgway jerseys around anyway as the team started using black as its third jersey well after Dave's retirement, but I'm betting it's the only one signed in a Minnesota family room.

The next morning, I was to take Dave to the airport. We have a guest bedroom in the basement and I could tell Dave was up in plenty of time to get ready. The shower wasn't quite ready, though, and the handle came off in his hands. Pretty embarrassing for us, but he's always a gentleman and things eventually worked out.

Dave was in Colorado for a few days, and called to say he'd been offered a great job with a telecommunications firm there. When I picked him up at the airport, he was pretty excited about it, and filled me in on some of the particulars. It was already evening, and we wanted him to stay the night, and head to Regina in the morning. However he decided to leave that night, armed with a basket of goodies from Maura.

I was on the lookout for a return package from Kent Austin, but days passed and soon I failed to think much about it, cursing my luck it had been lost in the mail.

The New Year of 2002 began for me at work with a flurry of rumours. Large companies had begun to send technology work overseas. The one I worked for was no exception. We also had significant numbers of workers from India employed as contractors and working in Minneapolis. Our technology department was huge, with hundreds of employees, and the inability of the American economy to quickly rebound from the events of 2001 made many people nervous about their ongoing employment.

The rumours were correct, as office tales sometimes are, and announcements of job cuts were made in late January. Dozens of jobs were being eliminated, including three in my fairly small group of about 30 people. It was explained firmly that jobs would be targeted, not individuals, there would be no early retirement offers and volunteers for job elimination could not come forward.

To hasten the story, I volunteered and was given a package anyone except Big Business would define as early retirement. My plans, with funding to back them, were to retire in 2004 when I became 55 and this just made it easier. This was a magic age of sorts at our company, since departure prior to that was considered termination, without retirement benefits of subsidized health insurance and continuation of certain

The Luckiest Man on the Face of the Earth

long-term incentives. At 9:30 AM on Friday, May 31, 2002, I left the office for the last time, having just taken over from Lou Gehrig as The Luckiest Man on the Face of the Earth. I was 53 years, two months and twenty-two days young, but just old enough for a package granting me retirement status at age 55.

If you are curious about my need to detail this in a book about Canadian football, rest assured I view this event as the final piece in a decade-long puzzle. The missing piece was a schedule allowing freedom to travel and, suddenly, the piece fit right into its slot. I was actually pretty nervous, but was certain I had worked the financial numbers correctly, and also had nearly two years of paid time to verify I was right on.

The 2002 CFL season saw some changes in the basic league structure. The expansion Ottawa Renegades were born, shying away from their predecessors' nickname. The former occupants of Frank Clair Stadium in Ottawa had folded in 1996. Their nickname had been the Rough Riders, two words, and the existence of two teams in a nine-team league with the same nickname can best be described as uniquely Canadian. In doing a bit of research, I discovered each team had their version of the name dating back nearly to Biblical times, and played in separate leagues until their consolidation in the 1950's. From that perspective, the idea of "double Riders" seems really perfectly reasonable.

The increase in teams from eight to nine also caused some adaptations in the schedule, with teams alternating byes throughout the season.

The Green Riders from Saskatchewan opened the season in Ottawa, playing in the Renegades' debut contest. Paul McCallum kicked a field goal on the last play of regulation to send the game to overtime. He then finished off the Renegades with a 54-yard effort as Saskatchewan won 30 – 27.

It was a great summer. I went the entire months of June and July and most of August without wearing long pants even a single time. The CFL schedule was out and I targeted a personal record of three games to attend. I was still coaching baseball, but we had moved to a league with a break in the first week in July, so a Rider game on July 5 against Calgary fit perfectly.

Shortly before we left, to my astonishment, the mail delivery brought the Kent Austin package, containing a nicely signed jersey and the program. I do not know the cause for the delay, but was very glad to get them back. I'm assuming they floated around in the postal system, but hope someday I will be able to meet Kent and hopefully share a laugh with him about it. I did meet Argos player Clifford Ivory at Grey Cup in 2005, told him the story, and sent a message to Kent that the jersey idiot from Minnesota said "Hello!"

The July 5 game was on a Friday evening, so we kept to the pattern and left home Wednesday morning, arriving in Regina in the late afternoon. Maura and the boys had not met Rob Vanstone, so we joined him on his supper break for the first of a few meals we've shared together. After dinner, we went shopping at the Superstore and, as things work, ran into Roy Shivers. He was about as surprised to see the four of us as we were to see him, but checked on our trip and made sure we knew when practice was the next morning.

There were several good things to get me fired up at practice. I had arranged to meet a person from the internet that morning, but was a bit apprehensive. The person I was to meet was Kelly Ramler; I'd not seen a picture of the individual, and realized the name could be either gender. Well, Kelly was in fact a guy and we had a great talk. I liked him immediately, and consider him now as a very valuable Regina friend. He and Maura got on very well also, and the two had a good conversation while I wandered around.

One of my favourite pastimes when I'm in Regina for a game is just wandering around at practice. It's only a short period of time, but the conversation opportunities are limitless. The affair is low-key and informal, and it's fun for me to watch reporters do their thing. People from the team are always around, and the first trip of the season always serves as a renewal of acquaintance with at least a dozen people. The players are always pleasant and now I always try to introduce myself to one or two new guys, just to get to know more people.

We also needed to see our new seats, and liked them immediately. The aisle factor was great, but being only seven rows from an exit meant trips inside during the game could be very quick – I've actually made a run to the men's room without even missing a play.

At this practice, I noticed a man whose appearance made me think he came right out of a book – in fact, Dave Ridgway's book. I checked with Roy to be sure I was correct, and walked up to introduce myself to Lorne "Shorty" Mitchell.

The Luckiest Man on the Face of the Earth

A devoted Rider fan and 41-year season-ticket holder, Shorty had helped out equipment manager Norm Fong for a number of years and was the subject of a touching story in *Robokicker*. The team had pitched in to get him to Hamilton for the 1989 Grey Cup game, and Dave told the story well. I knew Shorty meant a lot to Dave, and I'm always interested in meeting Dave's book characters, since they are a good cross-section of Rider times in that era.

Lorne "Shorty" Mitchell

Shorty was great; the first thing he did was to repeat the Grey Cup story, and it was my pleasure to hear it right from him. He wanted to know about Dave, and I was able to fill him in. We even took a photo together that I e-mailed to Dave. In the next year, I saw Shorty a few more times and he always snagged me right away to ask about Dave. Shorty passed away in 2003, and although I didn't know him well, I knew the Riders had lost a great fan.

I also met Rider defensive back Eddie Davis at this practice. He made me feel really old, although inadvertently. Eddie is the same age as my oldest son Chris, both having been born in 1973. As I mentioned, Chris attended Bradley University in Illinois, and Eddie had attended Northern Illinois University, just down the road, at the same time. I knew NIU was in DeKalb, Illinois, and impressed the heck out of Eddie for having that knowledge. I like the way the man plays and although I've only said "Hi" to him a few times, he's a current favourite and I was glad to see Eddie sign up for 2008.

My strategy for getting photos autographed isn't too

complex. I just bring them along the next trip, locate the subject and ask if they would mind signing the picture for me. I had taken a photo with Eddie but he had broken his arm by my return trip and wasn't around. As she always does, Liz Measner took care of me, and Eddie joined my collection.

Eddie Davis

We had a picnic lunch in Wascana Park, and that evening viewed a recently released film, *Spiderman*. When Game Day arrived, lunch with Will Chabun was on the menu, and we met a few friends from Riderfans.com for a beverage on the practice field before the game.

Intentionally, we went to our new seats early. I liked the fact they were higher up, giving us a better, wider view of the action. We all noted with glee that we were just under the upper-deck overhang, and in theory might be afforded some protection in the event of rain from the west. My happy feet accidentally nudged the back of the man in front of us and very legitimately he nicely let me know about it. It was the perfect time to lapse into the Dumb American mode, and I apologized while introducing the lot of us.

Joe and Nancy McNeill of Regina sit in front of us, and a family could not possibly have better Taylor Field neighbours. In the years since 2001, we have gotten to know them better and enjoy them a lot. Nancy brings extra blankets for us to sit on when it's a chilly day, and Joe helps me keep up to date via e-mail on breaking Rider news. The McNeills have joined our list of Regina dining companions, and we even put them in contact with our daughter Meredith for tips on their 2005 vacation trip to Washington DC.

It was our ninth family trip to the home of Canada's Team, and this time they didn't disappoint. Newcomer quarterback Nealon Greene was at the peak of his game, as the Riders jumped to an early 18 – 0 lead, fueled by a great play to watch, a 100-yard pass and run to Derrick Armstrong. Calgary came back, however, taking the lead 20 – 18, and I honestly wondered if these Minnesotans were in fact a cruel jinx for the Green Riders. Greene wasn't done, however, and he led the team to two touchdown drives in the final quarter, with Sedrick Shaw and Corey Holmes scoring on nice runs. The Riders prevailed 32 – 21 and the Minnesota Monkey was off their back.

Despite some difficulties on the previous Labour Day weekend, I was very eager to return for the 2002 Classic. Although the Riders had lost in 2001, the large crowd and general atmosphere in town during the weekend had made it an exciting time. Additionally, many of the friends I had made from Grey Cup and the websites are very likely to be journeying to Taylor Field for the Winnipeg match-up. Chris Melin agreed to join me; in fact we have now attended four straight Labour Day Classics together.

But the family summer trip was first, and we took a long driving voyage to Utah and Arizona, stopping on the way back at a condo in the Colorado Mountains. We capped the trip with dinner one night in Colorado Springs with Dave Ridgway, who seemed to be doing well in his new position, and finally a visit with our son Chris in Omaha.

Chris Melin and I headed out early on Friday morning, August 30. We had not seen each other for several months, and the initial portion of the drive passed quickly as we brought each other up to date. Chris' dad, Larry Melin, is actually close to me in age, and also worked at the same company. Larry was also retired, in circumstances similar to mine, and it was good to catch up on the older Melin as well. Arriving in Regina, we had dinner with Rob Vanstone, made a very brief and unsuccessful casino visit, and retired pretty early.

The Saturday of the Labour Day Classic is always one of my favourite days in any year of Rider football. It's a family day, with the team doing its standard day before the game walk-through, followed by player introductions and an autograph session. It's a weekend where natives of Saskatchewan (many from Calgary) and Winnipeg fans alike clog the highway in both directions in their quest to Regina for the Labour Day Classic. It's the time to see certain friends for possibly the only game in a season, and to be part of the usually civil, but relentless, bantering between Rider and Bomber fans.

At Taylor Field on Saturday morning, we quickly hooked up with new friend Kelly Ramler, and he and Chris were introduced. Bill and Cindy Wakefield had arrived from Calgary; Chris had met them at Grey Cup 2000 and the three were reunited. Govind Achyuthan, the knower of all things Rider, was also present from Cowtown, as was Gerard Stang.

Bill and Cindy Wakefield

Autograph lines are long at this event, since the Riders usually provide a team poster for the fans' enjoyment. The players are set up at tables, in an order that is seemingly random, but may be quasi-numerical. As much as I wanted to visit with folks, I did have a mission pledged to Carson and Connor back home in Minnesota, so I blended into a line.

After our visit at the Rider practice earlier in the season, the boys belatedly told Maura and I about a fine experience they had enjoyed. While Maura was talking to Kelly and I was just wandering, a player had approached them, and in their words, was "really nice to them." Now, Rider players are essentially always pretty nice, but for Carson and Connor to mention this, even multiple times, indicated something, and someone, possibly out of the ordinary.

My sons had described the player as a "big guy," certainly not quite a method of positive identification for a football player. They had noted that he wore jersey number 35; this was obviously enough to identify the man as Chris Cvetkovic.

One of my shortcomings as a CFL fan is that I have very limited exposure to Canadian college players. I had never heard of Chris, but a bit of research revealed he'd had a solid career at Concordia in Montreal (not too be confused with the *two* Concordias in Minnesota) and had signed with the Riders as a free agent rookie.

It's important to me to acknowledge the good things people do, and I wanted to meet Chris and tell him of the great impression he had made on Carson and Connor. As the line moved forward, I approached a tall, athletic looking player with number 35 on his jersey. Once the lines get rolling, they actually move quickly, and I am not one to hold them up. Thus, I briefly introduced myself, and told him the boys' story. An "Aw, shucks" grin came over his face, and he was a guy to like immediately. Chris and I have since become friends – he and Chris Melin and I try to get together for dinner on Labour Day Saturday when we can. Cvetkovic for me typifies the greatest resource of the Canadian Football League: the players. He's friendly, approachable, humble, and extremely appreciative of the fans paying the bills.

Ironically, Chris joined the rival Winnipeg Blue Bombers late in 2003, but I'm not the type to let that stand in the way of a good friendship. When I see him on Labour Day, he always asks which team I will be cheering for in the Classic. My answer of "I'm hoping you have the game of your life in a losing effort" covers all of the bases.

Knowing a Bomber isn't always without difficulties if a person is a Rider fan. I have had people, one in person and one on the internet, show some amount of displeasure that I would even consider associating with a hated Winnipeg player. I can only answer with a weak paraphrase of Martin Luther King, by replying I long for the day when my friends will be judged not by the colour of their uniform, but by the content of their character. I'll take the character of a Chris Cvetkovic any day.

Chris Cvetkovic

Saskatchewan was in the playoff hunt this season, but sorely needed a victory over Winnipeg to keep pace. Injuries had reared their ugly head and the offensive line was close to decimated. Worse yet, starting Rider quarterback Nealon Greene had been playing hurt, but a bad knee was to keep him completely sidelined this week. Backup Kevin Glenn was wearing a cast on an injured thumb. The choices at pivot then were rookies Rocky Butler and Jonathan Beasley. Coach Danny Barrett had not announced his choice, but the Taylor Field wags that day were betting on Beasley.

Family day finished, Chris and I had lunch with Kelly, wandered around Regina, and met Bill and Cindy Wakefield for dinner at Golf's, a fine downtown steakhouse. Sitting just two tables away was Winnipeg coach Dave Ritchie, but Cindy and I managed to keep Bill calm.

Game day dawned and we made sure to visit the practice field before the game, a scene of food, drink, live entertainment and some of the best people watching on the planet. It's customary for some fans to cut out watermelons and wear them as helmets, and these were out in full force. Winnipeg fans were everywhere, and they generally mix well, despite the great rivalry. Rumours were circulating that Rocky Butler would be the starter. The average Rider fan, although most would never admit it, had less than a great feeling about the outcome.

Since I had four tickets, I'd invited Kelly Ramler to sit with us. He's generally a resident of the east side of Taylor Field, but seemed to enjoy the change of scenery. The crowd was loud and Taylor Field was jammed. Back in 2002, prior to the installation of the Maxtron video board, tickets were sold for spots in the area past the south end zone. This location was generally used for seating only on Labour Day, and since patrons sat on the ground on a slight slope, it was known as Hemorrhoid Hill. On this day, the Hill was full, and we even saw fans on roofs of houses on the north side of the stadium.

Fans on Hemorrhoid Hill, September, 2002

There may have been more spectacular victories over the seasons at Taylor Field, but possibly none more unlikely as on this day. Rocky Butler did get the nod over Jonathan Beasley and he simply played his heart out. A game plan clearly designed to help him succeed worked well. Despite completing only nine passes and being sacked eight times, Butler ran for three touchdowns and Corey Holmes racked up an astonishing 304 all-purpose yards in support. Final score was Saskatchewan 33, Winnipeg 19. The atmosphere was just fantastic the entire game and I felt like I had finally been in attendance for "one of those games" the fans more seasoned than I always talk about.

For my friend Chris Melin, it was his second visit to Taylor Field and first for a Labour Day game. He's been my companion, without any hesitation, for many Labour Day Classic battles since. The Rider fans in attendance were understandably excited and hundreds stormed the field at the end of the game. Walking down the Taylor Field ramps to leave the stadium can be a long trip after a loss, but on this day, jubilation reigned. High fives, hugs and yelling were the order of the day, and it was fun to be in the midst of it.

To their undying credit, the vast majority of the

Winnipeg fans handled themselves with complete class. A true sports fan knows when to acknowledge an opponent's performance if it is so deserved, and the Rocky Butler Riders earned a lot of respect that day. As we left the stadium, an unknown young fellow wearing a Bomber jersey and a mournful face walked up to me, extended his hand, and said, "Good game, Saskatchewan." It was the type of gesture that embodies all that is good about CFL fans, and it meant a lot to me.

As it often is at Taylor Field, some key game action was directly in front of us that day. We're about on the 25-yard line and have a good view of any action in the south end zone. I had high hopes for a few of the pictures I had taken during the game. Timing is everything on sports action shots, and I was uncharacteristically "right-on" for a Paul McCallum field goal. It's probably my favourite action shot and Paul and Dylan Ching, his holder, both signed it for me on my next trip.

Paul McCallum field goal

Chris was still a relative rookie on the Roseville-to-Regina Grand Prix circuit, and had convinced me that we should drive part of the way home after the game. I don't care for this, but agreed in the spirit of co-operation. We have not done it since and I hope such folly is out of his system. Heading toward North Dakota, we encountered very severe thunderstorms and even tornado activity not far south of Regina. By the time we arrived at our destination and had dinner, it was already late, and we actually only spent four hours in the motel room before heading down the road the next day. Labour Day is essentially the end of summer in the Twin Cities, and most of the world was returning from northern Minnesota lake homes. Bumper-to-bumper traffic for 80 miles on the freeway is not fun, but would have been even more unpleasant without the Rider victory.

In the 2000 and 2001 seasons, the second Regina trip was also the last Saskatchewan football excursion of the year. Because of my newly found freedom, however, I had a third jaunt planned for the September 28 game against Ottawa, but was a bit nervous about the trip. Rob Vanstone of the Regina *Leader-Post* had spoken to me about doing an article on the Mad Minnesotan, and I was less than sure about it. I naturally would have preferred having Maura, Carson and Connor be a part of it, but, as my wife explained, I was really the fan – they just humoured me. Plus, a guy cannot request a particular time slot for media coverage, especially a guy like me.

Two of my baseball-coaching buddies, Steve Gustafson and John Becker, had planned on making the trip with me, but both had to decline for work-related reasons. Not only would I have to face the mighty scribe Vanstone, but I would even have to do it alone. With Maura's encouragement, I set off for the third trip of the 2002 season.

I actually enjoy driving very much and don't mind driving alone at all, since I can completely set the pace. The miles flew by, and I arrived in Regina with time left in the afternoon. I was staying at the Super 8 Motel on Victoria, since it offered a good price, and I was familiar with the area. As I checked in, I noticed a lady in the manager's office who looked somewhat familiar.

Sometimes it takes me a minute, but I nearly always can remember a face I've seen before. In this context, it was a bit easier, since this lady and her face were very likely to be part of a football past. I went to my room and, as I opened the door, remembered she was Marian Vollans, Maid Marian of Total-CFL.com fame and wife of Ron, whose handle was Ronbo the Rider Fan. I had met them, although briefly, at the Calgary Total-CFL.com event in 2000. Re-introducing myself, I found they were free for dinner and had a nice time with them, all the while thinking that the repeat sightings of people just never seem to end.

Rider Pride on the American Side

In late September of 2002, the Minnesota Twins were well on their way to a division title, just a season removed from almost disappearing by contraction. I had spoken to Roy Shivers briefly on the Labour Day weekend, and, since he's from Oakland, part of our conversation revolved around potential match-ups in the upcoming playoffs. When I returned home after the Butler Battle, the Twins were selling Homer Hankies, a follow-up to a successful stunt used in the 1987 and 1991 World Series Championship seasons. It was nothing more than a small piece of handkerchief sized fabric, with a logo on it.

Purchasing one, I folded it up in an envelope, addressed it to Roy and tossed it in the mail without a return address or note. I had actually forgotten about it, but when I entered the Rider Store on Friday morning prior to the team's practice. Liz saw me and immediately said, "We've been looking for you. Roy wants to see you!" I remembered the hankie and hoped it was the reason for the invitation.

Liz took me back to Roy's office, my first trip back in that area. He laughed when he saw me, later a commonplace event, and waved the hankie. Apparently I had not fooled him, and we had a nice talk about baseball, family and lots of other things. I was a bit nervous at first, but he's easy to talk to, and that day caused my relationship with the then Rider general manager to become a bit different than that of the average Saskatchewan football fan.

It is a part of Roy that I'm glad I was able to experience, and one he seldom received any credit for. He appreciates fans in ways the public doesn't always hear about. Roy has stopped in Calgary to see Govind Achyuthan at work and happily posed for Gov wearing a well-traveled cap at Grey Cup 2005. When Tara Stang, Gerard's wife, had on a full leg cast and was on crutches, the general manager approached her and offered to get her a wheelchair for the game. In a great gesture, Roy found time to celebrate with Nat and Marie Hrynuik when invited to their wedding anniversary party as a surprise guest.

It was time for practice, and Roy led me out through the locker room, where King Fong looked at the intruder suspiciously until recognition hit. Norm and I chatted about Dave and I showed him a photo of Dave, Maura and I from Colorado to prove the kicker was still on the planet. As it always is for me, practice was enjoyable and I caught up to

Chris Cvetkovic again, asking him to autograph a Labour Day weekend photo, and wishing him well. As he does each time we meet, he asked about Maura and the boys, and shrugged off any credit for his great demeanor with my sons, who had asked me to be sure to say "Hello" to that number 35 guy.

Rocky Butler multi-tasking, September 2002

    I also had another photo from the Labour Day Classic. It was my first attempt at combining two photos into one, and was actually a good learning experience for me. Merging a photo of one of Rocky Butler's three touchdowns with one of that same player leading sideline cheers gave, in my humble opinion, a neat effect. I presented Rocky with a copy, had him autograph mine, and a lot of players stood in the circle with us asking how it had been done. It was fun to do a tiny thing for Rocky after watching him on Labour Day.

    Rob Vanstone was at Taylor Field doing what media folks do, and he and I left after practice to get some lunch and provide him some story fodder. To be honest, I was a bit cautious because I realize my attachment to the Saskatchewan Roughriders is a bit unusual, and feared I could be portrayed as a fellow whose mind was about nine yards short of a first down. But Rob's reputation was certainly not such, and I for one really know that I'm quite normal.

    The interview was fun – although I already knew Rob a bit, he had never heard the entire strange story and took tons of notes. He mentioned a *Leader-Post* photographer would be taking some photos at the game the next day, and my nervousness returned immediately.

I had dropped by the Outdoor Hockey League offices to see Russ Matthews, and we set a date for dinner that evening. I told him about the interview with Rob, and he thought I deserved some press, so I felt better about it. Russ found out where I was staying, and said he would pick me up later.

Back at the motel, the phone rang. It's easy to panic when you are away from home and this happens. No one except Maura knew where I was staying and I had already spoken to her that day. I answered, and a voice I'd never heard said, "Is this Terry – the guy who's going to be in the *Leader-Post*?"

Russ Matthews and Wes Sunshine, September 2002

For possibly the only time in my life, I didn't bite. It hit me immediately Russ Matthews HAD to be involved, since he was the only person in Regina who knew about the article. Rusty was laughing in the background, and then took the phone, introducing me to a friend named Wes Sunshine, who just about had gotten me big time.

It was for me a typical encounter with the fine people who live in the province of Saskatchewan. I barely knew these guys, but they picked me up, bought me a meal and entertained me with great stories. They were as real as real can get, just like the overwhelming majority of other people I have met in the Prairie province. I don't know if it's something in the water or in the air or what, but people are different there, in a

The Luckiest Man on the Face of the Earth

very good way. That weekend was the only time I've ever met Wes and I have lost track of Russ, but they are on my list for rediscovery.

I had previously invited Russ to the football game, and Wes agreed to join in also. We decided to meet at the Superstore lot and then head over. Like my late September game a year before, the weather was beautiful, and I didn't even bring a jacket.

We met the photographer, Joshua Sawka, who took pictures for what seemed like an hour, but probably was only a few minutes. It was early and many of the locals had not yet arrived, so it was tolerable. Will Chabun also sat with us and on a fine day for football, the Riders beat the Renegades for the second time in 2002, winning this contest 29 – 11.

After the game, I met Kelly Ramler at Montana's, one of my favourite Regina eateries. We enjoyed a good meal over a Pilsner or two and he insisted on grabbing the tab. Especially with the Rider win, it was been a good weekend, one where I not only survived alone, but actually even flourished and I smiled most of the way home.

Rob's article appeared in the *Leader-Post* the following Tuesday. My fears, of course, were groundless. The portrayal was accurate to perfection and well-written as all his pieces are. I was incredibly flattered, but truthfully still wonder why anyone makes such a big deal about driving a few miles to a football game. Notes came from many internet denizens, and as things happen, a fellow in Saskatoon named Jeff Banow mailed me a copy of the Saskatoon *Star-Phoenix* version of the story. I had met him once or twice fleetingly, but appreciated the gesture on his part. Good old Chabun made certain I was well stocked with *Leader-Post* copies also.

Saskatchewan finished the season with a record of 8 – 10, 4th in the West Division, but good enough to qualify for the Eastern Playoffs as the crossover team. The crossover rule can be as confusing as time travel and programming a VCR, but essentially allows a 4th place team to qualify for the league playoffs in the other division if its record is better than that other division's 3rd place finisher. Or something similar to that, I think. Anyway, Saskatchewan's 8 – 10 record was better than Eastern 3rd Place squad Hamilton's 7 – 11 mark. The Riders thus headed for Toronto to play the Argos on November 10.

The Green Guys jumped off to a 12 – 0 lead, but the

Boatmen countered with a 76-yard TD on a lateral, and former Rider QB Reggie Slack helped Toronto pull away in the second half, as they bested the Riders 24 – 12. A week later, Montreal and Edmonton won their respective division finals for the right to compete for the Grey Cup.

I had attended my personal high of three CFL games, but as the Grey Cup approached, I was only at the halfway point for my pro football appearances in 2002, since both the CFL championship and the Aussies were on their way.

Chapter 11

Edmonton, Buffalo and the Pack

My Australian friend Terry McEvoy is a very intelligent man, successful in business, exceedingly street-wise from his days on the Adelaide Police Department, and as well traveled as anyone I have ever met. In 2002, however, he seemed bent on proving he is completely clueless about North American weather.

Brainstorms are his specialty, and his first of three that year was classic. Having visited the Football Hall of Fame, he was very eager to journey to Cooperstown, New York, to visit its baseball counterpart. An excellent choice, since it is a fabulous showcase, but he decided mid-January would be just an ideal time.

Many readers are likely aware that the seasons in the Southern Hemisphere are reversed from what we Northerners are accustomed to. Australia is also the beneficiary of a very mild climate in its "winter", mainly due to favourable latitude. Adelaide is nearly as far from the equator as one gets Down Under, but is about the latitude of Georgia in the U.S.; except at high elevations in outlying areas, temperatures below freezing are virtually unheard of. Down Under is a far cry from Cooperstown's location in upstate New York, a place where snow is measured by feet instead of inches.

However, facts just make the man more determined, so Maura and I spent an interesting weekend with Terry and Kerry in Cooperstown. The quaint little village is very beautiful, and that weekend a combination of fresh snow and few people gave it a very tranquil quality. We had a good visit and enjoyed the Baseball Hall of Fame. Although I had been there before, on this trip I noted a display about the All-American Girls Baseball League, and was surprised by the number of Canadians listed, including several from Saskatchewan.

We had just missed a storm, but Terry only cackled

about our obvious over-reaction to the grand New York weather, and pretended not to believe Maura's clear and ominous description of lake effect snow. Fired up, he was already hard at work on the next adventure before we even parted ways.

He outdid even himself on this next extravaganza. Terry and Kerry would be returning to the U.S. in December and his desire was to attend a football game at the Mecca of NFL places, Lambeau Field in Green Bay, Wisconsin. When the schedule was released, he jumped for joy, since the Minnesota Vikings, with our excellent friends Green and Culpepper leading the way, were scheduled to play in Green Bay on Sunday evening, December 8. Again, reality did not enter in to the equation, and any concerns about ticket availability were completely ignored.

Not content with just one NFL game, he scanned the schedule for the preceding week to locate another. His intent for his third trick was to find a good game, have Maura and I meet them in that city for the weekend, and then we would all reconvene at our place in Minnesota for the crusade to Packerland.

We do much of our traveling in the summer due to school schedules, but the idea of a quick weekend trip to a warm locale sounded like a great way to briefly escape the ugly, frozen Minnesota winter. As I checked the NFL schedule for the December 1 weekend, the availability of destinations such as Jacksonville, San Diego and New Orleans nearly caused salivation.

Terry called with his decision – Buffalo vs. Miami. Ecstatic for just an instant, I paused when I didn't recall having seen a game listed in Miami that weekend. The realization we were again headed to upstate New York, not Florida, slowly sunk in. The prospect of seeing Niagara Falls had won out over the possibility of being snowbound. Our Australian friend scoffed at that weather notion, scolding me for my apprehension. All I could think of was the old television commercial explaining one cannot fool Mother Nature.

As Terry explored the Green Bay ticket situation, I prepared to head to the Grey Cup, to be held in 2002 on November 24 in Edmonton. Chris Melin was coming also, and we looked forward to hooking up with friends Bambi and Arnie Fearon and their group on their home turf. Better yet, there was another Total-CFL.com "Meet and Greet" party scheduled, and we were able to get a hotel room at a group rate that had been reserved for followers of that website. Finally, game tickets were easy, since Bambi and Arnie snagged us two spots right near where their season-ticket seats are located in Commonwealth Stadium. At $140 each, a bargain, we felt.

We flew to Edmonton on Friday, November 22, again a direct flight from Minneapolis/St. Paul. Heading to the hotel, we immediately ran into Brad Lawryk and a number of other folks, and acquaintances were renewed. The location seemed fine, as we scouted out Riderville and Spirit of Edmonton and determined them to be an easy walk. We seemed to be on the edge of downtown, and our distance from the stadium was not significant since Arnie and Bambi had us covered for getting to the game.

The Total-CFL party was in the upper floor of the hotel, in a room perfectly sized for the group, with a nice view of the city. Like the party in Calgary, it was well attended by fans from throughout Canada, and many of those we had met in 2000 were again present. With bargain beverages and tasty eats, it was another one of those very fine Grey Cup experiences. I was able to meet many more people who had not been in Calgary and the good feeling of meeting fans who shared the CFL camaraderie carried over perfectly from the previous gathering.

Chris and I spent a decent amount of time with Jeff Banow from Saskatoon, who had mailed me the Vanstone newspaper article, and his friend Marty Neumeier. We discovered both were from Esterhazy, Saskatchewan, and had grown up there together. They remain in the inner circle of our Saskatchewan buddies, and are both great friends. I even put up with young whippersnapper Marty calling me "Grampa."

The organizers had done an incredible job, filling a large table with enough door prizes for everyone. Mine was very nice, if "Oskee Wee Wee" is your song, since it was a gift certificate to a pub in Hamilton. I can be mildly resourceful though, and looked around for a TiCat jersey to see if I could make a deal for a certificate to be named later. I located a smiling young fellow whom we had walked in with, and traded my gift for his T-shirt prize. As Grey Cup lore would have it, I have run into this fellow at most Grey Cups ever since. His jersey says "Swami," but I am quite sure I have never known his name. It is one of those actually darn near special Grey Cup things, sharing a laugh annually with a good man whose real name is not necessary for the moment to be a fine one.

The party wound down and we headed to Riderville en masse. It was a few blocks away, and an easy walk on a decent night. It was crowded, but we were able to get in, and I spent a while talking with Gerard Stang, "The Hold," and finally discovered the source of his handle, as I noted earlier. Gerard is one of my favourites – he lives in Calgary and I generally see him only on Labour Day, but sometimes also at Grey Cup. He's a nice kid and, as you will find later, a fine public speaker.

Jeff Banow, Marty Neumeier, Chris Melin – Edmonton 2002

Grey Cup Friday can be a long day, and this one fit that description. We decided not to try Spirit of Edmonton, knowing the hometown crowd would make it hard to get inside. Staying at Riderville until close to last call enabled us to meet up with a never-ending string of acquaintances and hear "The Last Saskatchewan Pirate," one of mankind's greatest tunes, done live for the first time ever for the Minnesotans.

We had planned to stop at another party on the way back to the hotel, and set off down the sidewalk, accompanied by several of Edmonton's Finest, some police officers who were interesting to talk with for a few blocks. However, they soon spotted an undesirable in an alley and decided they preferred his company to ours. Reaching the next party, we found the line was impossible, but it was late anyway, so we headed for

Edmonton, Buffalo, and the Pack

our room.

Grey Cup Saturday is always a great undertaking, and this day both Chris and I had signed up for an event called Snow Bowl. Organized by Jim Wolf, a Rider fan living in Winnipeg, this touch football classic pitted the boys from the Western cities against their Eastern counterparts in a contest for a year's worth of bragging rights. Jim had a website set up for online registration and a large contingent of players had signed up to play.

Note that I signed up, but certainly not to play. Remember – most of these guys are younger than some of my children, and I was never much of a football player anyway. I have all the tools - small size, bad hands and no speed, but great organizational skills, so I signed up to be the West's general manager. Since I had once been in Roy Shivers' office, I felt eminently qualified for this completely ceremonious position. Chris was an experienced rugby player and couldn't wait to get out there.

We grabbed a ride with Ken and Jacky Smith of Calgary, whom we'd met in that city in 2000, and their brother-in-law, Mike Allison. The venue was a high school field somewhere in Edmonton, and we eventually got to it, after a tie up caused by the Grey Cup Parade. Jim Wolf managed to get CFL fact books for all participants, and there were again a ton of door prizes, including some Ridgway items Dave had mailed to me to bring along.

Each team had some talent, and each team had a few players I might have been able to compete with. In a classic finish, the West scored on a last-second pass play from Brad Frunchak to a swift wide out from Quick Current (or possibly a quick wide out from Swift Current) named Darwin Gooding, whom I met that day for the first time. The brilliance of the West's general manager was evident throughout the contest, and I decided then and there to retire from football administration while still on the top of the pile.

Darwin won the Snowman Award as MVP and we all headed to a local pub to warm up and visit. He had traveled to Minnesota previously, and impressed me with his knowledge of the Minnesota Gophers, the university's football team. Of course, as you will soon realize, a few years later I came to wish he'd never heard of them.

West defensive stalwarts Dave Fulton (37), Chris Melin

Chris and I had arranged to have dinner with Bambi – she and Arnie had recently had a beautiful little baby girl named Courtney, and we had a good time catching up and talking about babies and football. She was going to pick us up at the hotel for the game on Sunday, and we finalized those arrangements. Best of all, Arnie had some way to get us into the Spirit of Edmonton party without waiting in line, and we were given directions on where to meet him.

Heading to the hotel where the Spirit was held, we were ushered into a waiting area and hooked up with Jeff Banow until we caught up to Arnie. Jeff pointed out Rider defensive lineman Shonte Peoples and BC Lions linebacker Carl Kidd. Remember, my Canadian football TV exposure is non-existent, so it's nice to have people point players out. Jeff didn't understand why I began laughing at Carl Kidd's name, so I quickly told the Dennis Green/Daunte Culpepper story, and decided to approach the two players.

Carl was busy, so I introduced myself to Shonte, who did not appear to be in a talkative mood. His reticence was fine with me, since that is his business and I was not about to force any conversation. By then Carl was alone, and I had better luck with him. He certainly remembered the Vikings day in question and agreed it was pretty remarkable he and I were standing in Edmonton, Alberta discussing it. I was wearing a Minnesota Twins wind jacket, and found that Carl grew up in Pine Bluff, Arkansas, also home to Torii Hunter, the fine Twins' centerfielder. It was a brief and fun conversation. Carl Kidd was certainly not the most popular player in the CFL, but I make sure I try to value people I meet by my interaction with them. By that alone, I enjoyed talking to the man.

Arnie arrived then and we slid in with him, miraculously bypassing a sizable wait time. It was a very large party, in a cavernous room, and we joined up with the Edmonton group we had met twice before. I went to purchase some drink tickets, and the line was long. Making conversation with the fellow with me in line, I discovered he worked for an oil pipeline company in Edmonton. Feeling like the Dumb American, I remarked that my next-door neighbour back in Minnesota had worked for a similar company in Edmonton for a few years. Of course, as you may have already guessed, it was the same company and this man had worked with my neighbour!!

I lasted until about midnight and headed back to the hotel, leaving Chris to fend for himself, which he did quite well.

Grey Cup Sunday dawned, and we had a pre-game treat in store. Will Chabun had once sent me a tape of a Canadian TV special highlighting Grey Cup Sunday by focusing on each CFL city, chronicling the celebrations of both large and small groups of fans. We had been invited to such a gathering, a party to be held at a community center, and attended by an extended group of the friends and family of our Edmonton acquaintances.

The TV special may as well have been filmed at this party. Bambi and Courtney picked us up, and all greeted us warmly as we arrived. The two Americans were likely a bit of a novelty, but the hospitality was tremendous, and left good memories. There was food and beverage enough for an army, and rides to the stadium had been all set up. Those attending the game piled in cars for the short ride to Commonwealth Stadium, and those remaining settled in to continue the party by watching the game on television.

The stadium area was packed, and Chris and I entered a long distance from our seats. The inside concourses were jammed with bodies, and I felt almost swept away with the crowd a few times. I had presence of mind to hit the restroom, a wise move since the crowds later made it essentially impossible. There's likely nothing much better for a CFL fan than to attend a Grey Cup game in their home stadium with their team in the game, and that was the treat the Eskimo faithful had that day.

Arnie Fearon bundling up, Nov. 24, 2002

I am not sure it's an annual Grey Cup event, but there was to be a jet flyover this day, and it was a breathtaking experience. The roar of the engines and the billow of the exhaust rev up the crowd and create a neat effect. Fortunately, in Vancouver in 2005 the flyover was accomplished during the Parade on Saturday, calming my fear about how this could possibly be done in a domed stadium.

To the consternation of our Edmonton friends, the Alouettes dominated the game's first half, leading by the very CFL - like score of 11 - 0 at the break. Edmonton's offence was sluggish, gaining fewer yards in the entire half than Montreal picked up on one play. This play, a 99-yard TD throw from Anthony Calvillo to Pat Woodcock, set a Grey Cup record for the longest pass play.

Shania Twain was the halftime entertainment and gave a good show, but one that was seemingly very quick. She looked good on the video board, bundled up for the crisp weather. We tried to make a restroom run at half time; it was hopeless, but at least the cold discouraged any beverage thoughts.

Like many Grey Cup games, action heated up in the second half. The Eskimos scored ten unanswered points in the third quarter to pull within one. Montreal countered with about 11 minutes left as Cavillo hit Jeremaine Copeland with a 47-yard TD throw. With time running out on the Edmonton crew, Ricky Ray hit Ed Hervey for a touchdown but the two-point attempt failed. With just a few clock ticks remaining, the Esks tried an on-side kick, but Copeland found a seam and returned it for a touchdown and the final tally in a 25 – 16 Alouettes win. A good game, the third such for us in three Grey Cup tries. Bidding Arnie and Bambi goodbye and armed with directions to get back downtown, we had dinner with Kelly Ramler, and checked off another successful trip on our CFL log sheet.

Game Day flyover, Grey Cup 2002

In the morning, I bought a couple of newspapers for airplane reading material, and we took the shuttle to the airport. One of the other van passengers was Krista Baker, the wife of Montreal kicker Terry Baker, the punter on the Riders '89 Grey Cup team. The retiring Terry had just played his last game, and I'd read an article over the weekend about him.

Of course, I decided to introduce myself, primarily because the article I had read brought back Canadian memories of the physically painful kind. The story noted the Bakers lived in Nova Scotia, in a town just down the road from my 1997 kidney stone adventure. Krista was great to talk with, and gave me their business card – they were now the owners of Admiral Benbow's – a gift shop in Lunenburg that I clearly remembered. When I returned home, in keeping with my pattern, I came up with a good picture of Terry, sent it to him with a note, plus the Edmonton sports pages from the game. Shortly afterward, he sent back a nicely signed photo, football cards and a friendly note. Once again, the reinsertion of a previous event into a later CFL-related one was interesting to note, but I was becoming used to it.

The week after Grey Cup at home was a madhouse, since Thursday was American Thanksgiving, and our trip to tropical Buffalo began the next day. Although I had thought I was prepared, I'd been cold at the Grey Cup game, and pulled out the heavy artillery for Buffalo: lined nylon pants and my Rider parka, the warmest jacket on earth. Our flight was through Detroit and uneventful. Terry and Kerry met us at the Buffalo airport.

The male portion of the Aussie duo was a bit of a smart guy, since the weather was fine, and our concerns about it were clearly unfounded in his estimation. We were staying right at Niagara Falls, on the American side, and the view was wonderful. A casino on the Canadian side and good restaurants filled out the experience. On Saturday, we drove to the Bills' stadium, a long haul from our motel, but worth inspecting for the next day.

American Thanksgiving weekend is a nightmare for air travel, and Maura and I had a 6PM flight back on Sunday. We decided she and Kerry would drop off the boys at the stadium, go shopping, and then pick us up at 4:00. We knew we would need to leave the game early, but had no choice.

Buffalo's tailgating is legendary, and we enjoyed walking right through it to enter the stadium. We were early, but Terry and I both like to wander around, and did so. Going down to field level from our seats, Terry noticed that the gate was open, and we snuck our bundled bodies right onto the field during warm-ups. I was a bit nervous, but Terry always pleads Australian ignorance – it's an even better defense than the Dumb American ploy.

It hit me then that former Calgary quarterback Dave Dickenson was on the Miami Dolphins' roster. For just an instant I was thinking about the giant coup I could score by introducing myself to him as a CFL fan from Minnesota while he was out on the playing field in Buffalo. A great story it would have been, but we basically chickened out, got some good photos and headed to our seats.

Lots of imbibing fans enjoy football in Buffalo, and we saw several ejected by very zealous security forces. Our seats were in a corner and the view wasn't great. Buffalo ended up wining 38 – 21 in a game in which Ricky Williams of Miami ran for 228 yards, but the game highlight for us soon became the weather.

Buffalo Bares, December 2002

Mother Nature had tired of the Aussie indifference to her power, and began to toss down the snow. By the fourth quarter, near-whiteout conditions had arrived, and we trudged through several inches on the way to the meeting with the ladies. Maura and I had little time to spare, but the airport was a good ways away, and driving was slow.

Terry and Kerry were driving to Minnesota to meet us in a few days, and they actually made it out of Buffalo just ahead of the worst weather. Maura and I had a delayed flight due to the blizzard, missed our Detroit connection, and spent the night in a Michigan airport hotel without our luggage. We were forced to detour through Chicago the next day, and finally arrived home over 24 hours after we had left Buffalo. Much to my frustration, Mother Nature nailed the wrong Terry.

The Australians arrived mid-week, and since Kerry had not been in Minnesota before, much sightseeing was in order, and the couple from Australia soon met our friends who had heard so much about them. Terry had solved the Green Bay ticket challenge in his own interesting way. He called the Packers' radio station from Australia, and the DJ put him on the air live, and allowed him to shamelessly beg for tickets.

Of course it worked, and we had four seats lined up. Terry and I, and my friends Tim Kurtz and John Becker, headed out on Sunday morning for the six-hour drive to Packerland. The only motel we could find was 40 miles west of Green Bay, so we checked in as we drove through, and met our ticket benefactors at 2 PM for the 7 PM contest.

These two couples must have Saskatchewan roots. They were just incredible – found us a place to park, and took us around tailgating until game time. When we left them, I felt like I'd known them for years.

Lambeau Field was in the midst of a large renovation project, but was a sight to behold, unless you had need of a restroom, since most were closed. The Pack edged the Vikings 26 – 22, but the big news was the triumph of Mother Nature over a large Australian. The night was cold, about 10 degrees Fahrenheit, or –12 Celsius. Warnings had been issued by experienced Northerners regarding the correct winter apparel, but Terry had purchased his parka in North Carolina, and was certain it would be fine.

Bottom line is John, Tim, and I took turns checking on him all during the second half, because he was seldom moving, and we wanted to be sure he was still alive. Frozen game over, we headed the 40 long miles to our motel. Aussie Terry managed a grunt once or twice, complaining that the foot warmer inserts I had so thoughtfully given him for his shoes had failed to work. Of course, when he finally took them out at the motel, they were almost hot enough to burn his hands - his feet were just too cold to tell. The final score of this great football season was thus Mother Nature 1, Australia 0.

Chapter 12

A Hall of Fame Kind of Guy

Football news continued as 2003 began. Aussie Terry called after Christmas – he had decided to attend the Super Bowl, but I had to decline, citing concerns about both budget and additional time away from home. Around the first of February, Dave Ridgway phoned one morning from Colorado with fantastic news. He had just been informed of his selection to the Canadian Football Hall of Fame, joining Edmonton defensive lineman Ron Estay, Saskatoon amateur football builder Ed Henick, Edmonton receiver George McGowan and Winnipeg offensive lineman Chris Walby as the Class of 2003 Inductees. It was exciting news, and I really appreciated being told well before the official announcement.

The Canadian Football Hall of Fame is located in Hamilton, Ontario, and 2003 marked the first year in its history the events of an induction would take a road trip from that city. Calgary, Alberta, had been chosen as the site, with the Hall of Fame Weekend scheduled for mid-September. Maura and I were on Dave's list of invitees, and it was literally a no-brainer to decide to attend.

Certainly, I'm a bit biased, but Dave's selection, in my mind, had been a matter of when, not if. Although at the time Edmonton kicker Dave Cutler was the only kicking specialist in the Hall, Dave's record in his fourteen years with the Green and White made him a very strong choice. It's easy to recall his career within the context of just one play in 1989, but that kick was really just a representative sampling of his career, and not at all the pinnacle. When he retired in the spring of 1996, Dave held a fistful of CFL records, several of which still stand now, a decade later. Importantly, even though playing in an era with a very impressive array of place-kickers, he was a Western All Star seven times and a CFL All Star on six occasions.

Rider Pride on the American Side

It was really pretty exciting to receive an official, personalized letter from Janice Smith, the Hall's Managing Director, inviting us to the event. We sent in the paperwork, and received our tickets in July. Making a hotel reservation at the Hyatt Regency where the induction dinner was to take place, we even managed some decently priced airline tickets. Brad Lawryk was also attending, plus some of Dave's friends whom I had met at his house a few years before, and of course, Dave's father.

Actually, for a retired player, Dave Ridgway had pretty decent stats for 2003. He'd met a nice lady who lived in Indiana, and Dave and Connie were married in the summer. We were looking forward to meeting her, since Dave sounded very happy.

Maura and I left on the last flight of the day to Calgary, but it was delayed and we did not arrive at the Hyatt until well after midnight. The first event of the weekend for us was the unveiling of the busts of the inductees, held at the Calgary City Hall on Friday at noon. We'd not yet caught up to Dave's group because of our late arrival, but arrived in plenty of time for introductions. Dave was busy, so we spotted a lady who had to be Connie and introduced ourselves, and also caught up with Dave's friends Troy Christian, Jim McLaren, Thom McInnis and Randy Pollack. A gentleman who looked very familiar walked up and asked if I was Terry from Minnesota, and thus we met Dave's dad and stepmother, Len and Toni Ridgway.

It was easy to understand why Connie had caught Dave's eye. She's attractive, funny, and a lady with a take-charge attitude whose voice has just a nice hint of the Indiana drawl I'd heard from my relatives who are from Fort Wayne.

The unveiling ceremony was to begin, and was hosted by Mark Stephen, Calgary radio personality and the radio voice of the Calgary Stampeders. Mark would not likely be a front runner in a popularity contest in Regina, but I've met him a couple of times since then at Taylor Field and found him to be a gentleman. He did a nice job as the host and it was a very moving ceremony.

Calgary Stampeder great Wayne Harris was in attendance, one of several CFL greats making an appearance. Wayne was assisting the inductees don their new Hall of Fame Blazers. Interestingly, when it was Dave's turn to receive his jacket, Hall of Famer and ex-Roughrider great Bill Baker stepped up and asked Wayne if he minded if an old Roughrider helped Dave with his jacket and he graciously allowed Bill to assist Dave. I spoke with Dave afterwards about that and he told me how much it meant to him that Bill Baker not only was in attendance but also wanted to help with the presentation of the jacket. It was also great fun to see Dave's dad, Len, meet Wayne Harris, since "Thumper" had been Len's favourite player.

    An autograph and picture session followed, and there was ample time for my favourite pastime at such an affair, so I wandered to my heart's content. I had met Chris Walby briefly in Regina the football season before, and he seemed to remember me. As I shook hands with this giant man, I marveled at the Supreme Being with enough imagination to make hands of the same species so different in size as Walby's huge mitt and my tiny palm with its short little fingers.

Busted in Calgary – from left, Chris Walby, Dave Ridgway, George McGowan, Mike Henick (for his late father, Ed) and Ron Estay

    The event was open to the public, and internet legend Calgary Rider Fan (our good friend Govind Achyuthan) had slipped away from work to stop by. Many people know Gov, but for those who do not, he's literally a walking, talking encyclopedia of Saskatchewan Roughrider information. I can hold things in my head pretty well, but Govind makes me appear to be a dementia patient when he begins reciting Rider facts. He talked to Dave for a long while, and the assumption our Grey Cup group later discussed was that Gov was going over, undoubtedly in excruciating detail, each one of Dave's 574 field goals.

The induction dinner that evening was right in our hotel, and I showed Maura around like an old pro, since it had been the scene of the Spirit of Edmonton party at the 2000 Grey Cup. The tickets indicated either western or business attire were preferred, a reminder of just where in Western Canada we were.

A reception prior to the dinner served to get me wandering again, and I spoke with Liz Measner and met her husband and son. Inductee Ron Estay, of course, was the Rider defensive line coach, and Roy Shivers, Liz and others had traveled to Calgary to be there for him, and also to see Dave inducted. Brad Lawryk arrived also, and it was very good to see him again. Dave had personally invited Brad since they had known each other for quite some time. Dave assisted Brad with his web site and the two men had quite a nice friendship and mutual respect for each other.

Troy Christian, Connie Ridgway   **Bob Poley**

Time came for the dinner to begin, and we were ushered in to our tables. Maura and I were right behind Dave's table, seated with Brad and Ridgway friends Jim Bostwick, Thom McInnis and Jim McLaren. Former Rider center Bob Poley was

A Hall of Fame Kind of Guy

to be Dave's presenter, and in meeting him, I discovered his Walbyish hands also. It was fun to meet Dave's high school football coach from Burlington, Ontario, Scott Smiley, who had made the trek west to join in Dave's celebration.

As these types of affairs often tend to be, it was a long dinner, with many speeches. I was very impressed with the nicely done video tributes to all of the new Hall members. Truly an emotional time for many people, and Dave was no exception. When he closed his speech with a stirring recognition of his father's role in his life, there were no dry eyes either at the speaker's podium or at our table.

With a long program, and several breaks, I of course found time for wandering. Mark McLoughlin, who right then filled the perplexing dual role of place-kicker/president of the Calgary Stampeders, was in attendance and recalled my 1998 autograph request, though he was a little surprised to have me wander up in this place and time. I was also able to meet a great Saskatchewan Roughrider legend, retired running back George Reed, the best ever in the CFL.

Ridgway HOF acceptance speech, 2003

As the event was winding down, I went over to the table where Liz and her family were sitting with Roy Shivers. Word had already reached us that the Roughriders, playing that evening in Hamilton, had lost in overtime, 27 – 24. Hamilton had scored a tying touchdown with less than a minute remaining to gain what would be the TiCats' only victory in the 2003 season. Roy was understandably upset, but was his usual gracious self – we made arrangements to get together when I would be again in Regina later in the fall.

The party was slow to break up, and there were plenty more opportunities for socializing. Maura and I met a lovely couple from Regina, Mr. and Mrs. Paul Dojack. Paul was himself a Hall of Famer as a field official, and knew Art McAvoy very well. I also spent quite a bit of time in conversation with Dave's high school coach, Scott Smiley, a very interesting man. Discovering he had taught Rider players Chris Cvetkovic and Phil Gibson in high school, I tucked this little piece of information away for later.

CFL Commissioner Tom Wright was also present, and seemed very happy to meet the two Minnesotans, convincing me once more of the magic of the CFL, since I'm not likely to meet the commissioner of the NFL any time soon.

Ron Estay

Chris Walby

The Ridgway group was the last to leave, finally forced out as the event staff took down the tables around us. It was a memorable evening; one Maura and I were thrilled to have been a part of. Parts of the ceremony were later televised in Canada; I still watch it occasionally and the excitement is always still there.

A Hall of Fame Kind of Guy

The weekend still had a lot of activity left in it. Nothing was planned during the day on Saturday; Maura and I had lunch with Bill and Cindy Wakefield, hearing Bill's classic tale of chasing Dave down the street near the hotel to get an autograph on a number 36 jersey. In the evening, we had been invited to a house party at the home of Dave's Calgary friends Barry and Marlene McCallum. It was a wonderful, relaxing way to socialize.

Our Calgary friends, Jacky and Ken Smith

Sunday was the Hall of Fame game, with the Winnipeg Blue Bombers providing the opposition for the hometown Stampeders. The new Hall members had an autograph session prior to the game, and our Calgary friends Ken and Jacky Smith had invited the entire Ridgway group to a famous pre-game McMahon Stadium tailgate. Maura and I rode out with Troy Christian, armed with some beer as our donation to the festivities. It can be a handy thing to be able to purchase beer on Sundays, another area where Canada is just a bit more progressive than Minnesota.

The tailgate was a great time and I was able to catch up with a number of Calgary folks I'd met in 2000, and also have Maura see what great people they are. One of the reconnects was with Rande Allison, Jacky's sister and the tattoo lady from the 2000 party. Rande and Mike's daughter Delaney had casts on her legs then to fix a problem condition, and I was able take a neat photo and get Dave to autograph it for them later. By the way, last I heard Delaney was an accomplished dancer, so the correction obviously worked.

Rande and Delaney Allison, with Dave Ridgway

A great perk for the Ridgway group involved passes for everyone to the stadium's Super Suite, an enclosed upper seating area. With nice seats, food, beverages and many CFL personalities present, it was a wanderer's dream come true. Dave had some extra tickets, so Brad and I invited Bill and Cindy Wakefield and Ken and Jacky Smith to join us.

Wonderful autumn warmth had become a victim of Calgary's shifting weather. A bitter wind arose, making me very glad we were indoors. George Reed was there, and I was able to chat with him for a bit and get my picture taken with him, another autograph I still need to get. The Grey Cup was also present and our group took a wide variety of shots with the treasured trophy. I also discovered this symbol of Canada's football past and present is carried around in a very nondescript looking hockey equipment bag, not the jewel-encrusted satchel one might expect.

It was a fine and memorable weekend, made possible by much hard work led by George Hansen, the Stamps alumni president at that time, and a large number of other volunteers. We were treated like kings, and it is a very favourite CFL memory for Maura and I, because we can easily recognize the experience was one the average fan will never have. Meeting the other inductees, Tom Wright, George Reed, Mark

McLoughlin, Bob Poley, Len and Toni Ridgway, Scott Smiley, the Dojacks, and a host of others, plus being there for Dave's big moment was clearly a once in a lifetime experience and was more than worth the trip for us.

Connie, Len, and Dave Ridgway and the Grey Cup

Chapter 13

Flat Out With the Elk Man

Pressure was on the Saskatchewan Roughriders as the 2003 season began. The Grey Cup was scheduled for Regina on November 16, an early date forced by the unavailability of lodging the following weekend due to the annual Canadian Western Agribition in Regina. An appearance in that game for the home team was clearly the goal as the season began.

Something like getting a motel room for a weekend many months away certainly seemed like a less-than-daunting task. I began searching shortly after we returned from Edmonton in November of 2002, but there were essentially no rooms at the inn for the entire Grey Cup weekend. Friendship jumped in one more time, as Kelly Ramler went door to door in Regina and was able to get us a reservation at our favourite spot, the Holiday Inn Express. Chris Melin was on board, since neither of us ever considered missing out on the fun of Regina's second ever Grey Cup week.

The entire Rider coaching staff was back, but the team had lost some key contributors from 2002 in defensive back Omar Evans and wide receiver Derick Armstrong. Solid linebacker Jackie Mitchell returned a bit late, after failing to stick with the San Francisco 49ers. The team would likely need to improve from its 8 – 10 mark in 2002 to advance in the playoffs, but optimism ran high as usual in the Queen City.

In Minnesota, we were preparing for our son Chris' wedding to Julie Chang, held in Honolulu, her hometown, on July 25. It was an easy decision to plan the Family Rider Trip for later in the summer, since the odds and ends of a long distance wedding needed time to tie together. We thus had our sights set on a game scheduled for August 17 against the Ottawa Renegades.

The Rider season began well, as they won at Toronto to

Flat Out with the Elk Man

open the campaign, and followed with a two-point victory over British Columbia in the home opener. Close losses to Montreal and Winnipeg followed, but the team then reeled off three wins in a row before losing to Ottawa to sit at 5 – 3 as we headed toward Regina.

We approached Regina from the west, having attempted an ill-fated camping excursion in Montana's Glacier National Park. Forest fires had plagued the park for some time, but had calmed down shortly before we arrived. The calm lasted only a day, however, and we bailed out early when the roads through the park were closed on our second day. Leisurely pointing the car toward Saskatchewan, we took our time and saw some interesting sights along the way. One overnight stay was in Medicine Hat, Alberta, where our server at Montana's was in fact a Rider fan. I even took his address and later sent him an autographed item from the 2003 Hall of Fame Induction, undoubtedly causing him to realize the older Minnesotan keeps promises made in restaurants.

Arriving in Regina a day or so earlier than planned gave me the opportunity to attend a regular mid-week practice for the first time. Kelly came also, and it was interesting to watch the entire proceedings. We caught up with Chris Cvetkovic, and I also met Rider trainer Ivan Gutfriend for the first time. Roy Shivers was out of town, but those things happen, since I was fairly certain he did not plan trips around our schedule. The whereabouts and well-being of Dave Ridgway were also a commonly discussed topic, and I was able to bring several of his Regina friends up to date on the adventures of Dave and his new bride. For Carson and Connor, the presence of more grasshoppers than any of us had ever seen brought a decent number of jumping contest opportunities.

The next day brought us to the pre-game day practice on a beautiful, hot morning. I missed a chance to meet Kent Austin, by then an Ottawa coach, at the Renegades practice, because it would have required dragging our entire crew back to the field a few hours later. We then spent a couple of hours at the Saskatchewan Sports Hall of Fame and retired to the water slides to escape the very hot afternoon temperatures.

On Sunday, game day, Kelly Ramler joined us for brunch, and it was off to the pre-game tailgate. The grasshoppers were out in full force, and afforded an escape for the boys from the boredom of a semi-adult event. On a beautiful, warm, clear day, a tailgate is a wonderful thing, and Maura was able to meet a number of the Riderfans.com faithful for the first time. I was pleased Darwin Gooding, whom I'd met the previous fall at Grey Cup, arrived from Swift Current in time for part of the tailgate festivities. We were able to visit with him again also, not realizing until a bit later that his stadium seats were very close to ours.

Chris Szarka (33), Richie Hall and Ron Estay watch a drill

The Renegades had defeated Saskatchewan in Ottawa just ten days before this upcoming matchup, and the Riders needed a win to get back on track. We had certainly arrived in Regina for an important contest.

Ottawa quarterback Kerry Joseph lit things up in the first half, running for two touchdowns and passing for another, as the Renegades jumped to a 25 – 16 halftime lead. The Riders exploded in the third quarter however, beginning with Kevin Nickerson's 96-yard TD return of the second half kickoff, and added a rare double return TD when Corey Holmes added an 87-yarder following a later Ottawa score. Chris Szarka also scored in the third, and the Riders led 44 – 26 as the fourth quarter began.

Kenton Keith then scored on a 5-yard pass from Nealon Green, and the Riders withstood two late Renegade touchdowns to leave with a 51 – 41 win in a game that was certainly an offensive battle and fun to watch. In section 102,

Flat Out with the Elk Man

my friend Mr. Gooding was kind enough to let the entire area know we were from Minnesota as he led an impromptu cheer into which he somehow worked the name of our state.

The Labour Day Classic was a scant two weeks after the Ottawa game, and even I didn't particularly enjoy the long rides essentially back-to-back. However, as we usually do, Chris and I spent time catching up on the drive to Regina, and it passed pretty quickly. Saskatchewan had lost in Edmonton in the week following the Ottawa game, and the annual end-of-summer showdown with the Winnipeg Blue Bombers had increased importance in the battle for a home playoff spot, since Winnipeg had won the first contest between the two clubs.

Chris and I were previewing our Grey Cup accommodations by again staying downtown at the Holiday Inn Express, but were immediately suspicious of a nearby bar/restaurant, where it took forever to just get a beverage, even though the place was empty. As we often do on the evening of our arrival, we enjoyed a good meal and some microbrew at Bushwakkers and headed to the annual family event on Saturday.

Family Fun at Taylor Field

This gathering again was a great time, and we were able to reconnect with a number of friends. Liz Measner again came to my rescue – I had cleverly lost a Rider banner I painstakingly had every player sign, but she was cheerfully able to replace it for me, adding to the tally I owe her. Chris Melin and I caught up with Chris Cvetkovic, who introduced us to Phil Gibson and said he would pick us up for dinner later that day. Phil had just come over to the Riders in a trade with Montreal, and delighted in recounting his Toledo Rockets' gigantic 38 – 7 upset of the Minnesota Gophers in 2001.

Cvetkovic picked us up at the hotel and we headed to a new spot (for us), Earl's, for dinner. Making small talk, since I didn't know Chris well, I asked where his hometown was, and was surprised when he answered it was Burlington, Ontario.

When I laughed, indicating Dave Ridgway had also lived there, Chris further surprised me by indicating he had not only attended the same school as Dave (Burlington's M. M. Robinson High School) but that Phil Gibson had also. This strange road had one final turn, as we established Dave and Phil had also both not only attended the University of Toledo, but began their CFL experiences with Montreal, then ended up in Saskatchewan.

Practice Field pregame, Aug. 31, 2003

It was a fun time with Chris, and we pledged to try to get together the next Labour Day. A trip to the Regina Rams football game filled the evening, and we made ready for the 2003 Labour Day Classic.

Sunday, August 31, dawned warm and bright and we headed to the tailgate fairly early. Things were jumping in the old Superstore parking lot, buoyed by Winnipeg fans and Saskatchewan fans returning home for the annual battle. The practice field was also very alive and well before the game.

Flat Out with the Elk Man

Aided by Grey Cup seat preparations, the Rider faithful numbered over 40,000 and were loud and proud, but not for long. Saskatchewan could not figure out how to stop the Bombers' Charles Roberts, who gained 124 of Winnipeg's 191 rushing yards. The Riders faced an early 17 – 3 deficit and never made up ground, losing 36 – 18. The Chicago Bears had released Henry Burris, the man missing to the NFL since 2001, in July. Signing again with Saskatchewan, he entered this game in relief of Nealon Greene in the second half. Burris was 11 of 22 for 130 yards and a TD, but remained third on the Rider QB list after Green and Kevin Glenn.

This game was a giant letdown for the Saskatchewan faithful, myself included. Winnipeg clearly had the emotional edge, and it cost the Riders since their momentum during the entire game was very limited. In the long run, the Blue Bombers' sweep of the season series would cost Saskatchewan the elusive home playoff game, since the two teams finished the season with identical 11 – 7 won-loss records. The Bombers' advantage in head-to-head competition gave them the home playoff nod over the Riders. Leaving the stadium, I tried to remember the Bomber fans' class in the previous year, and managed a few "Good Game" comments on my way out.

Chris Melin and I had hooked up with Bill and Cindy Wakefield and Kelly Ramler to head to dinner after the game. Our moods were not wonderful, and we decided to head back downtown and dine at the restaurant adjacent to our motel, the same slow beverage establishment of earlier in the weekend. "Fresh, not frozen" lasagna was highlighted on the menu, and the decision of all four of my dining companions to order it led to the first of this writing's two stories involving that Italian delicacy.

Despite the very slim post game crowd, the service was exceedingly slow, with the explanation given that the lasagna was not quite done. My meal arrived, and my friends urged me to eat, lest my food get cold. The long-awaited orders of lasagna arrived, but the waiter suspiciously hurried off. Frustrating football games can make fans hungry, and Cindy, Bill, Kelly and Chris all dug in. Looks of dismay sprang immediately from the starved faces, since the meals were still quite frozen. I personally thought the situation was ludicrous and hilarious simultaneously, but kept the second emotion to myself in deference to my furious companions. More steam rose from Bill

Wakefield's head than from the plates of food.

After our excursion to Calgary for the Hall of Fame Induction, I had one more Rider trip planned. My "Bus Buddy" friends, Harv Moen and Tim Anderson, were making their maiden CFL voyage with me for the Calgary game on Oct. 13. Tim, Harv, and I had met riding the bus to and from work in downtown Minneapolis a few years before, and our version of back of the bus sports talk had evolved into a good friendship and eventually this trip.

As we got to know each other on the daily bus journeys, I found Harv and I actually had two previous connections of a sort. His son Jeff had gone to high school with my daughter Meredith, plus Harv had been, again in a Rider-related coincidence, the quarterback on a very strong 1965 Madison, Minnesota, football team anchored by a big lineman named Tim Roth. Harv had put me in touch with Tim, who seemed amused by both my autograph request and my Rider fascination.

The game was on a Monday, Canadian Thanksgiving, and we left for Regina on Saturday. It was a trip with several things planned in advance, including a meeting with a character who had seemingly been lost forever.

Right before Maura and I had gone to Calgary in mid-September, the phone rang and a voice said, "I'm sure you don't know who I am – my name is Bill Donison." My reply belied his assumption, since I immediately shot back that Bill Donison was, in fact, the long-lost Elk Man, who had years prior encountered the Australian Terry McEvoy in an airport. Try as I might, I had never been able to connect with Bill in Regina, and had actually given up.

Bill had thought Terry was perhaps coming to Canada for the Induction, since the Aussie had mentioned that I knew Dave when they had met. I explained that Maura and I were heading to Calgary, and Bill and I arranged to meet on my next Regina trip. To say that I was amazed to hear from this man would be a gross understatement, but meeting Bill was easily added to the trip agenda.

Friends Harv and Tim had heard me speak glowingly for years about my CFL experiences, but bus talk is cheap and they were eager to see if my speeches had any rings of truth to them. They did not care much for the drive, but we soon settled in, had dinner, and met Will Chabun at Casino Regina

Flat Out with the Elk Man

for a bit. In the morning, we headed to practice, and good fortune smiled upon me in my mission of Rider conversion.

Arriving at practice, as I tell the story now, we were approached nearly non-stop by almost everyone I knew in Regina. My two friends watched as I related induction stories, brought people up to date with Dave's life, and even made a date for breakfast the next day with Roy Shivers. Just when they thought I had run out of acquaintances, I found Phil Gibson, reintroduced myself, and gave him an autographed copy of Dave Ridgway's book for Chris Cvetkovic. Chris was not on the active roster that week and wasn't at practice, but Phil promised to get it to him. We talked about Scott Smiley, the former teacher of the two young Riders in Burlington, who had asked me to say hello to both of them.

Harv and Tim could stand it no longer. When Phil left, they had a type of confession to make. Both had looked forward to the trip, it seemed, but had limited expectations things in Regina would be quite as interesting as I had so often described. The rapid succession of introductions, coupled with our presence on the actual playing surface during practice, a Regina reality they possibly thought I was making up, convinced them they could safely allow their expectations to move upward.

Traveling companions Tim Anderson and Harv Moen

Rider Pride on the American Side

As the confession ended, the Riders had departed, and the Calgary Stampeders were on the field. I spoke briefly with Stamps radio voice Mark Stephen, congratulating him on the fine job he had done during the bust unveiling ceremony during the Hall of Fame weekend, and then reintroduced myself to Mark McLoughlin. Mark was pleasant to talk to, and I was glad we had a few more minutes than we had been afforded at the dinner in Calgary. Former Rider QB Keith Smith was then with the Stampeders, and it was fun to touch base with him again, too.

The three Minnesotans left Taylor Field feeling upbeat; Tim and Harv because they had thoroughly enjoyed themselves and Terry because the Powers That Be had once again enabled a perfect alignment of the relatively few people I know in Regina.

With the two newcomers in tow, it was easy to find things to do, and we quickly filled out the day. Thanksgiving morning and Game Day arrived and we picked up Roy Shivers, who was a bit hobbled from knee replacement surgery, and headed to breakfast. World Series time was approaching, and much of our conversation involved baseball. Roy is a fine storyteller, and the Minnesotans tossed in a few of their tales too. Breakfast with the general manager was the final ingredient in Harv and Tim's conversions into CFL fans; the three bus friends have turned this fall trip into an annual event ever since this first 2003 sojourn.

The game itself had a happy ending for the Riders, as they clinched a playoff spot with a 24 – 22 win. It was hardly an offensive gem by either club, but the Riders held off five McLoughlin field goals and Omarr Morgan took a fumble back for a 56-yard touchdown in the third quarter. Paul McCallum won the game with a 17-yard chip shot with about 5 minutes left. The Saskatchewan club had a 9 – 7 record and was en route to its first season at .500 or better since 1994.

Harv and Tim enjoyed the contest, and asked a lot of great questions. We joined the exodus of over 46,000 fans from Taylor Field, heading down Albert Street to Earl's for the long anticipated meeting with one William Donison.

Earl's is a fine restaurant, and busy after Rider games. Will Chabun was also with us, and on the way, I wondered aloud how it would feel to meet another total stranger whom I was tied to in only the very loosest of ways. Any hesitation I had evaporated immediately, as Bill quickly proved to be a funny, talkative fellow, who engaged us all evening with interesting stories of past Rider glories and Grey Cup adventures. The five of us laughed nearly continually as I got to know a man who seemed like an old friend almost immediately, and who would prove to be a fellow whose heart was as big as Minnesota and Saskatchewan combined. We left Bill, with a promise to meet at Grey Cup, and the three Bus Buddies even almost enjoyed their long trip home.

The biggest trip of 2003 remained and the Riders still had a good shot to host the Grey Cup. Winning their final two games to finish at 11 - 7, they began the playoff slate by heading to Winnipeg for the third meeting of that season between the two teams.

Tim Anderson and Bill Donison

Chris Melin came over to our house, and we actually watched the game, not televised in Minnesota, by a complex computer feed from one of our Calgary friends. The picture was shaky and a bit behind the audio, but it was passable. The Riders were ready, and quickly jumped out to a 17 – 0 lead, on touchdowns by Kenton Keith on a 33-yard dash and by Matt Dominguez on an exciting 55-yard pass from Nealon Greene. Two TD passes from Khari Jones brought the Bombers within two as the 4th quarter began, but Kenton Keith became Player of the Week with a pair of touchdown runs in the last stanza, leading Saskatchewan to a 37 – 21 triumph.

Just one more victory, in Edmonton in the Western Final, would give Regina the coveted Grey Cup home appearance and likely also cause the best party in the history of this planet. It was not to be, however, as the Esks jumped to a 23 – 2 lead and held on for both dear life and the Grey Cup berth. Kevin Glenn replaced the faltering Nealon Greene in the second half, and led the Riders to three TDs in the final seven minutes, including one following the recovery of an onside kick. One kick recovery was all Saskatchewan could manage, though, and the Green and White lost the home Grey Cup dream by a score of 30 – 23.

Frankly, this loss was incredibly disappointing. Set to go to the Grey Cup, and with the possibility of Saskatchewan in the game, it seemed like all a person could want, but it just didn't work out. Since Resiliency needs to be the middle name of a Rider fan, Chris Melin and I knew we had to shake off the tough loss and get ready to head to Regina.

We had decided to fly for this important trip. The uncertainty of November weather combined with a Northwest Airlines promotion made the decision both easy and relatively painless. The hotel reservation was for four nights, so we made plans to leave Minnesota on Thursday, giving ourselves an additional day for the festivities beyond our usual Grey Cup pattern.

The Ridgway's were also coming, since Dave had been asked to do a ceremonial kickoff prior to the game. Better yet, they were scheduled to be on our flight from Minneapolis to Regina. However, things were amiss in the airline world that day, and although our flight waited for an hour for latecomers, Connie and Dave did not make it.

It was my first flight to Regina, and a very easy one. It was interesting as we circled to land to be able to spot landmarks, something I can seldom do successfully in the Twin Cities. A large fellow who looked quite familiar was seated across from me; only later did I determine it was 2006 Hall of Famer Bobby Jurasin, who undoubtedly would have been interesting to talk to. The disadvantage of the lack of TV coverage bit me once more.

Chris and I grabbed our luggage and headed for Customs and then out to the reception area, where Kelly Ramler was to be waiting for us. My friend was right behind me

Flat Out with the Elk Man

and, as I exited, I saw a couple of men with official Grey Cup committee identification and correctly assumed they were waiting to pick up the missing Ridgway's. After telling them Dave had not made the flight, I spotted Kelly, but then realized my friend Chris had disappeared.

Several minutes later, he came out the door, having evidently fit the bad guy profile and thus subject to a complete search of his belongings. I was certainly grateful I fit only the old guy profile, and had been ushered straight through. We were pleased to get a bit of VIP attention, as other Grey Cup Committee members were meeting the flights for hospitality purposes, and Chris and I received nice souvenir packets.

Kelly was working as a volunteer, and had to get to his post shortly, so we went to the hotel and had a quick lunch. He then dropped us off at Taylor Field so we could pick up our game tickets. The Rider Store was already hopping, so we said a quick Hello to Liz, made some obligatory purchases, saw Roy for a fast moment, and then walked back to the hotel. It's an easy walk, about a mile, and the day was certainly fine for the trek.

Our celebration needed to begin, and we had planned on meeting a number of friends at Riderville, the team's official hospitality area. In 2003, this event was held at the Agribition Grounds, about twice as far from our downtown spot as Taylor Field. A taxi seemed like the answer, but this mode of transportation on Grey Cup weekend in Regina is tough to find, and we walked up to the Delta Hotel on Saskatchewan Drive in hopes of finding some transport. Idling in the driveway was an official Grey Cup van, manned by a volunteer who had no apparent celebrities to chauffer at the moment. A reasonable man, he succumbed to the Dumb American ploy and gladly took us to Riderville.

Although it was still mid-afternoon, and a Thursday at that, many fans and partygoers were already present, and we soon found Govind Achyuthan, Jason Isaac, Marty Neumeier and Jeff Banow. Within a few minutes, Dave Fulton and Darwin Gooding also appeared, the latter lugging around a homemade replica of the Grey Cup itself.

It was great wandering time and I was in my favourite element. Chris and I were standing around, and suddenly we both saw the same group at the same moment, and burst in laughter. Spotting none other than the 1998 Ridgway

Discoverers, the legendary Three-Man Band, I bought them a beer, told them of the good fortune they had aided and updated the photo gallery.

The CFL Players' Association had a table at the party, and a number of recognizable players were in the area. I met Chris Szarka and Andrew Greene for the first time, and had a few seconds of conversation with Paul McCallum. Hamilton quarterback Danny McManus was there also, and interestingly, recalled our 1999 meeting. I'm always trying to think up a good conversational items to discuss with players, so I mentioned to Danny, a Florida State alumnus, that my wife had taught the younger sister of Seminole Heisman Trophy winner Chris Weinke, who is from St. Paul. With McManus was BC Lion QB Dave Dickenson, and a more pleasant person likely could not be found. Dave's brother had lived at one time in a Minneapolis suburb, and we spoke a bit about that. Once again, the ability of the average fan to interact with some of the league's marquee players was evident, and their willingness to do so is a real asset to their teams and the league itself.

Three-Man Band reprised, 2003 Grey Cup

We stayed for a long while, enjoying the friendship, the crowd and certainly the beverages. A number of volunteers were organizing audience participation games, and Govind and Chris were persuaded to pass an orange to each other, using only their chins to hold it. Of course, a photo of this intimate moment exists, but this is intended as a family book, and I am thus not able to publish it.

Marty, Jeff, Chris and I decided to return downtown for some food. Part of Scarth Street had been blocked off and a huge party tent erected, and we wanted to sample that celebration also. It was a lively place, and we soon caught up with many of the group who had been with us at Riderville.

Dave Dickenson   **Danny McManus**

As previously noted, I sometimes miss the very obvious. In this tent I had one of those interesting revelations. I had met Saskatchewan broadcast legend Dale Isaac on a few occasions and greeted him in the tent. Dale was with our friend Jason Isaac, and I finally realized the two are in fact father and son. The same last name should have given it away, but somehow did not.

The tent was a good time, but was crowded and also a bit smoke filled. However, there were many people we knew in attendance, and it made sense to visit. One of my very favourite Grey Cup friends, a man met in Calgary in 2000 and seen only on the Championship Weekend is the famous Eskinator, Brian Edwards. Brian and his wife Linda live in Edmonton and are in the elite of Grey Cup couples I have had the pleasure to meet. Even though Brian and Linda were also staying at the Holiday Inn Express, even on the same floor as Chris and I, we saw them this weekend only at some of the party venues.

Rider Pride on the American Side

Dale Isaac   **Jason Isaac**

The Spirit of Edmonton was next on our list, held in 2003 in the ballroom of the Delta Hotel. Since it was only Thursday, we were able to gain admittance easily, and Chris and I loaded up on free Grey Cup shirts that were available by the boxful. Many other acquaintances were at this party, including Ken and Jacky Smith of Calgary and the rest of the Fulton clan. It was fun for me to tell Tom Fulton, the group patriarch, about my discovery of Elk Man Bill Donison, since Tom was one of the persons with whom I had initially discussed this mystery in 2000.

A fun evening it was and we stayed put until the early morning hours. Our hotel was but a short stroll down Rose Street, and we awoke later Friday morning ready for more.

The agenda for Friday had Bill Donison at the top of the list, and another Riderville trip was the destination. Per the *Leader-Post*, former Rider center Bob Poley was hosting a gathering of Saskatchewan football alumni, which sounded like our type of fun. The Elk Man picked us up about noon, and he and Chris were introduced. At Riderville, the crowd was slimmer, but beginning to build. Bob, whom I'd met at the Hall of Fame Induction, told me Dave and Connie had finally arrived, but on the last flight, late in the evening.

Bill Donison had brought along the Nov. 27, 1989 edition of the *Leader-Post*, from the day following that year's Rider Grey Cup victory, and Bob was happy to sign it. CBC

Saskatchewan radio was broadcasting live, and I was asked to be on the radio, offering to George Reed, who was at another location, an unintentionally lame question that the Rider Hall of Famer answered very courteously. I was looking for Tim Roth, hoping to meet the man for the first time, but Poley indicated Tim had cancelled his trip at the last moment. *Leader-Post* sports writer Murray McCormick's daughter was one of the Rider cheerleaders, and was a bit surprised when I tracked her down and asked if her dad was around. I didn't catch up to Murray either and will hopefully meet him some day.

Bill, Chris, and I did catch up with someone I had on my short list of people to meet: retired Rider lineman Roger Aldag, who had entered the Canadian Football Hall of Fame in 2002. Despite my shortcomings in Saskatchewan upbringing, I did know the storybook tale of a man from Gull Lake, Saskatchewan, an exceptional player who finally won a Grey Cup ring late in his career.

Bob Poley and Bill Donison

A Hall of Fame player, but as we found out both then and later, he's certainly also an excellent man. Roger is always eager to talk to fans, and as I have come to know him a bit since 2003, always thanks me for coming up to support the Riders. In fact, in 2005 he had a great idea, suggesting the team should fly the Faithful Minnesotan to Regina whenever the Holy Grail of a home playoff game finally takes place. We know now that not every great idea gets implemented.

Roger also made a comment to me in 2004 that I love to

relate to Saskatchewan friends who may not know him personally, but certainly know of him. Joe Hadesbeck had asked me to be on the Rider pre-game radio show, and as I left the Green and White Lounge after my babble, I ran into Roger on the practice field. Since I had only met him once, at Grey Cup, I reintroduced myself. His eyes twinkled just a bit, and he said, "I was just driving in and heard you on the radio. I turned to my wife and said, "I know that guy!" Say what? The man who is often called Mr. Saskatchewan Roughrider telling someone he knows *me*!

Of course, when we had met Roger in 2003, a photo of he, Bill, and I had been in order. I had enlarged it, and had a couple of copies sitting at home, waiting for an opportunity to get Roger to autograph them. On this day in 2004, he indicated he'd be happy to do so, and later returned them, including for both Bill and I a signed 8x10 of he and Bob Poley hoisting the Grey Cup in 1989. A good man and I am glad to have met him.

Roger Aldag

Chris and I had lunch with Bill, and later spent the evening with our chauffeur Kelly Ramler, even threatening to get him an appropriate drivers' cap. A smaller "Meet and Greet" party was held, and Ken and Jacky Smith took the occasion to present me with a bottle of 2001 Montreal Grey Cup wine as their thanks for the Hall of Fall Game experience. After that, it was a pretty quiet night with a good friend, and we awoke Saturday rested and ready for the Snow Bowl.

Flat Out with the Elk Man

Grey Cup Saturday also brought the *Leader-Post's* Grey Cup section. Rob Vanstone needed filler for the 42-page special, and had called a few weeks earlier to update the Minnesota story. It was, as usual, well done, and I was able to snatch several copies for posterity.

The impact of the *Leader-Post* and its sports section in Regina is interesting to me. Here in Minnesota, both Minneapolis and St. Paul have large daily newspapers, with lots of competition for readers, and plenty of local sports teams to write about. I would have to rate special sections like the *L-P's* Grey Cup supplement and the 2005 Saskatchewan Centennial edition as journalism that is nothing short of excellent, and certainly at a par or better with my Minnesota experiences. The *Leader-Post* and its sports staff are continually beaten up by the online wags of internet message boards when the Riders are criticized, but I believe these online critics lack the perspective of comparison. Our local sports scribes at times are merciless and often make any criticisms by writers in the *Leader-Post* appear as mild indeed. Besides, if a person talks to Rob Vanstone or Rider football beat writer Darrell Davis for even twelve seconds, the realization sets in that these writers actually do know something more about football than the average cyberspace grumbler.

Chris was again playing in the Snow Bowl, and I was going along as a retired football executive. The game was held at a high school field on the east end of Regina and I was only mildly into it. A reprieve came in the form of a phone call from Dave Ridgway early in the game, inviting me to join he and Connie for a beverage. I convinced Darwin Gooding's lovely bride Deanna to give me a ride back downtown and joined Dave and Connie in the cozy lounge of the Regina Inn.

Being with Dave in a public place in Regina during Grey Cup week means a never-ending stream of people stopping by to greet him, and it was here I met Darrell Davis for the first time. We even spotted Commissioner Tom Wright, but he whisked through before we could hail him. Dave's friend Troy Christian also joined us, and the four of us relived some of our Calgary memories from two months prior.

Meeting Chris back at our hotel, he and I joined up with Edmonton friends Arnie and Bambi for a meal. Once again, Arnie, with the Minnesotans in tow, miraculously evaded the Spirit of Edmonton line. We spend the evening with our Alberta friends, and retired actually fairly early to be ready for Game Day.

Since season-ticket holders were allowed to purchase their regular seats for Grey Cup, I had done so, and later sold the two extras to a friend of Jeff Banow. The tickets were $159 each, a bit more than Edmonton, but favourably priced in comparison to Calgary and Winnipeg. Kelly picked us up and we enjoyed the practice field atmosphere, packed with people and concessions. Despite the crowd, we were able to hook up with most of our friends at one time or another before we entered the stadium.

Nearly 51,000 fans packed Taylor Field, including a large number of Edmonton fans eager to see their Eskimos atone for the previous year's defeat in this rematch with the Montreal Alouettes. Despite the crowd, Section 102 didn't feel much different than normal, since it's usually full anyway, and the overwhelmingly crowded feeling we had felt in Edmonton was not present. It was a bit disappointing that I missed Dave's ceremonial kickoff; it happened well before the start of the game.

Media hot air, Grey Cup 2003

The game was a good, although not great, championship contest. Edmonton scored on its opening drive and went ahead 14 – 0 early in the second quarter. The Als' offence then came alive, and scored twice in about two minutes to tie the score. The entire second quarter was great football entertainment as the teams combined to score 30 points in that period, with

Edmonton up 24 – 21 at the break.

Bryan Adams was the half time entertainer, and as I thought about The Summer of '69, I went searching for Bill Donison, but could not find his seats in the crowd. Montreal could not find its offence either, and scored only a single in the entire second half. Edmonton countered with a touchdown and a late field goal, spoiling the Als' attempt to repeat, and winning by a final of 34 – 22.

After dinner with Kelly, we headed back to the hotel to watch the highlights, enjoying a smooth trip home the next day as the culmination of being part of the fine effort by the Riders and the City of Regina as hosts to the 2003 Grey Cup.

Halftime at Grey Cup, Nov. 16, 2003

One more football task remained for 2003. I had Dave sign a copy of *Robokicker* at Grey Cup for Phil Gibson, noting the unusual and identical Burlington/Toledo/Montreal/Rider connections. I mailed it to Phil because a good man deserves a good book and was happy to receive a nice return note.

Ironically, in 2007 I met via email a man named Brad Frost, also a Burlington native and the women's hockey coach at the University of Minnesota. Brad is a bit older than Chris and Phil and didn't know them but seemed like just a good guy also. Those folks in Burlington, Ontario, all raised their kids well.

Chapter 14

Saskatchewan Nice

We all likely have a few movies that we can watch over and over again. One of mine is the great football movie *Remember the Titans.* A very favourite scene is a dramatic moment as the coaches prepared their team for the upcoming state championship contest. Coach Youst, played by Will Patton, stared at Denzel Washington's Coach Boone. Patton's character declared something on the order of "This isn't just about football anymore, is it?"

In a different context, we could say the same about our relationship with the city of Regina, the province of Saskatchewan and the Saskatchewan Roughrider Football Club. Over the years, and particularly in the past seven or so, the experiences we have had, the friends we have made, and the lessons we have learned really mean, in fact, it isn't just about football any more. It's about a broadening of the McEvoy horizons, about meeting people who matter and, importantly, about good old-fashioned fun. Let's take a look at both the interesting facets of life we have observed in our many trips to the Prairie Province, and also acknowledge some of those people we have been fortunate enough to meet.

In more ways than you might imagine, Saskatchewan and Regina are similar to Minnesota. I have mentioned my relatives who moved to the prairies, but have also met dozens of people in Saskatchewan who have Minnesota relatives. For example, we drive past a billboard in central Minnesota for Ramler Truck Repair and Kelly says it is likely he is related to that Ramler group. Al Christensen of Christopher Lake has Minnesota relations living near Alexandria, also in the central portion of the Gopher State.

Some of the similarities are even fairly unique on a broader geographic scale – in both Roseville and Regina, a person can ask for "pop" to drink, but in many other places I've visited, you had better order "soda." But more importantly, the values of the common folk are very close indeed in the two locations. A local expression, "Minnesota Nice," refers to the general friendliness and good demeanor of our residents here. It's sometimes used sarcastically, but often only means people most usually try to be nice to one another. I've seen a similar term also used in Saskatchewan, and it also certainly applies there. I've never lived in a small town, but St. Paul is often referred to as "the biggest small town in America," and at least part of that reference addresses the positive attributes of the population. In Saskatchewan, we've met people from farm and village, city and town, and the common factor, I believe, is that distinctively friendly first impression that nearly always hits us.

Right around the Labour Day Classic each year, the internet sites are filled with banter, much directed at Regina and at Saskatchewan by residents of Winnipeg and greater Manitoba preparing for their annual trek. Some is in good fun, but some is just nasty. To tell the truth, I really resent the negativity. Maura, Carson, and Connor have each spent the equivalent of more than a month in Regina since 1994, and I have spent over 100 nights in the Queen City. We may thus to able to comment on the merits of the city with a bit more actual evidence.

We like Regina, obviously. It is just large enough to afford many things to do, but still not of a size where traffic and general bustle impact a person's life as can happen here in our more congested part of the world. It's full of history, as clean or cleaner than other places we're used to, and is certainly a place where we've always felt safe. The abundance of good restaurants can even make the choice of a place to eat a difficult one. I have come to feel a bit like I belong and it's funny, but in a good way, when the voice of the Riders, Rod Pedersen, sometimes greets me with a "Welcome home!"

With all of those nights in motels, we often wonder why we have never picked a "favourite spot" in the Regina accommodations world. It's likely because there are a large number of lodging choices, and we have stayed in at least ten different places without a bad experience. Often, thrift enters the picture, and our choice may be made on price. When the boys were younger, we concentrated on waterslide-equipped locales, and usually still try to have a pool available. In our opinion, the location of the motel in Regina doesn't play a big factor. It's not hard to get from Point A to Point B, and even staying in the east end, where we like the Days' Inn, is an easy trip to Taylor Field and other attractions. Downtown works well also, especially when the boys are not along. Chris and I are particularly fond of the Holiday Inn Express, a neat old building with large rooms, a good continental breakfast, and an easy walk to the stadium. Our most recent family trips have pointed us to the Sherwood House, in our opinion a great value for our lodging dollar. In this age of corporate sponsorships, we would certainly entertain bids to enable an enterprising business to become the Official Regina Hotel of the Minnesota Gopher Family. Imagine your photo in the next book!

Restaurants in Regina are a treat for us, for multiple reasons. There are many of them, with a variety of specialties and a wide range of prices. Kelly Ramler once told me Regina leads the league in restaurants per capita, and I certainly wouldn't dispute it. It appears the competition keeps prices low, and we find meals priced about the same as here, even before the exchange rate factor. We have established a few favourites, with Montana's being on the top of my personal list. Carson and Connor like Boston Pizza, and nothing beats the Peking House for great Chinese. We don't often trip the light fantastic, but have very much enjoyed Golf's and The Lakeshore on special occasions. When traveling with Chris Melin, a required stop on the way to Regina is the Tim Horton's in Estevan, and he and I often enjoy a good meal and a brew at Bushwakkers. Chris can barely wait until his next trip, since the World's Largest Tim Horton's will be waiting for us.

French fries with gravy are certainly commonplace in Regina, but completely unheard of in Minnesota, where ketchup is the garnish of choice. We also do not have the pleasure of dry ribs, and Regina's Melrose Place restaurants are a favourite of mine for that delicacy. Caesar salad is much more common in Regina than here, and also much more likely to be misspelled as "Ceasar" on the many portable signboards.

Antique shops are often an entertaining way to spend some time, and the subtle, but distinct differences in the items in Regina's shops when compared to ours is interesting. I am always on the prowl for a 1989 Saskatchewan license plate, but the Rider success that season has clearly impacted the pricing of such an item. After the first edition of this book was

Saskatchewan Nice

published, I actually received this plate for Christmas. Meredith and Bill found it, of course, on the internet.

Day trips in the surrounding area have also been good to us. We all enjoyed the Tunnels of Moose Jaw, and the Western Development Museum was fascinating. I am even quite certain one of my great aunts is in a photo that is part of a railroad immigration exhibit. On the future list in this category is a trip to Regina Beach to determine if there is really a beach there.

On occasions, I have read something in the *Leader-Post* causing me to do some further investigation, since a fellow is never too old to learn something new. Late one summer, I saw an ad listing the Catholic elementary schools in Regina, and was amazed by the seemingly large number in the Queen City. St. Paul is a very Catholic place, but Regina has nearly as many Catholic institutions of elementary learning. Chabun again to the rescue, explaining that government funding is available to non-public schools in a much less restricted manner than exists here in Minnesota.

Although many words and phrases have universal meanings, we've certainly found a few that differ. In my mind, a bunny hug is what Elmer Fudd gives to Bugs, but it's evidently also a hooded sweatshirt. I learned what a toque in an embarrassing way, thinking it was pronounced "toke." It's just a stocking cap, anyway. By the way, I certainly enjoy a good cabaret, but here it's only an old movie with Liza Minnelli. In Minnesota, I've never seen a street with the tag "Crescent" following the street name, but seemingly everyone I know in Regina lives on one with that descriptor.

Beer is sometimes an ingredient to our experiences, particularly at Grey Cup parties. We've grown to like Pilsner, or "Pil," and I thought it was funny when it sold out at Riderville in Vancouver in 2005 and the local stores had no more. Maura and I also like Rickert's Red, a fine smooth beer. I have on occasion brought Minnesota beer to tailgates, but it has failed to impress. Most Canadians seem to prefer the native brews, but I do see a lot of Coors Light around also.

Pronunciation is one of our favourite Saskatchewan subjects. I noted earlier my lesson from Peter Lunde on the appropriate mouthing of the Province's name, but have found that to be just the tip (of the tongue) of the proverbial iceberg. One of my personal interests is the way various people say the name of the large Albertan city east of Banff, the one beginning with the letter "C."

Until we began going to Saskatchewan, I had never heard it pronounced any way except something like "Cal ga ree," said fairly quickly, and really containing just a single, extended syllable. I find it spoken two ways in Saskatchewan, both different from what I am used to. Some people say "Cal Gree," again quickly, but essentially dropping the "a'" we use. The other pronunciation actually set me back a bit the first time I heard it. This version is quite different, with the word said as "Cal Gary," two distinct syllables, and decent emphasis on each. The first time I heard it pronounced this way I was certain that the conversation was about a country western singer, first name of Cal.

Of course, I cannot let this topic go without a comment on the standard American perception that everyone in Canada ends every sentence with the expression "Eh!" The first time Chris Melin drove to Regina with me, in 2001, he pulled out a CD as we approached the border, and the car filled with the sound of Bob and Doug McKenzie's "Great White North," Eh! Despite Joe Canadian's rant to the contrary, there are a few "Eh's" and even an occasional "A boot" but I seldom notice them any longer. It is actually no different than parts of Minnesota, especially the state's central area around the city of St. Cloud, where regional dialects still vary some from the way we citified folks may say things. Besides, in Regina, I'm the foreigner and I'm sure many people wonder about my weird American manner of speaking.

Regardless of the phrases they might use, and their choice of pronunciation, Saskatchewan people are good folks, and some have on occasion done special things for the McEvoy family. I'd be remiss if I chose to ignore mention of these people and their deeds, since they have made our experiences "not just about football" and are very much "Saskatchewan nice."

First up are the people I have met who are officially associated with the Saskatchewan Roughrider Football Club. **Ryan Whippler** and **Kevin Clive** are always accommodating, put up with me at practices and are always good for a smile, a friendly greeting and often some good information.

President/CEO **Jim Hopson** is a newer addition to my group of Mosaic Stadium associates and does a great job in making me feel like I'm much more special than I know I am,

Saskatchewan Nice

and I appreciate the positive public face he has added to the business side of the Rider organization.

Tony Playter, the Riders' coordinator of football operations, is also always there with a warm handshake and words of welcome. As a man who likes to repay kindnesses, I was happy to be able to line up some Minnesota Twins tickets for a trip Tony made to Minnesota, an easy thing to do, but a rare occasion of payback for me.

The Rider ticket office personnel are wonderful on the phone, a very welcome island in today's world of ugly voice mail menus and offshore customer service. The manager, **Gail Mund,** did me a big favour in late 2005. I had purchased some Rendezvous Saskatchewan tickets in Regina, but somehow lost them when I returned home to Minnesota. After two days of searching, I gave up, and sent Gail a sheepish e-mail, wondering if the tickets could be replaced for the poor, old, and clearly senile Minnesotan. Shortly afterward, I received replacement tickets in the mail, a gesture that would never happen with the average lost ticket here. It wasn't a tremendous amount of money, but the thought certainly counted. Later, in 2007, my long-awaited home playoff tickets were apparently stuck in a mail truck somewhere and a quick email to Gail was all I needed to straighten things out.

In 2004, I was wearing my white Ridgway jersey at a game on a warm day, and the "G" in Dave's last name became stuck to my seat and peeled off. As a game worn artifact, it's my favourite Rider souvenir, and essentially priceless to me. But it needed repair, and I took it to several shops here in Minnesota that would not attempt the fix. Liz Measner sent me to Rider Equipment Manager **Norm Fong**, who expertly made it whole again, and seemed to enjoy doing it. My offer to pay was spurned, but at least Norm got a Minnesota Gopher shirt for his trouble.

Another Rider-related person I appreciate is the team's radio voice, **Rod Pedersen**. I still chuckle about introducing myself to him a few years back, and Rod responding with "You're the guy who sat next to my cousin Peter." A funny way to be known, but it has worked well. Rod is my internet host to a lot of Rider games, and I hope the Saskatchewan fans understand what a fine announcer he is. Especially appreciated by me is Rod's level of reality and lack of excessive "homerism" that is sometimes evident in other teams' broadcasts. Rod always warmly welcomes us, and I enjoy giving him grief about his attachment to a certain Twin Cities sports talk radio station.

Norm Fong   **Rod Petersen**

Some particular incidents stand out as well in terms of the kindnesses offered. In 2003, Maura, Carson, Connor and I visited the Saskatchewan Sports Hall of Fame on a day where a myriad of events were planned, including games, food, and lots of current and former Rider players. We met hall program director **Dale West**, a former Rider and also a hall member himself. I had a particular mission, since I had been told one of my cousins, Ken Orth, was a member, and wanted to find his display. Failing to find it, I mentioned it to Dale.

It was a very busy day at the hall, but Dale somehow found time to research my question, and tracked us down. He reported that cousin Ken was in fact a member of North Battleford's Saskatchewan Baseball Hall of Fame, and this revelation later helped me get motivated to track down some long-lost Saskatchewan relatives.

However, tracking down relatives requires more than Hall of Fame information. In late 2004, I noticed that a new member on Riderfans.com listed Rosetown, Saskatchewan as home. Since I knew my cousins were in that area, I took a chance, introducing myself via e-mail and asking if the cousins' surname of Orth was a familiar one. That began a correspondence with **Marilyn McIntyre** of Rosetown, who eventually hooked me up with the Orth brothers, Doug of Rosetown, and Ross of Swift Current. They are my second

Saskatchewan Nice

cousins, and Maura and I met them and their wives at Grey Cup in Vancouver in 2005. It's unusual for an old guy to meet relatives for the first time, and Marilyn McIntyre made it all happen. I was able to also meet Marilyn in 2005 and one of my many thrills of Grey Cup weekend in 2007 was meeting up with the entire McIntyre traveling troupe in Toronto.

One of my most interesting stories about Saskatchewan travels involves a truly thoughtful act by a complete stranger. Chris Melin, Jeff Banow, Marty Neumeier and I were visiting Riderville at the 2003 Grey Cup. Wanting to go back downtown and without a car, we debated our options. Walking was very unattractive due to the distance of close to two miles, and there were no cabs in sight. Suddenly, I spotted a woman who had been a volunteer at the festivities, and asked her if she would possibly be heading downtown, and if she could see her way to giving four louts a ride. She hesitated, although briefly, but agreed, correctly assuming we were quite harmless. We piled into her small vehicle, cramped but mobile, and she dropped us off downtown.

She did tell us her name, but we soon forgot it. The story was retold a number of times, including at the next Grey Cup in Ottawa. On the Saturday of that 2004 weekend, Marty and I were again rehashing the tale, and I even came up with the woman's name, which was Lorelei — or so I thought. That afternoon, at Rendezvous Saskatchewan, we were listening to the Rider Pep Band and for reasons I no longer remember, the name Lorelei was announced. Almost instinctively, I scanned the crowd.

There was a somewhat familiar face on the edge of the crowd – it was our 2003 benefactor. So I approached her and asked if she recalled giving any strange men a ride from Riderville the previous year. Recognition was immediate, and she introduced herself as **Laur'Lei Silzer**, and gave me her business card. We shared a hearty laugh at the extreme coincidence, and the boys and I have never forgotten the typically Saskatchewan good deed she had done for us. Chris Melin and I caught up with Laur'Lei in the fall of 2007 and enjoyed rehashing this fun story one more time.

A man deserving a lot of credit in bringing Rider fans together is **Shane Chapman** of Regina, the webmaster of Riderfans.com. For out-of-towners such as myself, this site is a good source of both news and friendships and Shane's talents and dedication in getting it going and keeping it moving forward are much appreciated. With a job, a family and school all in the mix, I don't know how he finds the time, but he makes a difference for a lot of us.

Shane Chapman, Riderfans.com

The McEvoys have met a number of fans from our association with Riderfans.com, and it is often hit-and-miss whom we will see on a given trip. Three lads in particular, though, are virtually guarantees, since they are also residents of Section 102.

Troy Souster and **Marcel Nogue**, also known as Sudsy and Nugsy, both live in Saskatoon. These gentlemen have organized a successful pre-game tailgate; an event so successful that even local law enforcement types eagerly felt compelled to attend. These two characters even sent out their own Christmas card, a greeting that had me laughing out loud when I opened it. It's not every day we receive cards displaying two smiling faces wearing Rider jerseys and each holding a beer. Our other Section 102 friend is **Darwin Gooding** of Swift Current, an enthusiastic fan who is the section's personal cheerleader. On more than one occasion, Darwin has pointed to us, and screamed, "Those people are from Minnesota – when I say Minnesota, you say Gophers" as the Americans try to crawl beneath their seats. He keeps the section alive and undoubtedly enjoys Rider football as much as anyone I've ever met.

Saskatchewan Nice

Marcel Nogue, Troy Souster   **Darwin Gooding**

Before the Labour Day Classic in 2005, I was approached by a man who presented me with a well-designed T-shirt acknowledging Regina as "Footballtown." It was a fun way to meet **Brent Magnus** of Regina, and his generosity was appreciated. Brent, his wife **Karen**, and their lovely daughter **Taylor** have become good friends. Maura was able to meet Brent and Karen in Vancouver and I also hooked up with them in Winnipeg in 2006. Chris Melin and I had one of our best-ever Regina evenings at their house during the 2007 season. They are a great family, fantastic Riders fans and always fun to be with.

Brent and Karen Magnus

Another man I originally met through Riderfans.com is **Joe Hadesbeck**, the fine host of several Rider radio shows, including the pre-game Touchdown Club. Joe treats me much better than he needs to or I deserve, and has honoured me a few times by allowing me to mumble on the radio. I'm amazed by his smoothness – I feel like I'm sitting in my living room as he asks his questions. Joe's sons Kris and Ryley are often around the lavish surroundings of the owner's tent where the pre-game broadcasts originate from. Joe's partner on the air is former Rider great **Bob Poley**, an always-enthusiastic man whose energy is very contagious. It's always a real pleasure to stop by to see these two on the practice field before the game.

Bob (left) and Joe on the air

The act of kindness I remember best came from a Rider player. In October of 2005, Terry from Australia was in Regina, and he and I attended practice on a chilly morning. Things were wrapping up and as kicker **Paul McCallum** headed back to the locker room, he stopped to say hello. I had met Paul a couple of times, but didn't really know him and was a bit surprised. The Aussie was introduced, and the three of us discussed polar bears, since Terry was on his way to see the bear migration in Manitoba. Since the game day forecast was on the cold side, Paul asked if we had something warm to sit on. We did not, and he insisted on giving us some Rider seat cushions, immediately going out to his vehicle to get them. This thoughtful act even earned Paul a coveted Robby award from the *Leader-Post's* Vanstone, winning for the best gesture toward a fan in 2005. I had certainly planned on returning the cushions to Paul, but that could mean he'd have the forfeit the priceless Robby. These cushions have come in handy multiple times since and I did track Paul down in 2006 to thank him again and give him a book.

As long as we are on the subject of **Rob Vanstone**, the *Leader-Post* guy is completely responsible for introducing us to the fine cuisine of the Peking House, and has certainly placed our names in his newspaper much more often than necessary or expected. He's a good friend whom we do not see as often as would be ideal, since he is always working!

The final group we'd like to recognize in this chapter will remain unnamed, but appreciated nonetheless. Our travels to Saskatchewan in the past fifteen football seasons have brought us in contact with hundreds of people, in every capacity and category imaginable. From food servers to priests, from sales clerks to ticket sellers, from cashiers to football players, we have rarely, if ever, met a bad apple. This says it all about the province and we thank you all for being forever Saskatchewan Nice.

Chapter 15

Vegetable Lasagna in the Nation's Capitol

The 2004 season appeared on paper to be one of high potential for the Saskatchewan Roughriders. The emergence of the team in reaching the Western Division Final the previous year had been encouraging, and the decent 11 – 7 regular season record had been the best in nearly a decade. A major downside was the move of wide receiver Matt Dominguez to the greener pastures of the NFL, where he attempted to crack the roster of the New York Jets. In May, quarterback Kevin Glenn, who had nearly pulled off a miracle comeback in the western final, was traded to the Toronto Argonauts, who immediately shipped him to the Winnipeg Blue Bombers.

But the quarterback position seemed secure, with Nealon Greene returning again, and Henry Burris expected to finally regain his pre-NFL form. Ian "Rocky" Butler, he of 2002 Labour Day Classic fame, was the third pivot on the roster. This security lasted less than a quarter, however, as Nealon Greene left the opening game in Toronto with a broken leg and would not dress for a game the rest of the regular season. Rocky Butler replaced Nealon in that opener, but the offence was ineffective. The Argonauts were buoyed by an early 105-yard touchdown return by Bashir Levingston after a missed field goal and won 21 – 10.

The Rider home opener followed in five short days, and the Riders tumbled again, losing to Calgary 33 – 10 in a contest that was close at the half, but saw the Stamps pull away quickly in the third quarter. Our Family Trip was planned for the July 2 game against the British Columbia Lions and it was clear the Riders needed to make some type of distinctive turnabout.

Maura and the boys had a treat in store, since they had not yet met Bill Donison, the Elk Man, and had on tap not only that introduction but also of a tour of Optimum Genetics, the

Vegetable Lasagna in the Nation's Capitol

elk and cattle business operated by Bill's daughter Rhonda Murray. Plans went awry immediately upon our Regina arrival, when we received a call at the hotel from Bill's wife Kathy. Our new friend had been hospitalized with potential heart difficulties, and a slowdown related to the Canada Day weekend would keep him at the Pasqua Hospital for several days. It was disturbing news, but Kathy indicated Bill seemed fine, and was not in any imminent danger. With regret, our introductions and tour were delayed.

At the Rider practice on July 1, it seemed like a good idea to get a trinket to cheer up Bill and then head to the hospital later to see him. We bought a football, and put out the search for Roy Shivers to ask him to sign it. Cindy Kistner was the team's football executive assistant at the time; she and I had met the previous season by telephone. Roy was then looking for some Vikings tickets for a Rider director who was going to be in the Twin Cities, and I showed my total lack of local connections by failing to obtain any decent seats for a sold-out Metrodome contest.

I asked the receptionist to tell Cindy her uncle from Minnesota was looking for her. She came out with a laugh, meeting Maura and the boys, and taking us back to look for Roy. The inner offices were in the process of being remodeled, and she gave us a quick version of the grand tour. The general manager was discovered back in the training area, and I was sent back there to see him. Ivan Gutfriend was working on Roy's new knee, but as always, Roy checked on our trip, gave his best wishes for Bill's recovery and signed the football.

The first trip of the season is always a great time, since it's an opportunity to renew acquaintances after the long off-season. Rod Petersen and Rob Vanstone were doing their media things, but had time for a quick "Hi" and a few words. Darrell Davis was also present and came over to meet Maura and the boys, and sit to chat for a bit. Carson, Connor and Maura had not yet met Phil Gibson, and we had an extended talk with the defensive lineman, checking up on Chris Cvetkovic. Phil thanked me again for the Ridgway book, and impressed Maura with his poise and sincerity. Carson and Connor liked his James Earl Jones-sounding voice.

Armed with yet another good Chabun suggestion, we toured the Legislative building after practice, and expanded by a good amount our knowledge of Saskatchewan governmental history and process. I then headed to the hospital, where a bored Bill Donison was glad to see me, needlessly apologized for disturbing our plans, and thanked me many times for the football.

Carson, Phil Gibson, and Connor, July 2004

Plans for game day on Friday included catching up with Jeff Banow, Marty Neumeier and Govind Achyuthan for a meal, and then a tailgate stop before the game. Once again, the Regina weather was about to have its way, and as we headed to meet our friends, the rain came down in a big way. Completely drenched even in a short dash from car to restaurant, we were able at least to join Jeff and Marty for a good Melrose Place meal while we waited out the storm.

Wait we did, arriving at a waterlogged Taylor Field with little time to spare. Mopping our seats with paper towels from the restroom, we attained a semblance of dryness as the weather made a nice turn for the better. Our seat neighbours Joe and Nancy McNeill were out of town, but we soon found that the man in their seats farmed directly adjacent to Bill Donison's Optimum Genetics, another interesting bit of Saskatchewan coincidence.

The Henry Burris of old was back. In a very fine game to view, he passed for four touchdowns and ran for a fifth. Saskatchewan capitalized on two BC turnovers early in the second half, scoring TDs after each and won 42 – 29. Casey Printers, a name new to us, passed for two Lion touchdowns,

Vegetable Lasagna in the Nation's Capitol

but it looked to me like British Columbia would be in for a very long season. As usual, the Minnesota Prognosticator would be incorrect.

The rest of our summer keyed toward another Australia trip. Realizing three-week jaunts would likely not fit well into the future schedules of two teenagers, we resolved for one more family trip Down Under. I had worked part-time for the past year for Dan Norris, the owner of a local exterior renovating firm, learning how to apply vinyl siding, replace windows and the like. I had always wanted to do something along this line, having spent my entire adult working career in an office, and can truthfully say I learned more from Dan in one year than I did in college in four. This part-time work also served to finance our trip.

We again had a wonderful visit, with excellent weather, as we stayed exclusively in Queensland. Terry and Kerry were scheduled to meet up with us, but had to cancel because of Terry's mother, who was having medical difficulties. It seemed strange to go halfway around the world and not see our Aussie friends, but we certainly understood their situation.

I had not heard from Regina friend Kelly Ramler for a bit before we left on our trip, something that was unusual since we communicated regularly. When we returned, and I prepared for the Labour Day trip, I finally received an e-mail explaining his cyber silence. He'd somehow contracted meningitis, and was recovering in the Wascana Rehabilitation Centre. Feeling much better, he hoped to be able to attend the game, and we made arrangements to help him get there.

The Riders had been inconsistent since the July 2 game, and entered September with a 4 – 6 record. They were coming off of a bye week, having been thumped in Edmonton 31 – 7 on August 20. The Blue Bombers were in a dogfight for a playoff spot and sat at 3 – 7. It was clearly an important game.

Chris and I had a relatively easy trip, filled with tales of Australia and the wonders of the workplace I no longer thought much about. Kelly was ready for the Fan Day activities, so we picked him up at the Rehab Centre and headed to Taylor Field. A typical Labour Day weekend scene was unfolding, with all of the out-of-towners appearing. Greetings were in order for Bill and Cindy Wakefield, Gerard Stang and Govind, among others.

Winnipeg was on the field, and I wandered over to see

Chris Cvetkovic and was also able to say Hello to Tyson St. James, since both of the former Riders were with the Bombers. We made a tentative dinner date with Chris for later. A crew from CBC was working on a documentary of Roy Shivers, as I found out when a fellow stuck a camera about an inch from my head when I innocently discussed the upcoming baseball playoffs with Roy. The GM asked about my friend Bill, and I was happy to report the Elk Man had but a scare, and was fine. Glen Suitor, former Rider safety and holder for the famous 1989 Kick, was in Regina in his role as a TV game analyst. I introduced myself, and was happy to meet yet another key Ridgway contemporary.

Chris Szarka, the bruising Saskatchewan fullback, had a leg injury and wasn't on the active roster, but said he hoped to be back soon. He gladly accepted, in fine Rider fashion, the giant responsibilities of helping out with a photo opportunity.

Erik Nickel and son Jacob, with Chris Szarka

I managed to screw up our dinner date, confusing the time and called Cvetkovic, who was staying in Moose Jaw with the Bombers, too late. Apologizing, we resolved to try again in 2005, and I wished him a good game. Chris and I hooked up with the Wakefield's and headed out for pizza and the largest pitcher of beer I had ever seen.

Game day dawned warm and clear, and Chris and I were invited to join the Donison family for brunch at the Hotel Saskatchewan. It was certainly a generous offer, and very enjoyable to meet Bill's wife Kathy and the rest of their family.

Vegetable Lasagna in the Nation's Capitol

We felt welcome and comfortable, marveling once more at how things seem to work out in Saskatchewan. Excusing ourselves a bit early, we headed to pick up Kelly. I often bring up St. Paul newspapers for the reading enjoyment of Will Chabun, and he met us at the Rehab Centre to obtain his bag of loot. Heading to the Superstore Tailgate, we prepared for the Riders, in this key game, to dissect the Bombers.

Emotions ran high at the party, with the many Winnipeg fans in town verbally sparring with the fans of the Green and White. Predictions ran rampant and Gerard Stang, our friend from Calgary, foresaw a long day for the Bomber quarterback, former Rider Kevin Glenn. We left the tailgate early and headed to the practice field to mingle with the masses there.

This was a Labour Day classic with no offence taken and little given. Both teams appeared a bit flat, and the Riders, in front of a capacity crowd of 30,220, led by the only-in-the-CFL score of 3 – 1 at halftime. Kevin Glenn stepped up in the second half, throwing two touchdown passes, while Henry Burris, although outgaining Glenn in passing yards, threw a pair of costly interceptions and also fumbled in the first half deep in Bomber territory. Trailing by only seven points midway through the final quarter, the Riders were stymied when Burris's badly executed pass was intercepted in the end zone. This turnover led to Winnipeg's final tally in their 17 – 4 win. Of all of the upsetting plays I've seen at Taylor Field, this pass stands out. It was right in front of us, at a very key moment, and there appeared to be no Riders in the vicinity of the play.

A late game streaker provided some comic relief, taken down by a security person with the fiercest hit of the day. At game's end, we filed out with the crowd, trying hard to remember the glory of the Classic two years prior, but burdened with the second consecutive distasteful loss. Meeting Kelly, we headed back to the car, catching up with Gerard Stang, who inadvertently broke our depressed mood.

Our friend from Calgary was on a roll and ranted nonstop about the Riders' feeble effort and the unlikelihood of Kevin Glenn, yes, THAT Kevin Glenn, making much of the difference in the contest. His soliloquy was passionate, but hilarious at the same time and, at least for me, helped ease the moment. I can easily still visualize Gerard, sitting on his tailgate, muttering Kevin's name, with a new and imaginative middle name added. It was the only pleasing memory on a long drive home the next day.

Saskatchewan lost again to the Bombers the next week in Winnipeg, but then rebounded by defeating Ottawa and Hamilton. The stage was set for another very important contest, scheduled for October 2 against the Montreal Alouettes, a team that usually made things difficult for the Riders. Wide receiver Matt Dominguez had returned to Saskatchewan after being released by the Jets, and had added some firepower to the receiving corps.

Tim Anderson would be making his second trip to Taylor Field with me, with Harv Moen having to decline due to a schedule conflict. Tim had a request before we left – he wanted to play golf while in Regina. I figured I had come full circle with Saskatchewan connections when I was easily able to set this up. E-mailing Dale Isaac, who I knew was a golfer, I arranged for Tim to play on the morning of the game. Tim and I set out on Thursday, September 30, and the miles flew by quickly. He had also recently been given a retirement package, and our discussion focused on how nice it is not to go to work every day.

Gerard Stang

We arrived late in the afternoon, greeted by a howling wind and falling temperatures. The breeze was mighty, with legend having it that the kickoff in a high school game at Taylor Field that night actually landed *behind* the kicker. In the morning, practice was chilly, but bearable, and I enjoyed meeting Saskatchewan safety Darnell Edwards, and wondered why God gave he and Roy such full heads of hair at my expense. Tim and I listened in at the press conference, had lunch with Bill Donison and a good Chinese dinner later at the Peking House with Rob and Chryssoula Vanstone.

Golf on Game Day had seemed unlikely, but the weather co-operated and Dale picked up Tim while I headed 10 miles south of Regina for the Optimum Genetics tour. Rhonda Murray, Bill's daughter, took me through the facilities, valiantly trying to put their livestock-related business in terms the City Boy could understand, and did very well.

Joe Hadesbeck had invited me on the Touchdown Club, the Rider pre-game radio show, and I walked to the stadium from downtown, a nice, easy hike. I had a great time, with Joe easily leading me through my personal Rider history, and I marveled at the power of the internet that allowed Maura and the boys to be listening back home. Tim was still golfing, so I had a lot of wandering time, and enjoyed, as usual, the practice field people watching entertainment.

I met Tim in the seats, and we settled in for what started out as a complete nightmare. Saskatchewan had defeated the Alouettes only once in the teams' last 17 meetings. The Alouettes could clinch the Eastern Division title with a win. With five minutes gone in the second quarter, the Als led 18 – 0 and we began to wonder why we were even there.

As Tim said later, the best football he had ever seen began right then. A Paul McCallum field goal finally got Saskatchewan on the board, followed by an electrifying 53-yard touchdown pass/run from Henry Burris to Chris Szarka. This remains possibly my favourite Rider play of those I have seen in person, as the big fullback ran over defender after defender as he willed his way into the end zone. Kenton Keith, who would rush for 145 yards, sped in for a 59-yard TD run and another late McCallum field goal put the amazing Riders up 20 – 18 at the half. The rebound continued in the third quarter, with the Green and White scoring two more touchdowns on the way to a convincing, and actually, shocking 35 – 19 win.

For me, this game rates at the top of my list, likely tied with the Rocky Butler Classic in 2002 for my best Taylor Field game memory. It also serves as a vivid reminder of the consistency the Danny Barrett teams have been able to show, but on such an inconsistent basis, if you know what I mean.

Tim and I were again at the Holiday Inn Express, and

walked back downtown with a large, happy crowd. Predictably, the Lasagna Nightmare restaurant had folded, and a new venture had taken its place. We were alone in the bar area save a pleasant man from Hudson Bay, Saskatchewan named Kevin. Inviting him to join us, we found he is a season-ticket holder who makes every game, and capped off a good day with this fine fellow.

My friend Chris Melin had opted not to attend Ottawa's Grey Cup, and I had been leaning toward passing also. However, the Saskatchewan momentum was contagious, and two victories following the Montreal contest had me scraping an itinerary together. Jeff Banow and Marty Neumeier offered to let me bunk with them, and a conversation with the expert Govind Achyuthan indicated tickets would likely be available once we got to Ottawa.

A Rider loss in Vancouver the last week of the regular season forced Saskatchewan to travel to the unfriendly confines of Commonwealth Stadium, and on Nov. 7 two Burris touchdown passes and a strong defence propelled the Green and White to a 14 – 6 win. For the second consecutive season, Saskatchewan would play in the Western Final for the right to go to the Grey Cup.

As I settled in to listen to Rod Pedersen bring the action via the internet to Minnesota, it seemed like it was exceptional good fortune that had caused me to reverse my Ottawa decision. The Riders played well, and led 24 – 21 with only six seconds to play. The playoff untested Duncan O'Mahony lined up for a nearly 48-yard field goal attempt, one I felt certain he could not make. He did, however, and put the Lions in the Grey Cup when he made another field goal in overtime, after Paul McCallum had missed an 18-yarder on the Riders' OT possession. BC won 27 – 25, but ugliness followed in the Prairie Province.

Since CFL coverage is very sparse in Minnesota, many of my friends never see or read much about the Canadian game. I have met a *St. Paul Pioneer Press* sports columnist named Charley Walters, and he happily inserts CFL tidbits I lob to him on the occasions when local ex-Gopher names such as Ryan Thelwell or Arland Bruce III have made some news. The Saskatchewan happenings following the loss to BC made my friends take notice, in a very unfortunate way.

Following the game, kicker Paul McCallum's Regina

Vegetable Lasagna in the Nation's Capitol

house was pelted with eggs, manure was dumped in a neighbour's yard and threats were uttered against his family and property. Acts as senseless and moronic as these finally caused CFL to get some attention in my home area, but this publicity was much to my chagrin.

Suffice to say some arrests were made, and the kindness of the vast majority rose to the surface in the next few days, as the McCallum household was overwhelmed with good wishes and floral arrangements. I'm sure most Rider fans, like me, realized we were dealing with a football game, not an event necessitating a response even remotely requiring threats and vandalism, and I for one am pleased to see that all have since moved on. I remember Dave Ridgway saying that if he had missed the final kick in the 1989 Grey Cup, it would have been difficult for him to continue to remain in Saskatchewan, and thankfully the basic goodness of people prevented that outcome for Paul.

Despite my early season prediction, British Columbia had advanced to the Grey Cup to play the Toronto Argonauts on November 21. I left on Thursday the 18th, transferring in Detroit for the flight to Ottawa. Jeff Banow was arriving nearly when I was, but my flight was late and I couldn't track him down at the airport. We were staying at the Sheraton Hotel downtown, the home of that year's Riderville and close to the Spirit of Edmonton also. Marty and Jeff were relaxing when I showed up; Govind Achyuthan and Jason Isaac were at the same hotel and soon came down to our room, with Govind carrying a gift for Jeff.

Now, Jeff Banow is a great kid and a good friend, but at the time may have been the poster boy for the phrase about the guy who sees every glass as half empty, rather than half full. He was constantly teased about the perception that he was a bit grumpy, and was known to complain on occasion. Thus, it was appropriate, and left us rolling on the floor in laughter, when Jeff was presented with a personalized bottle of Sourpuss Liqueur. The photo later led to my best joke of the trip, but hang on for that.

It's interesting that I used the past tense in my references to Jeff in the above description. As a man very interested in self-improvement, Mr. Banow has since lost weight, had laser eye surgery and has a generally lighter attitude about many things. He's the kind of person that I'd go through a wall for and I'm sure he'd return the favour if needed.

Almost our milk carton kid, Jeff Banow

I was a bit hesitant about traveling to my first Grey Cup without normal accompanist Chris Melin, but this frivolity set the tone for the weekend. Jeff and Marty were great roomies, and we shared some fine conversations in the partying down times.

With Riderville just a short elevator ride away, we headed down and joined the fun. It was early, so not much was happening, but we were able to solve our ticket issue immediately, thanks once more to my ongoing savior, Liz Measner. Liz set us up with Ron Taylor, from Calgary's Saskatchewan Social Club, and we snatched up end zone seats at half the normal price of $200 each. I knew Gov, Jason, and Dave Fulton would need tickets, and had actually thought ahead to bring enough cash to complete the transaction. While we might have done better on Game Day, we all agreed it was good to get this obstacle out of the way.

Later, heading a few blocks up the street, we finished the night at the Spirit of Edmonton party amidst lots of reunions and friendly faces. Marty somehow found a CFL game official in the crowd and peppered the poor man with rules questions. I just asked him to say Hello to Art McAvoy, retired

Vegetable Lasagna in the Nation's Capitol

from field officiating but still a man this fellow knew.

Jeff and Marty had arranged to attend a session of Parliament in the morning, and had disappeared well before I decided to tumble out of bed. I met up with Gov and Jason, and we joined Dale Isaac for a leisurely late breakfast. We were then off to a tour of the Parliament Hill area. Taking a building tour, we enjoyed the exhibits and went to the top of the Peace Tower. The token American was fascinated by the local collection of feral cats, living just outside of the Centre Building, and cared for by a group of volunteers.

In the afternoon, we went down to the Frank Clair Stadium area, visiting the attractions set up for Grey Cup and watching some of the field preparations. The evening was more of the same, as we met a number of Riderfans.com followers at the Riderville party, walked down to the Hamilton's Tiger's Lair party and back, then had dinner at a nearby buffet. I personally passed on the vegetable lasagna, not attracted at all by either part of the dish's name. Wisely, we turned in early, since our group was scheduled for the famous Spirit of Edmonton Breakfast at an early hour on Saturday.

It was to be my first appearance at this almost-legendary breakfast. Always a sellout, it features a nice breakfast buffet coupled with the main event, all the orange juice and vodka a person could possibly desire. It was an interesting experience that lasted a good share of the morning. Appearances by team dance squads, the Rider Pep Band, the Winnipeg Bagpipes and a host of others filled the room with noise and laughter. Jeff Banow, though, wasn't laughing much. He had taken ill during the night and was not doing well at the breakfast, even ordering soda in place of the vodka concoction.

Marty Neumeier, conversely, was the life of the party. He magically transformed from a staid accountant into the Most Valuable Partygoer of Grey Cup Saturday. He soon knew most cheerleaders and dance team members by name, and was even able to add some pointers to help them improve their routines. I came to realize this man was made for this day.

It's not often in life that an event deemed legendary actually lives up to that billing, but the Spirit of Edmonton Breakfast is able to make that claim. If you are a Grey Cup attendee and have not yet had the chance to partake in it, please do so, but order your tickets early.

We made a quick stop at the hotel before heading to the Rendezvous Saskatchewan party. Jeff had not improved, and decided to try to rest. Marty, Jason, Gov and I piled into a cab for the short ride to the Saskatchewan venue. As usual, this event was both jammed and alive. It was perfect for my wandering tendencies and I met many friends, both old and new.

Marty Neumeier of the Toronto Blue Thunder

Rod Petersen was the master of ceremonies, and slyly made certain I won a door prize by naming a U.S. driver's license as a qualifying ingredient. I introduced myself to newly named Saskatchewan Roughrider President/CEO Jim Hopson, and Marty suddenly appeared with Regina Mayor Pat Fiacco so I could meet him also. Toss in the chance meeting with 2003 benefactor Laur'Lei Silzer described earlier, a good band, and the result was a very excellent party.

Jim Hopson　　**Mayor Pat Fiacco**

Vegetable Lasagna in the Nation's Capitol

Eight-plus hours of partying beginning early in the morning were starting to slow me down. Fighting the onset of a cold, I crashed early, but the rest were not far behind. Jeff felt a bit better and had gone to meet some friends, so we were hopeful he just had a 24-hour bug. He was good to go in the morning, or so we thought, and left to meet more friends while Marty and I scouted the neighbourhood for some drugs for my nasal affliction.

Transplanted Reginans Craig and Kim McTaggart had invited us to a pre-game party at their house, very near the stadium. We headed down to meet our gracious hosts, joined by Steve Flynn, a university friend of Gov's. Once again, the friendliness we've found in our acceptance by total strangers was evident, and much appreciated. The proximity to the stadium made the sale of parking spots an attractive venture, and we even saw the Metrodome-like price of $40 successfully negotiated by Craig and Steve.

Jeff and Marty had purchased their tickets online, and had good seats in the main part of the stadium. After setting a spot to meet after the game, I joined Gov, Jason and Dave Fulton in climbing the steps to our end zone seats.

In nearly 50 Canadian football trips, I have very seldom come away disappointed, but these seats were a sad way to enjoy a football game. Sight lines to scoreboards were poor to non-existent, and we were unable to hear the public address system. Large speakers had been placed in the area, but they were located below the stands, and the sound seemed to be completely absorbed by the multitude of bodies clumped together. Possibly that is always the case with temporary seating, but our nearly total inability to follow the flow of the game made viewing a real challenge. Although I seldom do such things, I later sent an e-mail to the Renegades later to note my dissatisfaction. Paying full ticket price would have been even more upsetting.

In an interesting coaching decision, British Columbia coach Wally Buono decided to start veteran Dave Dickenson at the quarterback position. On the bench was Casey Printers, who had been named the league's Most Outstanding Player earlier in the weekend. But Printers had been banged up, and former Montana Grizzly Dickenson got the nod. The opposing Argos countered with 20–year CFL veteran Damon Allen, just 41 years young.

Rider Pride on the American Side

The Western champions struck first, leading 7 – 0 after the first quarter on a 12-yard touchdown pass from Dickenson to Regina product Jason Clermont. Allen moved the Toronto offence well in the second quarter, though, running for a TD and passing to Robert Baker for another. Adding a field goal, the Argos led 17 – 10 at the half. Damon Allen rushed for another TD in the third quarter, but a BC field goal and a 7-yard Dickenson gallop in the 4th quarter brought BC within range at 24 – 19 with a lot of time left. Going for the two-point conversion to narrow the gap to a field goal, BC took a pair of penalties before finally resorting to a kick and missing it. A Toronto field goal made the final score Toronto 27, British Columbia 19.

It was certainly a decent game, but not as exciting for a neutral fan as some other Canadian championship contests. Damon Allen's strong game was rewarded, as he won the game's MVP award for the third time, and collected his fourth Grey Cup ring.

As we filed out with our 51,000-plus friends, it was evident the only viable transportation back to the hotel would be the Shoeleather Express, since the streets were crowded to overflowing with pedestrians. Arriving at our prearranged meeting spot, we were surprised to see Marty, but not Jeff. Marty explained that Jeff's illness had returned, worse than ever, and his friend had been forced to leave the game in the first half to return to the hotel.

This was certainly awful news, but was soon to get even worse. We joined the crowd, walking back the mile or so to the hotel, and immediately went to the room to check on Jeff, since leaving a Grey Cup game early is an indication of more than ordinary illness.

The feeling I had when Marty and I entered the room is still a strong memory today. Jeff was not there, and clearly had not been there, since our "male mess" was undisturbed since our earlier departure. To our credit, we didn't panic, but there was very obvious reason for concern. As the old, semi-responsible adult, I suggested we find the hotel manager and seek help, since we did not really know where to start. Gov, Dave, and Jason were with us, and we headed to the lobby. I noted that at least we had Jeff's picture on the Sourpuss bottle to help with any identification needs.

The hotel manager, an imposing man with a German-sounding accent, was an incredible help. Correctly gauging our concern, he promised to start his staff calling hospitals in the search for our friend. By this time, it was about two hours after the game had ended and nearly four after Jeff had left Marty.

Marty called Jeff's brother, Ryan, in Saskatoon, hoping for news, but likely just adding one more person to the ranks of the people who were scared Jeffless by the situation. With little else to do, we packed for our scheduled early morning departure and finally the phone rang.

It was Jeff, much to our relief. Leaving the game, he had realized he was too ill to make it to the hotel and found help. Taken by ambulance, he was safe, but uncomfortable in the hospital, and was undergoing tests. For Marty and I, it was a giant relief, since it was easy to have bad premonitions about the ordeal. We let the other guys in Ottawa know, and Marty called Ryan back to reassure him also. Marty and I awoke at some ungodly hour, took a bus at 6 AM to the airport, and bade farewell until the next season.

Jeff's saga was far from finished, as he was eventually diagnosed with food poisoning, and had the opportunity to enjoy Ottawa for several more days. Suspicion was cast immediately at the vegetable lasagna, a convenient fall guy since apparently none of the rest of us had eaten it. To this day, that dish ranks above even ax murderers on the Banow Most Wanted List. Ever the analyst, Jeff later circulated a spreadsheet succinctly detailing the financial burden of the weekend in terms of lost wages, partially used game ticket, airfare penalties and the like. He did neglect, however, to show the priceless bottle of Sourpuss on the asset side of the ledger.

I joke a bit now, but it was frightening at the time, and we were all very glad Jeff was fine in the long run. It was certainly on my mind as I returned to Minnesota, and I felt better after I spoke to Jeff later in the week.

Interestingly, the very day after I returned, I had one of those very rare Rider experiences in the Gopher State. Walking through a parking lot wearing a Grey Cup sweatshirt, I was stopped by a fellow who related he had regularly attended Saskatchewan Roughrider games in the very early 1960s. He then proceeded to explain that his mother lived in Regina, and had sent him an article from the *Leader-Post* detailing some guy from Roseville who had — can you believe it — Rider season tickets. I explained he was in fact talking to that particular madman, and we shared a good laugh and some fine Saskatchewan stories.

Right before Grey Cup, CBC had aired a documentary on the life of Roy Shivers. Titled "Roy Shivers: Football First," it was a close up look at Roy's formative days in Oakland, his college career at Utah State, life as an NFL player and, most interestingly to me, a good amount of perspective from his wife, Carol. Both Kelly and Marty had sent me copies of it; the film was fun to watch, for a couple of reasons. First, I enjoy learning the detail and background of things, and this was a great look on the challenges Roy and Carol have dealt with, plus a multitude of information about Roy's career that was new to me. Also, it is always a treat to see on film places and people that a person is familiar with, and the documentary had plenty of both. Some of the scenes were from times when I had been in Regina, and many of the people with cameo roles were people I knew and recognized. Tim and Harv even came over one evening, and we watched it together.

As the page turned to Next Year, the Rider faithful were prepared for a big campaign, since it certainly appeared everything was in place for a Grey Cup run in 2005.

Chapter 16

Happy Birthday, Saskatchewan!

The year 2005 was only a few weeks old when another jacket-related Saskatchewan coincidence took place. Driving on a street close to home, I spotted a man walking down the street wearing a winter jacket adorned with the unmistakable Rider "S" logo. Traffic was heavy, but I quickly turned around after I had passed him, and stopped as he approached. Hailing the man and his companion, I asked where he had obtained the jacket.

Logically thinking I knew nothing about Saskatchewan, he began to explain the logo. Swirling traffic forced me to cut him a bit short, as I had the car in a bad spot. This gentleman, Pastor Greg Heidorn from Rochester, Minnesota, had attended seminary in Regina in the mid-1970s and had been given the jacket by a friend. He had been a fan while in Regina, and we had a brief, though very pleasant, conversation. Rider jackets are amazing items occasionally.

Jeff Banow led an early 2005 charge toward Grey Cup tickets and offered to be the point man for arranging them for the contest to be held in Vancouver. Chris and I joined in, and I arranged for a pair, since the plan was for Maura to make her Grey Cup debut this season. Lest you think I had just been running off without my wife to be with the boys in the past, there's actually just a little more to it. Maura is a teacher, with a schedule that makes time off during the school year both difficult and discouraged. However, the Vancouver event was on the Sunday of American Thanksgiving, and made things easier, since she would only need to cover the following Monday, due to the Friday school holiday.

Mr. Banow doesn't mess around when football is concerned. Our group snagged great seats, very close to midfield, although close to the top of the second deck. They were $252.50 each, but in a strange way that was fine, since we paid for them in March and had time to recover before the other expenses hit.

In Regina, change was in the air. Quarterback Henry Burris, after extensive negotiations with Saskatchewan, bolted in February to sign with the Calgary Stampeders. Large portions of the Rider faithful were more than miffed, and Henry's return to Taylor Field with Calgary in October was circled on many a Green and White calendar.

2001 Grey Cup MVP Marcus Crandell was signed as an extra quarterback, however, and the Riders went to camp with decent experience as he joined Nealon Greene and Rocky Butler at that spot. With Matt Dominguez on tap for the full season, there was lots of optimism as camp began. Edmonton would be tough, with the return of quarterback Ricky Ray in May from the NFL, but many of the preseason prognosticators picked the veteran Riders to finish first or second in the West.

We had the most aggressive Taylor Field attendance plans to date on the McEvoy travel docket. Our family trip was set for the home opener on June 25, and the Labour Day and Thanksgiving matchups were on my list also. A late-season treat was in store, since Terry and Kerry from Australia were to be vacationing in Canada, and a get-together was planned in Regina for the October 23 Burris Bowl, as Henry's return had been named.

Saskatchewan's home opener was set for June 25, and we headed north on the 23rd. The new Maxtron scoreboard and video screen was to be unveiled, and enthusiasm was evident throughout Regina. Practice on the 24th was of the typical first trip variety, as we greeted lots of our Regina friends. The Winnipeg Blue Bombers were the opponent, and were around too, so all four of us were able to greet our friend Chris Cvetkovic and catch up with him. He had not seen Carson and Connor for two years, and both were by now as much man as boy, with Carson towering over Dad by then.

Maura coached Connor's soccer team, and in 2005 had a new assistant coach, a fellow interestingly named (from a Rider perspective, anyway) Mark Shivers. We had a good laugh with Roy about this, and asked him to sign a mini-football for Mark. I mentioned to Roy that Mark, who is white and pronounces his surname as "Shy-vers," was likely not related to the general manager. Looking as me with a sly grin, Roy responded, "Didn't we all start with Adam and Eve?" and he certainly had a point.

Rob Vanstone and Winnipeg's Jon Ryan, June 2005

The new video board was big news, and Rider media man Ryan Whippler steered me toward an interview about it with Global TV Sports. I was pretty nervous, and you can certainly tell from the tape, later provided thoughtfully to us by Taylor Field neighbour Joe McNeill. But it was fun to have 15 seconds of fame and I had just a belly laugh the next day in the Cornwall Centre when a couple who had seen the interview on Global stopped me to ask about the drive from Minnesota.

Maura had time to talk with Roy while I was stammering with the TV people, and mentioned how much we had enjoyed the CBC documentary. He thanked her, and said he was pleased by it, even adding maybe a tear or two had run down his cheek when he saw the finished product.

After practice and lunch, it was off for the 2004-cancelled tour of the Donison elk ranch. Maura and the boys had not yet met Bill Donison and his wife Kathy. We accomplished that at the motel before we followed them out to Optimum Genetics. Bill's daughter, Rhonda Murray, gave a perfect G-rated tour, an imposing task when the subject matter is considered, and we enjoyed a fine evening of steak and companionship.

Rider Pride on the American Side

Game Day came with another interesting weather forecast. Potentially severe thunderstorms were predicted but we were sure we would not get rained on for the second consecutive year. A pregame meal was planned, and we met Kelly Ramler and Jeff Banow at Boston Pizza. Joining us were Troy Souster and Marcel Nogue from Saskatoon, whom we were meeting for the first time. As things so often unfold, these guys were good fun, and we were all friends within an hour.

Troy and Marcel were initiating a new attempt at a tailgate, and invitations had been posted on Riderfans.com. They left early to be the good hosts, but by the time we were ready to depart, the weather had that Saskatchewan Storm Face showing. Hustling to our parking spot, we stopped quickly at the tailgate, but it packed up early since there was no question any longer about the upcoming rain.

We made it inside Taylor Field quickly, and just in time. The heavens opened, and delayed the start of the game for a half hour. For us, it worked out well – Troy and Marcel sit very near us, and Darwin Gooding does also, allowing some good visiting time. I spotted Joe and Nancy McNeill; they joined us also, as did Nat Hrynuik and his son Damian. Nat is another Riderfans.com acquaintance, and serves an important purpose on that website as one of the few who admits to being older than I.

The rain finally stopped, and the evening became quite pleasant. The football was even more so, as Corey Holmes electrified the home crowd by returning the season's first kickoff for a touchdown. Saskatchewan had lost both of its pre-season games, but had certainly come to play this night as the Riders jumped to a 22 – 8 lead at the halfway mark.

The Maxtron debut was flawless and added immensely to the game viewing experience. Calgary friend Bill Wakefield was the very first fan to be interviewed on the screen after the game began, a fact that will be a great trivia question some day down the road.

Nealon Greene tossed touchdown passes to Matt Dominguez and Elijah Thurman in the third quarter, and the Rider defense dominated as the team coasted to a 42 – 15 win. From what I could see, Bomber long snapper Chris Cvetkovic had played well, so it was a perfect night for me

Back in Minnesota, in an interesting turn of events, one of the local Twin Cities independent television stations was doing the impossible and had actually scheduled CFL telecasts on Saturday evenings.

The Rider game at Hamilton was on tap for July 2, and was the first CFL game I had seen on television here in Minnesota since the 1997 Grey Cup game. It was a new, interesting feeling for me, seeing players in my living room who I had actually met. The exhilaration was short-lived, as the CFL experiment lasted only a few weeks. Poor ratings caused it to be replaced with *Magnum P.I.* reruns, evidently a guaranteed ratings winner.

Saskatchewan won in Hamilton, but the victory was extremely costly. Matt Dominguez tore a knee ligament and would not return the rest of the season. As the season progressed, additional injuries would plague the team, with Kenton Keith, Neal Hughes, LaDouphyous McCalla, Nate Davis, Jeremy O'Day and Karsten Bailey down at various times early in the campaign. Rider coaches refused to allow the injuries to be an excuse, citing team depth as an asset while the squad tried to play through the misfortunes.

As I follow other sports, it's interesting to me how football seems to emotionally deal with injuries. We have all come to expect gridiron coaches to say, "Injuries are part of the game" and other such platitudes, but it's my observation that in other sports the impact of injuries is often more straightforwardly admitted. An impact player like Matt Dominguez isn't easily replaced, yet the 2005 Riders, like other football teams everywhere, seemed to be hesitant to make that statement. It seems to me that, for example, in baseball, injuries to key players are bemoaned as the crucial event they are. When a Curt Schilling, a Francisco Liriano or a Ryan Howard goes down, any help received from their replacement is viewed as a bonus. For some reason, in football, that help is viewed as an expectation. I often wonder about the realism of that thought process.

Despite the injuries, the Riders initially made the best of things, losing to Toronto but defeating Hamilton in a rematch on July 17 to boast a 3 – 1 record. On July 23, a sea of Rider Green invaded McMahon Stadium in Calgary with high hopes of viewing the visiting Saskatchewan squad dole out punishment to the disliked defector, Henry Burris. Smiling Hank, however, had the first of multiple Last Laughs, as he led his team to a 44 – 18 shellacking of the Green and White, the first in a series of five consecutive Rider losses.

As Chris Melin and I prepared to head to Regina for the Labour Day Classic, the Riders were reeling. At 3 – 6, they were seriously behind British Columbia, a team that had started the 2005 season with a long undefeated streak. Chris convinced me to fly this trip, cleverly setting me up just days after Maura, the boys and I had returned from a 4,600-mile driving excursion to Utah, Arizona and New Mexico. We took the early flight on Friday, September 2, renting a car and trying the east end Holiday Inn, since we were not able to reserve a spot downtown. The hotel proved very nice, and a straight flush at a video lottery terminal quickly recouped half of my airfare.

In addition to football, this weekend was also the Saskatchewan centennial celebration, and many special events were on tap as part of that significant provincial milestone. I had been looking forward to this weekend since I had realized the centennial would be part of it. We would not be disappointed.

Saturday dawned both bright and decent, with a warm sun blanketing Taylor field for the annual fan gathering. Reunions were the first order of business. The Blue Bombers had arrived, and we quickly rounded up Chris Cvetkovic, setting up a dinner date for later. I had brought along a Saskatchewan Wheat Pool mini-football, and had Chris introduce me to Jon Ryan, asking the Bomber punter, a Regina product, to autograph it. Sometimes I just don't think until it's too late – I should have tried for the signature of Winnipeg kicker Troy Westwood, well known for disparaging Saskatchewan, even allegedly referring to its residents as "banjo-picking inbreds" before the western semi-final in 2003. Ryan's signing in early 2006 with Green Bay makes my choice look better, though.

The fine day brought out a big crowd, despite the recent slide of the team on the field. I presented Roy with a photo of myself taken on our recent trip, leaning on a directional sign pointing to his Utah State alma mater. Rather than jumping to the obvious conclusion that I am daft, he seemed to enjoy it and we talked about the beauty of that state for a while. Friends Govind Achyuthan, Kelly Ramler, Gerard Stang and the Wakefield's were around, and it certainly fulfilled all of my high expectations for a Labour Day Saturday. I snuck through the autograph lines to greet Rider safety Darnell Edwards, and

Happy Birthday, Saskatchewan!

introduced myself to defensive back Dustin Cherniawski by taking a picture of him.

Darnell Edwards

The Blue Bombers were staying in Moose Jaw to avoid the friendly, late-night attentions of the Rider legions, so we headed west for dinner. Tracking down Chris Cvetkovic, we also met Bomber linebacker Neal McKinlay. Both players' lady friends had driven in from Manitoba, and the six of us made small talk as we looked for a place to eat. In a scene reminiscent of "Do you know Suzy from Saskatchewan?" Cvetkovic's friend and future bride Ashley Wawryko mentioned her cousin had played hockey at the University of North Dakota several years earlier. Everyone save me was surprised when Chris Melin revealed that this cousin, Russ Romaniuk, had actually been a Grand Forks party acquaintance in his college days. The strange happenings just never seem to end.

Dustin Cherniawski signing autographs, September 2005

Rider Pride on the American Side

After a good visit, we lamely wished them a good game on the morrow and headed back to Regina. Meeting up with Kelly Ramler, we went to an outdoor concert featuring Tom Cochrane. It was a beautiful evening with a nice crowd, cold beer and good company. The ability in Regina to mix easily and feel secure was evident, as we had to walk several blocks from a parking spot. We also ran into multiple folks we knew, including radio host Joe Hadesbeck and his sons, and I was even familiar with the Cochrane signature tune, "Life Is A Highway." All night long, for sure.

Sunday was also warm and pleasant, and the new tailgate party was in full swing. I left for a bit to be on the Touchdown Club radio show, but returned to mingle. Another visit to the Practice Field followed, and we headed to our seats, hoping the Riders would get the momentum a playoff run required. In a surprise move some fans felt was long overdue, Nealon Greene, who had struggled during the losing streak, was replaced as the starting quarterback by Marcus Crandell.

Crandell responded well, leading the Riders to a 45 – 26 victory. As he had done in June, Corey Holmes again started the scoring, this time with an 89-yard punt return. Kenton Keith had 170 rushing yards, including a 75-yard touchdown run in the fourth quarter. Fans who appreciate good football players, regardless of team affiliation, had a treat this day. Winnipeg's Milt Stegall set a CFL record for career TD receptions, as he scored his 118th and 119th receiving touchdowns.

Happy Birthday, Saskatchewan!

Happy Birthday, Saskatchewan!

A huge fireworks celebration was to be held after the game, so Chris and I filed south with the stream of vehicles to a parking place west of Albert near the Legislative building. After a decent walk, we had a great spot for seeing some amazing pyrotechnics, and were happy to have been in Regina for a small bit of history. It was interesting for me to think just a little about my great aunt Emma and her journey from Minnesota exactly 100 years earlier. As now expected, we ran into folks we knew, Joe and Nancy McNeill, who we'd left just moments before at the game.

Labour Day was a "jump start" for the Riders, but we all knew they needed some type of run. The team did just that, peeling off victories in the next four games, and climbing back into the playoff picture with an 8 – 6 record before heading into the Oct. 8 game in Regina against the Montreal Alouettes.

Friend Tim Anderson was the traveling companion this trip, for the third consecutive year. With the Thanksgiving weekend contest set for Saturday, we were scheduled to leave on Thursday. Two days before, we had a huge storm in Minnesota, with over five inches of rain falling in the Twin Cities. Newspaper reports indicated some snow in North Dakota, but the accounts I read indicated it was in the northeast corner, not exactly in our path. Checking Thursday's predicted temperatures along our normal route, I saw projected highs well above freezing and felt we would have no weather issues.

Tim and I chatted away as we sped toward North Dakota. We recalled the Rider comeback in the 2004 Montreal game, and planned the weekend. As we sailed past Fargo, Tim casually mentioned the Interstate had been closed the previous day due to snow and wondered if we would see any evidence of the storm. This was the first I knew of the storm's severity and I hoped we would somehow avoid the worst of it. Of course, Tim could have also chosen to mention things sooner.

Just north of Jamestown, the city where we turned on to two-lane U.S. Highway 52, the snow line began as if a tarp had covered the landscape as the flakes fell. We went from dry pavement with no snow to a foot or more in a distance of less than a mile, and much of the road was still snow and ice covered. The snow deepened as we approached Minot, with the radio indicating a depth in the vicinity of two feet. Trucks and car scattered the ditches, and in more than one case, partially blocked the road.

To be honest, we were fortunate. We nearly went off the road on two or three occasions, and were lucky there was very little traffic. Our progress slowed to a maddeningly crawl, but we had little choice but to continue and were eventually able to arrive in Regina after close to a 15-hour trip, much longer than normal.

A good meal with Joe and Nancy McNeill at the Peking House and the familiar comfort of the Holiday Inn Express did wonders, and we were refreshed enough to head to the Rider practice in the morning. It was chilly and the players were bundled up for their walkthrough. I rounded up Dustin and Darnell, and gave them a copy of the photos from Labour Day.

Tropical North Dakota, October 6, 2005

Tim and I headed under the stands, where the media types huddled to stay warm, and we sat through the press conferences of Danny Barrett and Montreal coach Don Matthews. The two are an interesting contrast, the smooth, soft-voiced Saskatchewan leader contrasting with the head Alouette's more clipped, right-to-the-point responses. Coach Matthews was in the process of manipulating his team's defensive schemes and, when asked for his players thoughts about these changes, he basically said it did not matter, since they were professionals and needed to adapt — or words to that effect. I have only a small bit of experience hearing Coach Barrett, mainly from Riderville videos, but doubt that he would have answered quite in that almost-brusque manner. But as we know, it takes all kinds.

Happy Birthday, Saskatchewan!

Friday evening, we were having dinner in a downtown restaurant, and prepared to leave. The service had been extremely slow, but finally we had the bill and placed our cash on the table. While I visited the restroom, Tim decided to engage the two sinister-looking ladies at the next table in a bit of clever conversation, failing to notice their two male acquaintances then helped themselves to some of our funds. Not a huge deal, since their take was only a small amount, but annoying nonetheless. The power of the internet allowed me to e-mail the particulars to several friends who we would see on the next day, and Tim was very perplexed when total strangers came up to him and asked him about his two lady friends from the previous evening. I realize now that I had not explained *why* I'd asked people to query Tim, but several just did the favour anyway.

Game Day temperatures were cool but reasonable and the tailgate was alive. The Fulton brothers and dad Tom were there, and it was good to see Dave, Kevin and Warren at a time other than Grey Cup. A gray overcast sky gave a good backdrop as a tailgate dance duo swayed to the music on an impromptu dance floor, in this case the roof of a pickup.

Dancin' on the Truck, October 8, 2005

Montreal jumped on the Riders again, leading 14 – 0 after only seven minutes. Two Crandell TD passes and a McCallum field goal put the Riders up 17 – 14 late in the half, and it began to look like deja vu all over again, since the story of the 2004 Alouettes game was being closely followed. A momentum-changing play happened right before halftime as Montreal's Reggie Durden picked off Crandell for an easy touchdown.

In the third quarter, the Riders gave away points when they were penalized on an Alouettes' field goal attempt for having too many men on the field, giving Montreal a first down and leading to an eventual touchdown. As the game continued to see-saw, Saskatchewan countered with two touchdowns in the third quarter, but Anthony Cavillo completed a 62-yard pass on second and 31 to head the Als toward what would be the winning touchdown, as the Easterners prevailed 38 - 34. It was a frustrating game to watch, as the Riders twice overcame double-digit deficits but still saw their winning streak end.

Bill Donison had viewed the game with us, and he, Tim and I capped a very forgettable day with a really poor meal at a restaurant best purged from our memories. With the snow, the poor result in the game and the sad meal, this did not rank as one of the best Regina trips, but those things sometimes happen. The drive home was made a bit easier by an exciting 18-inning baseball playoff win by the Houston Astros, in a game we followed by leapfrogging from station to station, possibly the highlight of that weekend.

A record fourth trip of the season was still to come. Terry and Kerry McEvoy, our Australian friends, had planned to visit Canada, touring the Rockies by train, and spending a weekend in Regina on their way to Churchill, Manitoba, for the famous polar bear migration. Give Aussie Terry a good nature show on TV, and he can easily turn it into a trip, so Maura and I planned to meet them. Add the long awaited Burris Bowl, a potential meeting finally with Plaza of Honour Inductee Tim Roth, and a reuniting of an Aussie/Elk friendship made five years earlier in a German airport, and you have the stuff of which dreams are made.

It was again the October long school weekend in Minnesota, so Maura was able to clear her schedule. Our flight arrived in Regina a few minutes early, and we waited just a short time until Terry and Kerry came in from Calgary and then headed towards downtown Regina.

I had ordered Terry a Rider jersey similar to my own for the occasion. My birthday/Father's Day gift had been a new green jersey, and I had MINNESOTA put on the back name

Happy Birthday, Saskatchewan!

panel, with 49 as the number, signifying my year of birth. The Aussie's was to read S. AUSTRALIA, with number 57, the year of his birth. Liz and staff had it all set, and we were able to make introductions all around, including Roy, who was nice enough to spend time with us even as he made ready for the Plaza of Honour Dinner.

We met Bill and Kathy Donison at the Lakeshore, a very fine restaurant, and spent a great evening full of catching up and fun stories. In the morning, Terry and I went to the Rider practice. I was looking forward to finally meeting Tim Roth, who had invited us by e-mail to attend a Plaza gathering on Saturday afternoon. By now, you won't be shocked to learn that as we pulled up to Taylor Field Saturday morning, Tim and his family were getting out of the car next to us. As he introduced his wife and daughter, I realized Tim's daughter had been in the seat in front of me on the flight the day before, a type of double coincidence, I'd guess.

Tim Roth is a very large man and had been advertised by my friend Harv Moen as a special guy. The former lineman was just that, and we very much enjoyed getting to know him just a little that weekend.

It was still early and bitterly cold on the field. The Riders came out very late, and we kept warm back under the stands. Introducing the other Terry McEvoy to broadcaster Mitchell Blair, we heard a story from Mitch about meeting a fellow named Blair Mitchell, proving I'm not completely alone in strange happenings. Aussie Terry was a bit nervous, not sure it was all right for us to be where we were. I thought back to our trip to Canton, where *his* boldness had made me nervous, and congratulated myself on my progression in five short years.

Kerry McEvoy was not feeling well, so Terry, Maura, and I made just a short afternoon trip to the Plaza of Honour party. A short trip, but sweet, as I did get the chance to meet Tim's fellow Plaza Inductee Jeff Fairholm, who was one of my first Rider favourites. Jeff is a great fellow, and we had a good talk about days of old. As it always is, the feeling of meeting a person I never really hoped to meet was a very good one.

Joe Hadesbeck, good soul that he is, had asked the two Terrys to be on the pregame show and, with lots of help from his partner Bob Poley, wound us through a fun conversation with a multitude of topics. One of the topics was our matching jerseys, and Joe noted Aussie Terry was wearing Bob's old number 57. Had I been thinking, I probably could have spun a great yarn about how well known and revered Bob Poley is in Australia. We had time to introduce Terry and Kerry around at the tailgate, and I even squeezed in two other meetings.

The first was with none other than CFL Commissioner Tom Wright, who was also on the Hadesbeck/Poley show and remembered our Calgary meeting. The other was with Marilyn McIntyre of Rosetown, a Riderfans.com acquaintance who was in the process of doing me a fine favour. We will get to that shortly.

I'm grateful for the good things that happened that weekend, but the football game was not one of them. The Riders jumped to a quick lead of 21 – 3 and had a chance right before half time to score again. A fumble, one of eight Saskatchewan turnovers, gave Calgary the ball, an unexpected field goal, and some momentum. The second half merits little discussion here; the Riders failed to score even a single point and lost 29 – 21. A disappointed crowd left Taylor Field, as Henry Burris's return to Regina had not turned out nearly as the local throngs had hoped. The Calgary quarterback ended up with Last Laugh number two. Even so, it was good to see the Australians and fun to see the Elk/Aussie reunion.

Tim Roth   **Jeff Fairholm**

Maura and I returned home, but a Grey Cup trip was just over the horizon. Before that, though, bad things happened in Saskatchewan. Rider linebacker Trevis Smith was arrested on a charge of aggravated sexual assault on Oct. 28, a case needing no further coverage here save to note that it was ignored in the U.S., belying the internet wags who were certain it would cause the CFL to be ripped apart by the American press.

Winning its last game in British Columbia to finish 9 – 9 and make the playoffs as a crossover team in the East, Saskatchewan's season ended painfully and quickly in Montreal on November 13. The Riders fell behind 24 – 0 and lost a 30 – 14 decision. A week later, Edmonton and Montreal advanced to the Grey Cup for their third matchup in the last four championship games.

However, not all of the news I heard from Regina before Grey Cup was of the disturbing variety. An annual large fundraiser for the team is an event called the Saskatchewan Roughrider Touchdown Lottery. A campaign selling $100 lottery tickets gets under way each fall and offers a number of large prizes, including trips, cars, and a grand prize of $100,000.

The 2005 drawing was on November 3, and the winners were posted on Riderville.com the next morning. The headline read, "And the Grand Prize winner is....Bill Donison of Regina!" I laughed for about ten minutes before calling Bill to congratulate him. Here's hoping the elk received a few extra carrots.

Team turmoil and the rapid playoff tumble did not sit well in the Prairie Province. Rumours seemed to run in all directions, as the shock of the Smith situation combined with the unrealized lofty expectations of the season in a bad way. In some reports, the Shivers/Barrett regime was on thin ice, and an announcement right before Grey Cup that any final decision was being postponed did not serve to clarify the issues.

Armed with that confusion, I hoped to be able to pick up some more information in Vancouver. Chris Melin, Maura and I headed out on Friday, Nov. 25, with Maura and I traveling in flyer miles seats, a welcome reprieve from the $600 cost of an airline ticket. We had two interesting meetings on tap in addition to all of the usual festivities associated with the championship weekend.

Marilyn McIntyre had helped me track down two second cousins whom I had never met; Doug Orth and his wife Polly of Rosetown plus Doug's brother Ross Orth, and his wife, Dianne Miller, of Swift Current. Dianne and I had corresponded by e-mail, and plans were made to get together.

Strangely enough, I had located yet another Terry McEvoy, this fellow being a Vancouver-based writer, director and producer of film and television productions. With time and determination, anyone with an e-mail address can be tracked down, and we much enjoyed a breakfast on Granville Island with Terry III on the morning of the game. Later, in 2007, Rider ticket manager Gail Mund told me of the double take she did when she happened to be introduced to Vancouver Terry at a film event in Regina.

Of course, when you are anxious to get somewhere, there are always delays. Our flight arrived well over an hour late, and the lines in Vancouver to pass through customs stretched far as the eye could see. Making small talk with the fellow behind us, I discovered he was the father of Edmonton defensive back Davis Sanchez, a good player who was injured and would not be playing in Sunday's game.

We checked into the hotel and headed out for a quick walk that eventually ended in a late lunch. Arrangements had been made to have a very informal Riderfans.com get-together at the Riderville party at 5:00. Chris and Maura headed over there while I returned to the motel to retrieve a forgotten camera.

Walking toward Riderville, held right near BC Place stadium, I met *Leader-Post* sports writer Darrell Davis crossing the street. He was in a hurry, trying to catch up to Roy Shivers for a story, so we talked just briefly and I moved on.

I had entrusted my companions with the heavy responsibility of purchasing my annual Grey Cup cap. They did well — actually almost too well — snagging a $42 number, and giving us our first glimpse into the Vancouver pricing structure. Meeting Maura and Chris at Riderville, we found many of the Usual Suspects already present, and greetings and conversation overflowed.

My bride, at her initial Grey Cup party, was amazed. I had tried to describe the events, but mere words sound pale in comparison to the actual experience. She spoke for days about the friendliness of a bunch of young guys who treated her like they had known her for twenty years. There was actually a pretty decent turnout from Riderfans.com, and we met at least fifteen or so folks for the first time. Dave Fulton pointed out former Rider player (and former CFL President) Bill Baker, a man I would have liked to meet, but he was always busy and I didn't get the chance.

Maura was not the only lady making her debut at Riderville for the first time. Marie Hrynuik, wife of Nat, had also come to her first Grey Cup, and she and Maura were clearly kindred spirits. Nat, by the way, had a dream goal for the 2005 CFL season, making plans to attend every Saskatchewan Roughrider game, home and away. This incredible fan had his plan thwarted by a back problem eventually requiring surgery, but it's our expectation he will attempt this worthy quest again in a future season.

Maura and some of the boys, Riderville 2005

We stayed for a long while, but finally decided to try the Spirit of Edmonton. It was a walk of a mile or so, and felt good. Chris, Maura and I walked up with the Fulton brothers, stopping along the way at a few of the booths set up beside BC Place. The Edmonton party was filling up, but we gained immediate admittance. However, the Minnesotans decided food was needed, and a leisurely meal in a nearby restaurant meant a very long line to re-enter the party, so we crashed early.

The Grey Cup Parade was on Saturday's early docket and, although chilled by the wind, we really enjoyed it. Standing near a couple of obvious Rider fans, we introduced ourselves to Al Christensen of Christopher Lake, Saskatchewan, and his son Darren of Calgary. It took about four seconds to determine Darren's wife knew our friend Govind, but so does nearly everyone else, I sometimes think. Al was interesting to talk to as we waited for the parade – he was planning a trip to Australia and New Zealand, and Maura and I tried to pass on a few pointers.

As the parade wound down, we headed to the Rendezvous Saskatchewan party, held in a huge tented area close to the stadium. Many of our friends had been at the Spirit of Edmonton Breakfast, arriving with that special glow only early morning vodka can bring. This was the event where we were scheduled to meet our Saskatchewan cousins, and I was pumped up for it. We had received a phone message that they had been snowbound in central BC but they expected to make it to Rendezvous and would meet us there.

Roy Shivers was the scheduled master of ceremonies, but Bob Poley was taking his place, and did a fine job. Roy's absence and the other constant vibes about his future, beginning a week or so earlier, made me uneasy, and I was hoping I would somehow run into him to get the data right from the GM's mouth. Small chance, but a guy can hope.

Marie and Nat Hrynuik

It was a fine party, as this event always is. We quickly found Arnie, Bambi, Rob and Sheila, our Edmonton friends, and I was thrilled Maura had a chance to meet these fine folks for the first time. She was also able to meet Roger Aldag, and greetings were passed also to Jim Hopson, Kevin Clive, and even Mayor Pat Fiacco for the second consecutive year.

With a ring of the cell phone, we heard from the cousins, and designated a spot in the huge area to meet. I am likely too sentimental, but it was a huge thing for me to meet Doug and

Ross and their wives, especially in this roundabout manner in a faraway place via a few layers of Saskatchewan Roughrider coincidences and acquaintances. Family is important and I have precious few relatives; finding new ones was a bonus a person cannot possibly expect. Hugs and handshakes flowed, and I noticed immediately that Ross, the Swift Current Orth, had a real resemblance to my brother Bob. Rather than try to socialize in the crowded and noisy party, we made a dinner date for later.

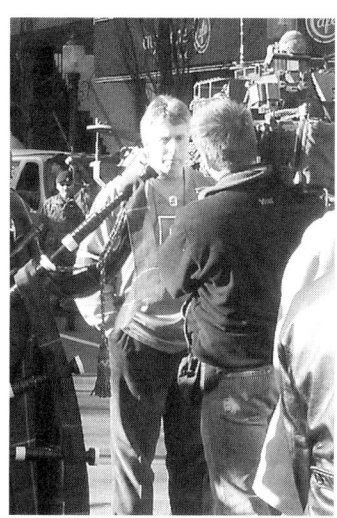

BC Lion great Lui Passaglia, GC 2005 Parade

    With a bit of time to spare in a fast-paced day, Maura and I decided to slide back to the motel to warm up, since we had essentially been outside or in the cool tent for several hours. We had a long, enjoyable meal with Doug, Polly, Ross and Dianne, exchanging family tree information and getting acquainted. To make up for lost time, we also set up a get together for after Sunday's game, and finally turned in, reflecting on a really fine day.
    Occasionally, I wake up in the middle of the night, with a thought of something I should have done. The brainstorm this night was minor, but I realized I should have captured the address of Al Christensen, our parade-viewing companion, since we have reams of Australia literature he could probably use. My fears, of course, were groundless, since when Maura and I stopped at Riderville before the game, Al and Darren were the first people we saw. After all of these years and all of these

coincidences, possibly I will eventually trust the reality that no Rider fan is ever met just once.

Pregame time was also good wandering time, and the plaza area west of BC Place was filled with fun and folks. As Maura and I strolled, I noted Danny McManus, working this day as a TV analyst, moving directly toward us. He was happy to sign my cap, adding true value to the steeply priced souvenir, and recalled once more that we had met on multiple Regina occasions. Danny was traded to Edmonton in a move announced a few days later, and later in the off-season was dealt to Calgary, and I'm guessing I'll run into him again.

It was time to head into the game, but the line for our gate was long and unmoving. We heard later that the presence of the prime minister caused extra security precautions, and we waited a good 45 minutes to get in. Still with plenty of time, we were in no hurry and joined our companions Chris, Marty and Jeff well before kickoff. Chris had been rooming with Marty, Jeff, and Marty's brother Dean, and by all accounts it worked well, yet one more indication of what great friends these guys are.

As we settled in, Jeff and Marty had some news. On their way to the seats, they had run into Roy Shivers, stopping to talk to the Rider GM, and offering him their support. Jeff mentioned Maura and I were sitting with them, and Roy gave Jeff his seat location and asked him to send me down. With nearly an hour until kickoff, I headed toward Roy's section, wondering all the while why things like this just keep on happening.

The usher was a bit of a challenge, since Roy's location was a prime spot, but admission was gained when I promised to both be good and not stay too long. Roy was finishing up a conversation, but greeted me warmly and I took a seat. My question of "How are things?" brought a long response, with some interesting information that must remain between Roy and I. Like Jeff, Marty, and the vast majority of *Leader–Post* letter writers, I made sure to tell Roy fans like me wanted to see him back for a big year in 2006.

During the conversation, a couple of Rider fans stopped by, having *me* take their picture with Roy, a type of "coming full circle" experience for the camera-crazy Minnesotan. Roy introduced me to Adam Rita, the Argos general manager, and not wanting to overstay my welcome, I headed back to our group.

Grey Cup 2005 – from front – Marty Neumeier, Jeff Banow, Chris Melin, myself, Maura

The festivities were beginning, and our seats had the fine view we expected. Interestingly, BC Place reminded us very much of our local Metrodome, especially from the exterior. The Metrodome has private boxes all around the top of the lower deck, causing a steeper grade for the second deck, but the resemblance was distinct. We had heard that the BC Place sound system was suspect, and those rumours were correct. We could hear a bit, but without any consistency. It was not nearly as bad as the Ottawa experience, but still really quite a disappointment. It's certainly true I don't hear perfectly, but the youngsters had the same difficulty.

As noted, this was the third meeting of these two squads in the preceding four Grey Cups. Articles had been written stating this as a concern, since the game potentially lacked the variety of opponents necessary for continued freshness. From my perspective, if the Riders aren't there, I don't have strong opinions about the teams that do make it. Having seen the previous two Alouette/Eskimo contests in 2002 and 2003, I was at least reasonably familiar with the respective rosters in 2004.

I've read accounts stating the opinion that the 2005 Grey Cup game was the best ever played, but have to disagree. It had a fun, entertaining second half, with a heart-stopping ending, but the first thirty minutes were quite ordinary. Edmonton led 10 – 1 at the half, as Montreal had difficulty getting things moving offensively.

The Als would gain only 69 yards rushing on the day, but Anthony Calvillo's arm would get Montreal moving in the third quarter. With two touchdowns and a field goal, the Eastern team went ahead 18 – 13, but Tony Tompkins' exciting 96-yard kickoff return thrust the Eskimos back into the lead.

As the fourth quarter got under way, Montreal recovered a fumble in Edmonton territory and scored four plays later. Now up by five, the Easterners forced 3rd down on their own 50, but Eskimo quarterback Ricky Ray hit a 35-yard pass to keep the drive alive. With help from two pass interference calls, the Western champs scored and added a two-point convert for a three-point lead with just a touch over a minute to play.

A CFL minute can be an eternity, and Calvillo drove deep enough for a game-tying field goal as time expired. Overtime in the Canadian Football League is the same format as the NCAA in the U.S. – teams alternate drives beginning with a first down from the opponent's 35-yard line until one prevails. In the first overtime, both teams scored touchdowns and the score was knotted at 35 apiece. Defences stiffened in the second overtime and the Eskimos, scrimmaging first, collected a 36-yard Sean Fleming field goal. The Als' possession opened with a heart-stopping play, as Calvillo's pass was deflected, but directly back to the quarterback, who then threw a strike to Kerry Watkins, alone in the end zone. The pass was dropped, but the deflection made the play illegal anyway. A sack on the next play made Montreal's chances slim, and these changed to none as Calvillo's desperation punt was corralled by Edmonton for the tense victory.

A very, very fine game, with an absolutely thrilling overtime conclusion, but the slow first half kept me from declaring it the greatest ever. The Grey Cup was awarded amidst a shower of green and gold confetti, and we headed to another dinner with the cousins, then a smooth trip home to complete the 2005 season

A few days after the Grey Cup weekend, the Riders announced Roy Shivers and the football staff would be back for the 2006 season. I for one was glad to hear that news.

On the long flight from Vancouver to Minneapolis, it struck me suddenly that, in a 24-hour period, I had met new

Happy Birthday, Saskatchewan!

cousins, breakfasted with yet another Terry McEvoy, was greeted by Danny McManus and shared time with Roy Shivers in his seat before the Grey Cup game. A guy could almost write a book about all of those things.

Chapter 17

The Winds of Change

So I did just that in the following months and the first edition of this book was published in May of 2006. To be completely truthful, I was a bit surprised I could do it; it was a tremendous learning experience and actually quite fun. Certainly a lot of hard work too, but writing about times of enjoyment made it a pretty pleasurable task.

As the 2006 CFL season approached, multiple changes were in the works. The Ottawa franchise suspended operations on April 9, making necessary a draft to disperse the Renegade roster to the rest of the league. Other changes included the beginnings of a salary management system and the first use of instant replay in the Canadian league.

The CFL replay system is just a bit different from that of the NFL. Each team has two challenges per game, to be used before the last three minutes of the second half. An unsuccessful first challenge has no ramifications, but a second failed challenge will cause the loss of a timeout. Any challenges raised in the final three minutes of the game will come from the replay official in the CFL booth. As many of us learned at the 2007 Grey Cup, teams are NOT allowed to challenge a challenge!

In June our family signed a new free agent player to a contract. Nathan Beardslee, our third grandchild, was born to Meredith and Bill. Nathan was about a month premature and there were several anxious moments, magnified by the distance, since this part of our family lived in Washington, DC at the time. All was well soon, though, and today's he's a smiling, happy little toddler.

In Saskatchewan, there seemed to be a greater sense of urgency for success in 2006. The Shivers-Barrett regime was in the final year of their contracts, and extensions had not yet been offered. More so than other years, I felt a hint of "put up or shut up" for the Riders, and thus Roy was not sitting still on his roster by any means.

The team had lost a number of players due to a number of reasons as the Ottawa dispersal draft date of April 12 approached. Gone were Paul McCallum, Nealon Greene, Elijah Thurman, Daved Benefield, and Travis Moore. Defensive back LaDouphyous McCalla later joined the exodus, retiring shortly before the start of training camp. Offensive coordinator Marcel Bellefeuille, an embattled soul in the minds of some fans, also left for a position in Montreal.

The plum of the Ottawa dispersal was clearly Kerry Joseph, the Renegades mobile quarterback. Hamilton held the first draft selection and I admit to being taken quite by surprise when the Riders traded the popular Corey Holmes, Scott Gordon and a draft pick to the Ti-Cats for the rights to grab Joseph on April 12. Saskatchewan also chose receiver Jason Armstead with their own first round pick, creating what appeared on paper to be instant 2006 offence for the Riders. With the pending return of standout receiver Matt Dominguez from his knee injury, the Green Guys had clearly moved up to a better neighbourhood in their passing game.

Saskatchewan also acquired veteran defensive back Almondo Curry from Montreal in exchange for Nealon Greene. Curry started eight games, but was eventually replaced by rookie James Johnson, a player Mosaic Stadium neighbour Joe McNeill immediately recognized as a keeper.

Rookie Luca Congi won the kicking job, with Dominique Dorsey slated to handle the return duties vacated by the Holmes departure. Tommy Condell, Joseph's offensive coordinator at Ottawa, was hired to replace Bellefeuille. With a veteran offensive line and an established defensive crew, Saskatchewan seemed poised to make the run that might extend the contracts of its football management group.

The Riders played a home and away pre-season series with Edmonton and won both games. There was clear reason for enthusiasm as the team traveled to British Columbia for the regular season opener against the host Lions on June 16. Dave Dickenson put a temporary halt to that euphoria as he passed for five touchdowns in the Lions' 45 - 28 thumping of the Riders. Kerry Joseph played adequately, but had two turnovers. Saskatchewan lost both of its attempted challenges in the regular season debut of the instant replay system.

Rider Pride on the American Side

The sudden departure of Ottawa had caused a total revamping of the Canadian Football League's 2006 schedule. The Winnipeg Blue Bombers had moved to the Eastern Division to level the numbers of teams in each division and I'm guessing a dartboard was used to determine the needed corrections to the rest of the overall schedule. Saskatchewan was actually scheduled to play BC three times in the first five games, including the home opener for the Riders on June 25.

Maura, Carson, Connor and I headed north on June 23. This trip had a couple of neat extracurricular events planned and we were eager to get to Regina for both the home opener and these extra bonuses.

The first bonus was getting together with our newly discovered cousins, the Orth brothers and their wives. We'd kept up during the off season and were really looking forward to getting to know them better and also having them meet the boys. Our second bonus of this first 2006 trip, our 13th family trip to Rider football, was a really unexpected pleasure. I received an email from Trevor Bothorel, a Riderfans.com acquaintance who worked as a cameraman for Global TV in Regina. Our family saga had interested the story planners and Trevor had set us up to be the subjects of a news feature. A bit of a scary thought, but it certainly sounded fun.

On our way up, we were carrying a load of books for the Rider Store. My venture into the realm of publishing was proving to be as costly as expected, and it made sense to save the shipping costs by bringing the books along. This required applying for a Canadian tax number and paying GST at the border, but the officer was incredibly helpful and we had only a short delay before arriving in Regina. We decided to try the Sherwood House motel, where we had stayed just once before, on one of our very first trips to Regina. It was in a central location on Albert Street, the rooms were spacious and the price was a bargain. It seemed as if many of the other guests were construction workers and the like, and it was much quieter than one would expect from a place on the lower end of the cost spectrum.

We went directly to the Rider Store and delivered the books. It was great to see Liz and fun to hear that book sales were steady. At the team walkthrough the next day, I was disappointed to discover that Roy was out of town but we caught up with several friends; I also gave Rocky Butler a copy of the book, since his day in 2002 had been one of the most enjoyable parts for me to write. Returning later to the BC practice, I gave one also to Paul McCallum, a new Lion, in a mild repayment of the seat cushion affair. Former Rider Vic Stephenson was also at the stadium then, and we met and compared notes on the pitfalls and pleasures of book publishing. Vic was in the process of creating a children's book and it was enjoyable to meet him and trade notes and ideas.

Trevor had indicated that someone from Global would call on Sunday morning to set up the TV feature. A pleasant fellow named Ryan Ellis did ring us and we arranged to meet him later at the Rider Store. I could tell that Carson and Connor were getting a bit uneasy, but from my perspective it was a once in a lifetime privilege so we had to go for it.

The Orth families were pulling in Sunday morning, and we met Doug and Polly and Ross and Dianne for a great brunch at the West Harvest Inn. Stories were traded and we had also brought up a photo album of my grandmother's that had pictures of their dad, Ken Orth, as a young child. I guess I am no longer completely surprised by the good things that happen to us in Saskatchewan, but the discovery of these cousins is something I always still chuckle about. We arranged to have them meet us for part of the TV filming later and eventually headed to the stadium.

Polly and Doug Orth   **Dianne Miller and Ross Orth**

Ryan Ellis was the enthusiastic TV reporter scheduled to give us our Andy Warhol moment. He explained what he had in mind and the filming began in earnest. In the Store, on the field, up in our seats and in the front of Taylor Field we all pretended that it was just another trip to the football game. The Orths then joined us and we all went into to Green and White Lounge for a spot with Joe Hadesbeck and Bob Poley on the Touchdown Club. It was then off to the tailgate for some further shots and interviews before Ryan felt he had enough material and headed off for the processing.

We certainly know nothing about how TV spots are put together, but we'd been with Ryan and his cameraman for close to three hours and knew they had just a ton of material. The finished result, which aired as the lead story on the 6 and 11 PM news, was just amazingly well done. The various pieces and interviews had been mixed in a very coherent flow and I for one was completely impressed. It was also pretty fun to have the Orth story told as part of the feature, and Ryan did a neat job of weaving in our discovery of unknown relatives as part of the McEvoy story.

After the TV folks left the tailgate, we had some time to meet some new folks, catch up with lots of old friends, and wind down a bit from the stress of our media adventure. It was a very pleasant day and enjoyable to be outside getting ready for the game. By this time, I had sold a few books myself and a couple of the people present at the tailgate were folks who had purchased copies and I would meet for the first time. I remember my excitement when I received my very first book order and was thrilled at this tailgate to meet that purchaser, Brad Ruston of Moose Jaw. He's a fan extraordinaire and it's been fun to catch up with Brad on multiple other occasions since, including Grey Cup in both 2006 and 2007. I was also able to deliver a green Mohawk wig discovered at a St. Paul costume store by super fan Rick Gallinger, Regina's own Caped Crusader.

Game time on this day was at 6:00 PM, late for a Sunday contest. We'd been at the stadium since about 1:00 and it was a bit of a relief to finally get inside, greet Joe and Nancy McNeill, and settle in as the Riders tried to avenge the drubbing they'd received the week prior. As we sat down, I spotted Roy walking across the south end zone, but my powers of persuasion were not sufficient to convince the field-level usher to allow me access to greet him.

It was no longer Taylor Field that we entered to watch the game. The world of corporate naming rights had reached Regina, and a recent press conference had introduced Mosaic Stadium at Taylor Field, recognizing the $3.75 million contribution of the Mosaic Company. Speaking just for myself, I was pleased to see the "Taylor Field" title had remained and was thrilled to read that the descendents of Piffles Taylor had enthusiastically embraced the name change also.

Brad Ruston   **Rick Gallinger**

A realistic Rider fan had to be concerned about this game. The Lions had dominated in Vancouver just a week prior, and consecutive losses would mean a poor start to a pivotal season. Saskatchewan struck first, on Luca Congi's first CFL regulation game field goal, but Dave Dickenson came back with a TD pass on third down to defensive tackle Tyrone Williams, playing tight end in a goal line formation. Kerry Joseph had a better game, passing for 211 yards and rushing for 92 additional. BC led 15 – 11 at the end of the third quarter and the teams traded touchdown passes in the first ten minutes of the fourth as the Lions held to a 24 – 18 lead.

The Riders needed a big play and received one from Jamel Richardson. The big receiver grabbed a short toss from Joseph and rambled 49 yards through multiple tacklers for the score that put the Riders ahead for good. Add in an interception return for a touchdown by Eddie Davis on the Lions' ensuing possession and the result was a solid 32 – 24 victory for the Riders in their Mosaic Stadium debut.

Sometimes I'm not sure what gets into me. When I read that the 1966 Grey Cup Champion Roughrider team was having a 40th reunion the weekend of July 7 and 8, it just seemed like I should be in Regina for that event. It was only two weeks after our family trip, but the prospect of potentially meeting some of the '66 players was a hard temptation to ignore. I was able to line up a book signing for Saturday also,

Rider Pride on the American Side

and figured that certainly was at least partial justification for the trip.

Before that, though, the opportunity to meet another Rider fan down here in Minnesota arose. I'd received an email from a fellow named Allan Scheirer through Riderfans.com. He is from Saskatchewan but now lived and worked in Winnipeg and was going to be in the Twin Cites on business. Allan and I hooked up at the Mall of America for some pleasant conversation one evening; he'd not been to Regina for a game in years and I convinced him to join me for the Calgary game on July 8. Something I always have trouble explaining to people in Minnesota is how Rider fans have a commonality that just simply pervades relationships; the Green and White bond seems to make strangers turn into friends with magic haste that is difficult to describe.

Allan was not coming into Regina until game day on Saturday, so I was on my own until then. I feel forever fortunate that we've been able to meet so many people in Regina, because being on my own doesn't really mean that anymore. I headed off on Thursday morning excited about the weekend and looking forward to what it might bring. Although I seldom take the route using U.S. Highway 2 going east from Grand Forks, I decided to use it this trip since I had just made the standard drive two weeks prior.

Thinking of many things, but not terribly concerned with directions, I somehow missed the exit in Grand Forks and had gone 20 miles out of my way toward Winnipeg when I realized the error of my ways. Since I like to think I'm the type of person who is able to poke fun at their own stupidity, I made sure to tell Scott Schultz, who attended school in Grand forks, that it is indeed possible to miss the only significant exit in a long stretch of freeway. I'm not real certain he thought I was serious, though, since no one could really be that directionally challenged.

Managing to arrive in Regina in late afternoon anyway, I again stayed at the Sherwood House and a bit later walked down to Earl's for dinner with Rider Dustin Cherniawski. It was a fun couple of hours for me, learning a bit about Dustin and I left convinced that he's a man destined for success in whatever his chosen field may be.

The 1966 team was scheduled to be at Mosaic Stadium on Friday morning, and I was one of a decent sized crowd also present. There was ample media coverage in the *Leader-Post* that day and I had read an article about Bob and Rob Kosid prior to heading to the stadium. Rob, the younger, had recently returned from service in Iraq and was his father's guest that weekend. The article had included a photo, and I was able to speak to Rob for a bit after recognizing him. It's fun to tell someone that you enjoyed hearing a bit of their story.

I had also brought along my Rider share with the hopes of getting George Reed and Ron Lancaster to sign it, and spotted George immediately. It seemed like he remembered me from Calgary in 2003, and he was glad to sign both my share and a photo of he and I taken in 2003 at the Hall of Fame Dinner. He's a man who just exudes class, in my opinion.

Ron Lancaster

But the man I really made the trip to meet was Ron Lancaster, the legendary quarterback called "The Little General." As noted previously, I had messed up my chance in 2000, but did not plan on repeating that oversight this time. As I recall my earliest Rider memories, likely from seeing a game or two in the 1960's, Lancaster was the name I best remembered. Somehow, in a fan career where I had been fortunate enough to meet and talk to a decent numbers of CFL celebrities, Dave Ridgway and Ron Lancaster had always stood out and I waited my opportunity to talk to Ron with a pretty nervous feeling circling through me.

Once he was alone, I approached him and introduced myself. The nerves immediately settled; he made me comfortable with his first words. He's a soft-spoken man, and clearly very appreciative of his career and the fans who admired his play. We talked for several minutes; I even told him about Pastor Greg Heidorn who had watched him play and still clearly remembered Ron's career. As you might now guess, I was able to get a photo with Ron and later sent it to Hamilton to get it autographed. When I received it back, Ron had taken the time to write a letter thanking me for being a Rider fan and indicating that he was glad we had met. By the way, I was able to get an autograph for Pastor Heidorn also and that made the entire encounter all the more fun. Ron Lancaster is a man I won't forget meeting.

Saturday was a beautiful day, clear and warm. I had a fairly busy schedule for the hours before the game, since I was slated to sign some books at the Rider Store and also wanted to make an appearance at another 1966 team event at the Saskatchewan Sports Hall of Fame. The entire team was signing autographs and I had promised Kelly Ramler at dinner the night before that I would grab some for him. He actually dropped off his Rider share for signing as I waited in line to enter the building. As he drove past, we executed a rolling handoff that any NASCAR fan would have admired. I was able to get the signatures Kelly was looking for and then had a bit of wandering time. As luck would have it, the first person I encountered was CFL commissioner Tom Wright.

The league had just announced a few days prior that Mr. Wright would not seek to have his contract extended. Thus, his term as commissioner, which began in late 2002, would end at the conclusion of the 2006 season. I had read the news with a bit of a sad heart, since I felt the league had done well under Tom with strong increases in both live attendance and broadcast numbers. The CFL is certainly not immune to the concept of office politics and Tom was aware it was time for him to move forward elsewhere.

My first thought when I spotted him was probably a bit silly. Here I am, just a guy from Minnesota, about to speak to the Commissioner of the Canadian Football League for the *third* time. Perhaps my concept of the size of the world is a bit messed up, but my good fortune in having these types of events occur in my CFL life never ceases to amaze me. Tom and I had a nice chat and to be honest it was a satisfying feeling to tell him in person that I felt he had done a great job.

He thanked me and mentioned that his CFL work had been wonderful for himself and his family.

Tom Wright

My book signing session was fun and decently attended. There was plenty of time after it ended for some tailgating and even a visit to the practice field. I had met up with Allan Scheirer at the tailgate and could tell he was really enjoying finally meeting in person a number of Riderfans.com cronies. The weather was still very pleasant when the game began at 6:00 PM and we looked forward to seeing Saskatchewan put it to Calgary and the smiling face of one Henry Burris.

However, for the third time since he'd left the Riders, Mr. Burris had his own plans. Calgary jumped out to a 17 – 3 lead, but Saskatchewan fought back with a strong second quarter to tie the game at 20 when halftime arrived. The stanza following was all Stamps as they scored 16 unanswered points on the way to a convincing 53 – 36 triumph. Sandro DeAngelis kicked six field goals to help the Stampeder cause; Kerry Joseph had a great day in a losing effort, passing for 334 yards and three touchdowns and rushing for 62 more. Coach Danny Barrett, never exactly the comic type in my mind, did come up with a good quip after the game. Referring to the horse that gallops around at Calgary home games after touchdowns, Barrett said "Good thing it wasn't over there – the horse might have had a heart attack."

Allan and I shook off the disappointing loss and headed for a late dinner with a large contingent of tailgate cohorts. It was loud and friendly, the service was terrible, but no one seemed to care. We finally headed for some sleep, but I had planned on an early departure to attempt to beat the Minnesota end-of-weekend traffic. Biding a sleepy Allan adieu, I left Regina in the darkness of a Sunday morning.

Arriving at the border before 6 AM, I expected the usual questions and a short delay. I had all of my personal items in the back seat, just a few clothes and a half dozen copies of my book. The officer asked me to open the trunk, and spent what seemed like an eternity poking around in it. I was driving Maura's car, and knew the trunk contained just the basic junk that typically accumulates in that compartment.

For whatever reason, I evidently failed that day's exam. I was asked to pull to the side and come into the building. Questions were asked on many subjects, but seemed to concentrate on the amount of cash I was transporting. While a group thoroughly searched the car, I was led to a back area and asked to empty all of my pockets and hand over my wallet. As the wallet was examined, the spare car key I was carrying was discovered and the man seemed certain he was on to something. When I pointed out it matched the other vehicle key and was carried in the wallet only to protect against my own potential carelessness, he seemed genuinely disappointed. All of the currency questions were again repeated, with the same innocent responses from the increasingly shaken Minnesotan.

Finally the vehicle search ended and my books were brought into the room. I explained I had followed the Roughriders for a long time, and had written this book about my CFL adventures. The gentleman paged through it quickly, and said "I bet that would sell pretty well up there. Have a good day." Gathering up my meager pile of loonies and toonies from the counter, I stuffed my possessions back in my pockets and left. I wish now I would have asked what they were up to, but heading south was then my only coherent thought. It could have been a training exercise, they may have picked me randomly, or, as a Canadian officer told me later, they may just have been trying to pass the time at the end of their long shift. Whatever their motive, it was pretty nerve wracking for a guy like me.

Things were also nerve wracking in Saskatchewan in the next few weeks. The team failed to show consistency, beating the Lions again, losing to Toronto, splitting two with Calgary and then losing to Edmonton on August 11 to sit at 3 – 5 for the season. Newspapers and internet sites overflowed with

The Winds of Change

rumours and even the Riders 46 – 15 pasting of Hamilton on August 19 did not serve to squelch them. It was hardly astonishing on the following Monday when the Saskatchewan Roughriders announced that Roy Shivers had been released from his contract. Two days later, on August 23, the team announced the hiring of Eric Tillman as the new general manager.

The positives and negatives of these events were discussed in great detail in the Canadian media and I certainly have nothing of any value to add to those details. I had developed a good friendship with Roy Shivers; I enjoy the man and he treated the McEvoy family very well. But, to be honest, a general manager in any professional sport is a pretty precarious position. The Rider board and administration felt they needed to make a change and had both the authority and the responsibility to make the moves they did. The reasons can be debated forever, but it's undeniable that the situation was not working as well as would be needed for the team to quickly take the next step toward a different level of success.

But Roy's departure still hit me as a shock. Even though I was almost expecting it, in fact was getting more convinced daily that it could logically happen, the finality of it was upsetting. Jeff Banow had been the first to send me a note when he saw the news; ironically, he and I had sat on my deck just two months prior discussing the very possibility.

Jeff had noted at that time that Roy's departure might have a different, more personal, impact on me than on many others. The youngster was right again; I felt bad for all concerned that things had not worked out better, but also had a sad little feeling pretty inwardly directed.

I'm not here to add my two cents to what happened. I'm not going to say who was right, who was wrong, and who could have done things differently, since I do not know the answers to those questions. My intentions are not to point at this group or that, this media guy or another, or to second-guess anything that happened or was said or left unsaid. It just didn't matter to me who played what card, what the Shivers era Rider record has been, or whether the Board is doing the right thing.

It was more personal than all of that to me. A man I truly liked, who I definitely enjoyed speaking with, a guy I connected with positively from the start in 2000 would be around no more. What hard-core Rider fans thought of him or what the Regina and national media thought of him just was not part of my thought process. I didn't need to go any further than what I thought of Roy Shivers.

I think of the first time I met him, in August of 2000. Somehow, even though I was really nervous, we seemed to hit something off immediately. Maura and the boys enjoyed him too, and as my trips continued I always checked in with him. I'd love to be able to boast that he did all sorts of exciting favours for us, but that never needed to be part of the equation. We talked about baseball, our families, and he always made me feel welcome and just a bit special. To me, my family, and my traveling circus of friends he was a man who was gracious, irreverent, and enjoyable to be around. My real regret was that I would be unlikely to see him again and that our serious conversation in Vancouver would be our last.

Reality always jumps up to bite people and the reality here was that this man was gone. It was time to move on, time for the new Eric Tillman era in Saskatchewan Roughrider football to begin. In my balding little mind, I wished the Riders the best, Eric Tillman the best, and certainly also wished the best for my friend Roy Shivers.

With all that said, the Riders thumped hapless Hamilton for the second week in a row and the Labour Day Classic of 2006 was just around the corner.

Chapter 18

Eric Who?

Despite the apparent turmoil in the Prairie Province in the late summer of 2006, I was very much excited about making the annual Labour Day Classic trek to Saskatchewan. I had taken a part-time office job at Roseville Area High School in the spring of 2006, and this trip would be a good way to end off the summer before the school year began. Maura, the boys and I had visited Yellowstone National Park in mid-August and I had time to work just a few days during the school orientation before it was time to head north.

Others were traveling in 2006 also. Saskatchewan visitors were plentiful at our home in Roseville. Jeff Banow arrived first, in June, to attend a Tom Petty concert with Chris Melin. I picked Jeff up at the airport, and after a good visit and breakfast with Maura, handed him off to Chris for the concert. Marty Neumeier was next, as he and his wife Melissa stopped for a couple of days on their way east on an extended camping trip. The Chabun family followed shortly, spending an enjoyable summer evening at our house while touring the area. Our final group was an entourage coming down to see the New England Patriots play the Vikings in a Monday night game on October 30. Josh Shaw and Quinn Broda are guys I knew from Riderfans.com, and they stopped by for some burgers and brats with friends Matt Exner and Chris Sastaunik before heading to their hotel. It goes without saying that not too many years ago I would have bet my retirement that the McEvoy's would not receive fours sets of Canadian guests in the same season, but it was fun to see all of them on our home turf.

Labour Day and a Rider game meant that Chris Melin would again be my traveling companion. By 2006, he had me. The idea of flying gets more attractive, especially since I'd already driven to Regina twice and had a third trip planned for later. If you've flown on the Northwest Airlines route between

Rider Pride on the American Side

Minneapolis and Regina, you know that the plane is small and tight and the fares are expensive. But a Cash and Miles promotion gave us a steep discount with the use of some flyer miles and we were set for our Friday departure.

Chris and I both like dry ribs and thus our first stop after grabbing a car was Melrose Place North. After satisfying our urges, we checked into the ever-popular Holiday Inn Express. Our weekend schedule included picking up Bill and Cindy Wakefield at the Regina Airport when their flight from Calgary arrived. As a person used to dealing with a giant airport like Minneapolis-St. Paul International, I find the Regina airport to be just a great place. The concept of parking within sights of the doors is foreign here, and the compactness of the Regina counterpart makes it feel pretty comfortable. As we walked to meet Bill and Cindy, we spotted Mayor Pat Fiacco and stopped to say Hello. In 2006, I had begun donating some extra tickets to the Big Brothers of Regina at Pat's suggestion and thanked him for the tip.

The Wakefield's deplaned right on time and it was great to see good friends who appear in our lives unfortunately infrequently. We made a shopping stop for some weekend necessities for them and then had a great dinner on the patio at Tony Roma's.

As previously mentioned, the Saturday prior to the Labour Day Classic is possibly my favourite football day. I love the bustle of the crowd, the accessibility of the players and the presence of lots of good friends. A book signing was scheduled also, adding to the fun. As Chris, acting as my PR man, and I settled in at a table in the Rider Store, Jim Hopson passed by, asked if we had what we needed, and then said, "Oh, we told Eric about you. He'd like to meet you."

Density is often one of my most noticeable qualities. With other things on my mind, I just had no inkling of who this person Jim referred to might be. After a distinctly long pause, I finally gave up and said, "Eric Who?" Jim, patient as always, explained that the Riders had a pretty new employee with that particular given name and I finally, shamefully, got it. Chris' snickers were reportedly heard in White City.

With a break in the signing, we headed out to the field. The players were just being introduced and we greeted Dustin Cherniawski as he awaited his turn. When the players retreated to their autograph stations, I began my search for the

Eric Who?

new GM of the Saskatchewan Roughrider Football Club.

Some people are easier to spot in a crowd than others. Eric Tillman is not only above average in height, but he is easily distinguished in a group by his distinctive red hair. Sure, maybe I didn't recognize his name immediately, but it only took me about two seconds to spot him on the field. Eric ended a conversation just as I approached, I gave him a book, and we had a nice chat. To me, it was impressive that he was out milling with the masses just a few days into his job and he's certainly proven to be an incredibly open and accessible GM.

Rider GM Eric Tillman

An old photo also was finally signed that day. Waiting patiently in line with a flock of little kids, I was finally able to get Gainer's signature, paw print and all, on my photo from the 1998 Grey Cup. Chris and I continued to mingle a bit, I signed a few more books, and we then headed for lunch with Bill and Cindy Wakefield and the Saskatoon Souster family of Troy, Kim, Mikayla and Hannah. Our destination was Montana's and we were able to sit on the patio in the fine Regina weather of the day.

Bill Wakefield's ability to discover the largest beers in creation never ceases to amaze me and his schooner this day was the size of a small rowboat. The ability of Rider fans to have a good time together is also always a nice revelation and we all enjoyed our conversation and meal. The young ladies certainly found the dessert appealing.

Chris and I again had our traditional Labour Day "Dinner with a Bomber" plans and we headed to Moose Jaw in the late afternoon to hook up with Chris Cvetkovic. The

Winnipeg team stays at the Temple Garden Spa Hotel and it seems like a pretty swank place. We rounded up Chris and had a good dinner, catching up on families and football. Since both Chris Melin and I were planning on attending the Grey Cup game in Winnipeg, we made tentative plans with Cvetkovic to track him down in the Manitoba capital also.

Mikayla and Hannah Souster

Since Bomber players need their rest, it was still early when we returned to Regina. We gave Kelly Ramler a call and met him at Brewster's for a beer and a visit, noting that even the youngster Chris Melin seemed ancient in the youthful Saturday night crowd. On Game Day, we happily accepted an invitation for brunch at Joe and Nancy McNeill's home, enjoying some good home cooking.

This Labour Day Classic was an important contest for the Saskatchewan Roughriders. On the heels of two decisive wins, the Riders had evened their record at 5 – 5 but had not yet convinced many that they were a team to be reckoned with. Marilyn McIntyre of Rosetown, my Orth cousin discoverer, was joining us in Section 102 that day. She and her daughter Natashia proved to be serious fans, but it would be a year later when it became clear just HOW serious.

Kerry Joseph had been resting a bruised knee in the two Rider wins against Hamilton, but was back for this game. Winnipeg had lost three straight after a decent start, but the Bombers were also getting back a healthy quarterback in Kevin Glenn.

Shortly before game time, there was a general heightening of noise in our part of Section 102. A person heading to a seat in the row directly across the aisle from me seemed to be the benefactor of a lot of attention. Clearly he was someone many people recognized immediately, but Chris and I, despite a great look at him, had no clue. Of course, a Dumb American is allowed to ask, and we quickly found out that the new spectator was Lorne Cardinal, who plays the police officer Davis Quinton on the CTV comedy *Corner Gas*. This program is now available in the U.S., but on this weekend in 2006, Lorne Cardinal could have been Brent Butt and I would not have known the difference.

Well, I'd guess both Lorne and Davis enjoyed the next few hours. Kerry Joseph showed a little rust, but displayed a lot more skill. He ran for two touchdowns in the first quarter and passed for two in the second as Saskatchewan built a 28 – 12 halftime lead enroute to shutting out the Bombers in the second half. The final score of 39 – 12 included a touchdown scored by Kenton Keith on an impressive 31 yard scamper after hauling in a shovel pass from Joseph.

An easy trip home on Monday after breakfast with 2005 Grey Cup acquaintance Al Christensen and his wife led to the start of a new school year in Minnesota. Both of the boys were in key years, Carson as a graduating 12th grader and Connor as an incoming member of the 9th grade class. It was my first year working at Roseville Area High School at the beginning of the school year and it was a busy place.

It didn't take long for a couple of Rider-related connections to come up. I discovered that Roseville football coach Chris Simdorn had a tryout with the Riders at the end of his collegiate career at North Dakota State University. Chris had followed former Rider Jeff Bentrim as the Bison quarterback and won the Harlon Hill Trophy in 1990 after leading his team to an undefeated season and the national title. I always seem to confuse North Dakota (Grand Forks) and North Dakota State (Fargo) and so excitedly told Chris that I knew Scott Schultz, only later realizing that a Bison didn't really care about a Fighting Sioux.

The second connection involved a shirt, of course. Carson and Connor have a number of Rider and Grey Cup shirts. They wear them to school regularly, with essentially no recognition or other reaction. Carson was amazed when he walked in a new class wearing a Rider logo shirt and heard his teacher exclaim "That's a Saskatchewan Roughrider shirt!" This teacher of physics, Owen Zeumer, is from northern Minnesota and watches the CFL on TV when he goes home to visit.

The fourth trip of the 2006 campaign was aimed at the September 30 game against the Edmonton Eskimos. Saskatchewan had continued its season trend by dropping the Banjo Bowl in Winnipeg, but then narrowing defeated BC again. At 6 – 6 as the Evil Empire came to town, the Riders needed to rack up some consecutive wins again.

The season's last trip involves my bus buddies, Harv Moen and Tim Anderson. Harv had missed the past two trips, but was on board for this one. We always get a suite at the Holiday Inn Express and thus have plenty of room for the three of us. The drive was uneventful and we headed to Bushwakker's for dinner. There we met a fun food server named Donna Maloch, who convinced the brass to buy a beer for these fans who had travelled so far to see the Riders. Donna received a book in trade and I even checked in 2007 to be certain she had received it.

After dinner, we decided to invade Casino Regina. We were all tired and planned to stay only a short time. Tim fancies himself as a craps player and his eyes lit up when he saw the table just inside the door. Harv and I wandered around for a bit and Tim told both of us that he was heading back to the hotel soon. I left with Harv for the short walk back to the Holiday Inn Express and we went to bed, knowing Tim would be back soon.

We both fell asleep, as older folks tend to do. I awoke about 12:30 and noticed immediately that Tim was not to be found. Harv came alive at about the same time and we both wondered where our other friend might be. After a short discussion, we were concerned. We both thought Tim was on his way back when we left, since he'd insisted he was not going to stay long. Memories of a lost friend in Ottawa hit me hard and we shortly decided to go back to the casino.

Although Casino Regina is not far from the hotel, the street connecting them isn't too warm and fuzzy late at night. We actually looked around as we walked together, hoping Tim had not been discovered by some bad guys on his way back. When we entered the casino, we both immediately saw the back of Tim's head, gyrating and urging the dice to comply with his needs on the craps table. Relieved and annoyed at the same time, we left without him spotting us.

Next morning, the seating for the upcoming Rolling

Eric Who?

Stones concert at Mosaic Stadium was fully in place and blocked the door where we usually entered the stadium to watch the walkthrough. However, we saw an opening, the door was open, and so we walked onto the field. Ends up that Coach Barrett wanted part of practice closed and we were politely asked to leave. Milling with the media and other fans outside the south end of the field, we traded barbs with Mitchell Blair until the door in the fence finally opened. The mass of humanity had taken no more than a dozen steps when we were again asked to leave temporarily, giving Harv, Tim and I the distinct pleasure of having been booted twice in the same day!

I introduced my friends to Dustin Cherniawski, who was a bit amused that they too were from Minnesota. After practice, we went to the Cornwall Centre where legendary receiver Don Narcisse was making an appearance and met both he and Kerry Joseph. Don was incredibly friendly, gave me his card, and we've corresponded a few times since. Kerry was great also and it was fun to meet him. He mentioned he's a friend of Minnesota Vikings running backs coach Eric Bieniemy, so since then, I always remind Kerry that the Minnesota Vikings could use a quarterback. It was worth a laugh until the Argos needed one also.

We had some items for Will Chabun, so drove east to the *Leader-Post* to deliver them, and Will joined us for lunch. With an evening to kill, and because we are at times slow learners, we headed back to Casino Regina. Once again, Harv and I left after a short period of time, hopefully wiser this night to Tim's tendencies. In a classic story sure to be repeated every trip for years, Tim finally wandered home in the wee hours and tried to climb into *my* bed. I ejected him quickly, as you might imagine. In the morning, he was all excited since, when he had mentioned he was from Minnesota, a fellow player at the table figured out that Tim was in Regina with me. Tim's description lacked a bit of detail, but I eventually determined this man was Craig Robinson, a Riderfans.com and tailgate acquaintance.

The game was late on Saturday and we killed time until the tailgate. Harv and Tim seemed to enjoy themselves and mixed easily and well. The weather was decent for late September and we watched an even first half that ended tied at 17. The almost uneventful third quarter saw Rocky Butler replace an injured Kerry Joseph and the Riders take a five point lead heading to the final stanza.

Rider Pride on the American Side

A Luca Congi field goal gave the Riders a 25 – 17 lead with about seven minutes left. But Edmonton was fighting to stave off elimination from the postseason for the first time in 34 years and fought back. Two field goals and an eight yard Ricky Ray run put them up 30 – 25 with 42 seconds left on the clock. As time expired, Rocky Butler was sacked near centre field, and the three Minnesotans, like most others present, thought the game was over.

In an exciting play that nearly became legend, the Riders somehow had kept the ball alive. Charles Thomas, Andrew Greene, Butler, Kenton Keith, Corey Grant and then Keith again played keep away all the way down to the four yard line where Keith fumbled and the Eskimos recovered. It was an exciting play, and happened right in front of us. Unfortunately, instead of an exciting win, the Riders took a tough loss but gave the Minnesotans something to discuss on the way home the next day.

Saskatchewan split its final four games to end the season with a familiar 9 – 9 record. The Riders defeated Hank and the Stamps in the West Semi-Final, but lost again in the Western Final to BC by a lop-sided score of 45 – 18 after being outscored 26 – 1 in the second quarter. It seemed like Coach Barrett's last chance for a new contract melted away like the Vancouver fog on a sunny day.

With the 94th Grey Cup to be played in Winnipeg, Chris and I had planned all along to attend. It was close and would thus be less expensive than some, even after our $226.83 second deck tickets. My traveling partner surprised me a bit when he decided to fly, but I chose to drive and headed north in the early morning of Friday, November 17.

Winnipeg is an easy drive from Minnesota and I made good time until I approached the home of the Bombers. It's a slow drive in on the long Pembina highway approach to downtown and Chris reached the motel before I did. We had picked a place downtown, very close to the Convention Centre where many of the parties would be. Maura and the boys and I had stayed at this motel many years before, but in 2006 it clearly was in need of a giant makeover. The room was amazingly small, and had almost no floor space, but at least the price was right.

We decided on lunch, finding a nearby Irish pub with decent food but also the slow service we were to find the entire weekend. By then it was mid-afternoon, and time to head to Riderville. We'd been at this facility before, in 1998, and navigation was easy. Mayor Fiacco and his wife were the first persons we saw and we shared a few thoughts with them. The room began to fill and familiar faces began to arrive. I sometimes forget that I too am a familiar face to some and was very surprised when a gentleman I'd met on the practice field in Regina wandered up and introduced himself as Joseph Genoway. In Regina, I had discussed my book with him; he had bought a copy and this day shared some kind thoughts on my literary efforts. As the conversation progressed, he revealed his true identity – Joseph Genoway by day perhaps, but the temporarily retired Cousin Leonard in his spare time. This man is a great guy and true fan, who has indeed now become my personal sales person of Regina Rams 50 – 50 tickets.

Joseph Genoway

More of the regulars began to file in, including Calgary pals Govind Achyuthan and Jason Isaac, who had come this year only for the festivities and were flying home Sunday morning before the game. The Boys from Esterhazy, Marty Neumeier and Jeff Banow also strolled in, Marty fresh from his work stint in Yemen. Eskimo fan Brian Edwards also was in attendance and we talked about his appearance, along with his wife Linda and Calgary fans Ken and Jacky Smith, in a Grey Cup TV fan special scheduled to air the next day.

Since we had some history in Winnipeg, I was also on the lookout for yet another appearance by the legendary Three

Man Band. It's easy to assume things, but I was pretty sure these guys would be around. For once I was correct and I spotted the trio across the room.

One of the greatest feelings about writing the first edition of this book was the reaction of various folks who had been a part of it. These guys were a key part of an important story and clearly had enjoyed seeing their role in print. For me, it was fun to hear them talk about it and thank them again for their part in my life in this very building eight years earlier.

**The Three Man Band in 2006
Andrew Beckett, Darryl Spanier, Darryl Rieger**

As it usually always does, Riderville this Friday afternoon in Winnipeg was proving to be a great place to meet and greet. Brent and Karen Magnus, our Footballtown friends, were in the room as were lots of old and new friends from Riderfans.com and the Riderville.com websites.

One of my book sales in the spring of 2006 had surprised me. This buyer was one Jack Bedell, with a shipping address in Louisiana. The name sounded very familiar, so of course I had only to Google it to find out more. The results came back identifying one Dr. Jack Bedell, a Professor of English at Southeastern Louisiana University and an accomplished author of poetry. While I was imagining my book being used as an example of how NOT to write in a college English class, I stumbled upon an entry for Jack that explained the familiarity of his name. Jack Bedell also writes for the Canadian Football League official website, CFL.ca, and is the author of a column cleverly titled *Rouge, White and Blue*. Jack is an incredible fan of the CFL and I was able to share dinner with him that night, a real pleasure for me. As had happened at lunch, our server disappeared for a long while, causing further suspicious thoughts about dining traditions in Winnipeg that we Americans did not understand.

Saturday morning brought the Spirit of Edmonton breakfast, held this year in a hotel far from downtown Winnipeg, right in the vicinity of the airport. I volunteered to be the Designated Driver, so Chris and I picked up Jeff, Marty, and their friend Walt Hawrysh, who proved to be good guy but one hobbled by the unfortunate fact of being a Bomber fan.

Marty excels on Grey Cup Saturday and 2006 was one of his finest performances. Our table was at an end of the room and close to a service exit where large quantities of the breakfast beverage were stored and readily available for clandestine snatching. Clad in a turban, Mr. Neumeier kept the table very well supplied throughout the morning and ended the event by starring in the conga line. In the shot of our table shown below from late in the festivities, I'd argue that the Designated Driver is readily identifiable.

Spirit of Edmonton Breakfast, 2006

This event lasts the entire morning, giving party-goers a good run for their money. I was even able to sneak out for a bit and visit Ken and Jacky Smith in their nearby hotel. We'd missed each other in Vancouver the previous year and it was a good chance to catch up a bit with them. The Smiths moved to Creston, BC in 2007 and I hope to eventually take them up on their invitation to visit there.

Rider Pride on the American Side

We headed back downtown and naps were in order for most of the Breakfast Bunch. I headed over to Rendezvous Saskatchewan, which was already underway at the Convention Centre. As always, it was a great party, full of life and fun people. Our Edmonton friends were there and as always it was great to see Arnie and Bambi Fearon, Rob and Sheila Gaudreau and the rest of their crew. One of their group, Tom Von Stackelberg of Winnipeg, was even thoughtful enough to later send me a copy of a DVD he made of the weekend.

Rendezvous was winding down and we decided it was time to test the Winnipeg restaurant scene again. Jeff Banow is very familiar with Winnipeg's downtown and he led a merry parade seemingly to Brandon and back that culminated in a decent Asian restaurant with exceedingly slow service. By the time we returned to Riderville, the line to enter was beyond our waiting patience and we called it a day.

Game Day began with breakfast with our favourite Bomber, Chris Cvetkovic. We followed him out of downtown to a popular spot apparently not afflicted with the downtown service disease. He talked of his off-season job and excitedly of a baby due in 2007. It was a good visit with a good guy. By the way, when Chris and Ashley's daughter Payton was born in 2007, she received a cute little Rider green bear from Minnesota, complete with green Rendezvous beads.

As usual, there was time to kill before heading out to Canad Inns Stadium. We had decided to try mass transit, and met Marty, Jeff and Walt at a nearby bus stop. After a short wait, we boarded a bus which soon was jammed and passed hundreds of waiting fans at bus stops on the way to the stadium. The weather was just a bit chilly, but fine for a bit of pre-game wandering.

As we entered the stadium, I spotted former BC Lion and Hall of Famer Lui Passalglia waiting in a beverage line. He's a man I have always wanted to meet, so I quickly introduced myself, mentioning that I am from Minnesota. Lui was cheerful and glad to chat for a bit, mentioning some of his former teammates from the University of Minnesota.

We wound our way up to our seats, in the very corner of the second deck. Shortly after we arrived, there was a bit of an incident directly behind us. The occupants of some of those seats ended up having counterfeit tickets, by their own admission purchased from a scalper outside the stadium.

Evidently even the CFL is not exempt from such dastardly deeds.

Grey Cup, 2006, Winnipeg Manitoba

The game matched the BC Lions with the Montreal Alouettes in a contest of perennial CFL powers. It was a game with limited excitement as both offences struggled to score touchdowns. BC prevailed 25 – 14 on the strength of 19 points from former Saskatchewan kicker Paul McCallum, who several of us felt should have been named the game's outstanding player. As we filed out, I was even able to grab a leftover game program from a seat near us and thus had an instant free souvenir for Dave Ridgway, who always appreciates such items.

The bus ride home was slow and crowded. Chris and I returned to the hotel and went out to grab some dinner quickly, since he had a very early flight back in the morning. For reasons we never uncovered, the service this night won the weekend lottery for the Worst Possible and it took us three hours to have a beer and a sandwich. We were tired and getting cranky, but finally got out with some insincere apologies from a manager lacking basic customer service skills.

Chris left for the airport in the wee hours and I followed shortly after. My drive back to Roseville was pleasant and easy. It gave me ample time to reflect on the massive changes that had taken place already in Saskatchewan football and speculate on those still to come for the 2007 season. After a

Rider Pride on the American Side

Christmas trip to Germany to see Bill, Meredith, Fiona and Nathan, we began the New Year with no clue whatsoever how significant 2007 would eventually be in that place called Saskatchewan.

Chapter 19

Kerry On

It did not take long for Rider GM Eric Tillman to make some significant changes. Speculation reigned on the football websites about the future of Saskatchewan head coach Danny Barrett, whose contract had ended. Many fans felt he would be back, but I was just as sure his days in the Prairie Province were finished. He'd had his shot, for seven seasons, and it was very clear in my little Minnesota mind that it was time for a new kid in town.

On December 6, Tillman made his decision and announced Kent Austin as the new head coach of the Saskatchewan Roughriders. The need for an offensive-minded coach was apparent, and Austin fit that description perfectly. As a quarterback who led the Riders to their last Grey Cup victory in 1989, Kent was hard-working and demanding of himself and his teammates, and these would be excellent attributes for a head coach. He and Tillman had worked together in Ottawa and all these factors made Austin a very logical and deserving pick by the Rider GM.

We made a decision also, dropping down to two season tickets from the four we had purchased since 2001. Carson would be in college in the fall of 2007, a great step for him but a large financial consideration in the U.S. The upward movement of the loonie had changed the economics of our Regina trips also and thus our decision was made. Working around summer jobs, we made our family trip plans for the home opener on July 8, with arrangements made for the boys to sit with Jeff Banow to experience the East side in person.

Maura and I had celebrated our 35th wedding anniversary in April and decided treat ourselves with a trip once the school year was finished. We decided on a combination destination of Las Vegas and the north rim of the Grand Canyon and left in late June. The heat was unbelievable in Las Vegas; the outside temperature was 107 degrees Fahrenheit or just about 43 Celsius when we arrived. We spent an evening with our friends Mark and Sue Quam and arranged to have lunch at the MGM Grand with another friend who lives in the area.

We were waiting in the lobby when his familiar profile showed its outline in the brilliant sunlight. It was great to see Roy Shivers again. The three of us headed toward our restaurant, catching up with each other the entire way through the giant hotel. Our lunch was very leisurely and he entertained us with multiple stories of Las Vegas past. The conversation drifted toward football only once or twice. I could tell he missed some facets of pro football greatly and missed some others not at all. Hopefully his new position as BC's Director of Player Personnel will focus on those parts he enjoys.

Maura and Roy Shivers, June 2007

As training camp approached, the Riders had some big gaps to fill in their lineup. Running back Kenton Keith signed with the Indianapolis Colts, made the team, and proved that many in Regina don't know as much as they would like to think. Omarr Morgan, Davin Bush, Nate Davis and Jackie Mitchell were gone for the defence, Andrew Greene was released and Rocky Butler was traded to Hamilton for offensive lineman Wayne Smith. Other new players expected to make solid contributions included receiver D. J. Flick, cornerbacks Airabin Justin and Tad Kornegay, and right guard Mike Abou-Mechrek. A key trade sent Rob Lazeo to Calgary for Wes Cates, who was immediately projected as Keith's replacement. The

Riders won both of their pre-season games, but on the eve of the season opener in Montreal, the starting quarterback was still a mystery for Saskatchewan.

Friday the 6th of July was blazing hot in Saskatchewan. We were greeted with the exciting news on the radio as we approached Regina that the temperature was, in fact, the highest ever recorded on that date. Braving the heat, we walked a few blocks down Albert and met friends Nat and Marie Hrynuik for a very nice dinner.

The heat abated only slightly during the night and the day was already quite warm when we headed to Mosaic Stadium for our annual family appearance at the team walkthrough. We greeted a few folks and settled in with Govind Achyuthan to watch the proceeding.

A person would need to know Gov to understand his passion for the Saskatchewan Roughriders. He lives in Calgary but attends virtually every home game. His knowledge of Rider history is legendary and he is the person usually turned to when some obscure bit of football information is needed. I was hoping to meet Kent Austin as the players filed back to the locker room, but it looked like he'd be tied up with the media types.

Kent Austin   **Govind Achyuthan**

Govind and I were standing on the edge by the field when fullback Chris Szarka walked past and greeted Gov by name. Lineman Gene Makowsky was next, warmly renewing acquaintances with my Calgary friend. I was not surprised in the least, since I was aware Govind is not just your ordinary

Rider Pride on the American Side

fan, but have to admit I did a serious double take when the Riders' new coach then walked past. Pausing, he said, "Govind! How are you?" Once again, friendship had its rewards as I was able to introduce myself to Kent, grab a quick photo and have a brief chat before he hurried off to his pregame press conference.

Maura and I shared a mid-afternoon beverage with Bill Donison and then the four McEvoy's joined Joe and Nancy McNeill for dinner later. We kept a tradition alive by heading to a movie, *Transformers*, and Maura and I hoped we were not too much of an embarrassment to our sons, since we were the oldest viewers by many years. Despite the crashing and exploding, I did sneak in a short nap in the cool theatre.

Doug and Polly Orth, our cousins from Rosetown, were in Regina for the game and we met them at the Regina Inn for a fine brunch. The weather was still warm, but comfortable, as I joined Bob Poley and Joe Hadesbeck on the radio, giving me a public forum to use to whine about the exchange rate. Making a short stop at the tailgate, we greeted Marcel "Nugsy" Nogue and Troy "Sudsy" Souster and lots of others.

On the practice field, I had a mundane experience that nonetheless says a lot about the Saskatchewan franchise. Enduring a half hour wait to make use of one of only three portable bathroom units on the entire field, I mentioned this oversight later in an email to Rider President/CEO Jim Hopson. In my opinion, the fact that the Average Terry can directly email Jim is pretty impressive in a world where many CEO's do all they can to keep away from the paying customers. Better yet, Jim answered quickly, apologized for the oversight, and assured me it would not be an issue again. Good customer service sometimes can be judged by how a problem is addressed and the quantity of small plastic buildings was not an issue for the rest of my trips in 2007.

When we reached our seats, there was a family already sitting to our right, in the season seats we'd vacated. The adult male of the group looked a bit familiar, but when you are my age you have seen so many people that nearly every face rings some dull mental bell. As Sudsy and Nugsy scampered past heading to their seats, Marcel paused and whispered, "That's Brian Towriss next to you." Even the Dumb American recognized the name of the very successful University of Saskatchewan football coach and it didn't take me very long to make his acquaintance. Brian was fun to talk to and incredibly knowledgeable about football, helping me to understand a strange play or two. We've kept in touch and I'm hoping to take him up on his invitation to visit in Saskatoon some day. It was not very hard to understand why he is so successful.

Head Husky Brian Towriss

Every game at Mosaic Stadium is fun, but the home opener is always pretty special. The anticipation for a successful season is always evident and in 2007 the fresh start seemed even more complete. On this sun drenched day, Hank finally met his match in Regina. Kerry Joseph showed the consistency he would display all season, as he passed for four touchdowns and 244 yards in Saskatchewan's 49 – 8 romp. Two of these scoring passes were to newcomer D. J. Flick. This nimble receiver had impressed us even at the walkthrough the previous day, where Maura noted the great skill in his hands during a simple game the receivers were playing on the sidelines. In the Calgary contest, Flick made a terrific one-handed TD grab around a defender and my bride, for one, wasn't at all surprised to see him do it.

New running back Wes Cates ran for 58 yards and two touchdowns and the tough Rider defence blanked the Stamps in the final three quarters while registering three sacks, a forced fumble, and interceptions by James Johnson and Airabin Justin. The long ride home was better than usual.

Carson and Connor enjoyed their debut on the east side, indicating that Jeff was a great host. They told the story of a tall gentleman very much into the game, beating on his drum excitedly and generally verbally blasting the hapless Stamps.

Rider Pride on the American Side

They were confused by my zealous laughter, not realizing that they had described Darryl Spanier, the famed "Spanky" of the Three Man Band.

The Saskatchewan fans were excited, but their enthusiasm was doused by losses in the weeks following to BC and Edmonton. The Edmonton game was a frustration in Riderville, since the Eskimos rallied to win 21 – 20 after trailing 20 – 1 at the half. However, in a turnabout unfamiliar in the recent Saskatchewan football past, the Riders then snowed under the Eskimos 54 – 14 on the strength of two rushing and two passing touchdowns from Kerry Joseph. The quarterback from McNeese State was flourishing in the Austin offence, playing with fire and restraint at the same time.

Back in Minnesota, I found myself able to see Rider games for essentially the first time in a decade. Marty Neumeier sent me software for a contraption he had hooked up in Alberta. Called a Slingbox, it enabled me to view CFL games on my home computer. The picture wasn't bad, especially from across the room, and his thoughtfulness in thinking of Old Gramps was very much appreciated. Family changes were necessitating football changes also. Carson had graduated from Roseville Area High School in June and would be starting at Hamline University in St. Paul in the fall. He was going to be living in a dorm and move-in day was slated for the Sunday before Labour Day.

Family comes before football and Chris Melin understood. Although I had been in Regina for the past six Labour Day Classics, I would be missing this one and Chris and I rescheduled our annual trip for the game on September 22. Our Cvetkovic dining tradition was on the ropes anyway, since the Bomber Chris had dislocated his elbow and was out of commission.

The Riders continued their good play, defeating BC and Toronto in the next two games. Their record of 5 – 2 had the province buzzing and fans flocking to Mosaic Stadium. At home, we enjoyed a visit from stadium neighbours Joe and Nancy McNeill, who stayed with us for a couple of days in late July. Their visit had an eerie moment – in giving them directions, I had advised them in their travels about town to avoid a particular bridge that was being repaired, since the traffic was moving very slowly in its vicinity. Joe and Nancy left our house on August 1, the day that bridge, the I-35W span over the Mississippi River, collapsed.

Our family summer trip was to Colorado, where we visited with Meredith's in-laws, Bill and Nancy Beardslee in Fort Collins and then stayed for a week in a ski condo in Keystone. This was our fourth trip to the area and there's plenty to keep a family busy. It's also an incredible bargain in the summer, since we were in the off-season of the skiing economy.

More progressive than Minnesota, Colorado has a cable channel called Altitude that broadcasts CFL games. I noted that the Riders game against Edmonton on August 18 was scheduled to be shown and also that the condo's common area had a 52" big screen TV. Our college friends, Tim and Bev Johnson now live in Colorado and had come up to spend the day with us. Since the Denver Broncos were also on the tube that night, I was afraid we might have competition for the choice spot, but the four of us settled in without any NFL interlopers present.

Tim is a great sports fan and was interested in seeing our Riders. The first half was good football, with Saskatchewan holding a slim 24 – 22 lead. It was very enjoyable seeing Mosaic Stadium, and even pointing out on the big screen to Tim and Bev the location of our seats in section 102. Things were not quite as much fun in the third quarter though, as Edmonton moved to a 32 – 27 lead. They held this margin into the fourth quarter; Scott Schultz recovered a fumble at centre field and the rains came down in a BIG way, although I'm sure there is no connection between those two events.

Just as I was explaining to Tim and Bev that our first trip to Regina in 1994 had included a storm of similar proportions, the TV in Colorado went dead. We waited long enough to learn that lights were out at Mosaic Stadium and the game was delayed. The Johnson's left, and I waited in vain for the game to return, finding out the next day that I could have waited forever but also that Saskatchewan had won 39 – 32. A delay of about an hour had cooled the Eskimos, but not several thousand diehard Rider fans, who braved torrential rain, lightening and a power failure to savor the victory.

In the weeks that followed, I heard many incredible stories about this game. Those who waited it out will remember it forever and I'm sure it completely overwhelmed our 1994 experience in Saskatchewan football weather stories. My favourite story is from friend Karen Magnus of Regina. Karen and Brent's daughter Taylor is a great young fan who accompanies her parents to games. When the power failed, Taylor needed to use the restroom, a scary thought in the dark inner reaches of a stadium without power. Wearing her Matt Dominguez jersey, Taylor went with Karen to a room illuminated only by the faint light of cell phones. A lady commented on Taylor's attire, and then introduced Karen and Taylor to her companion, who just happened to be Mrs. Matt Dominguez.

With a 6 – 2 record and this memorable victory in their pocket, the Riders enjoyed a bye week before taking on Eastern Division leading Winnipeg in the Labour Day Classic. Carson's first day at college was an all-day event, and the game was already in progress when I fired up the Slingbox. Saskatchewan played a mediocre first half, trailing 18 – 10 at the break and still down 26 – 24 when they scrimmaged after a Bomber punt with 1:34 left.

Kerry Joseph ran for 13 yards and then completed four straight passes for a total of 49 yards. Already in winning field goal range, Joseph handed off to Wes Cates for a couple, and then fooled Winnipeg completely with a 27-yard TD scamper on a quarterback draw. It was a great call, perfectly executed, and Saskatchewan won 31 – 26. It would have been great to be there, but that wasn't to be and I did at least manage to watch the game here in Minnesota.

The Riders had won five straight heading to the Banjo Bowl in Winnipeg on September 9. That streak ended with a bust as the Bombers routed Saskatchewan 34 – 15. Kerry Joseph had a rare off day and was replaced by Marcus Crandell in the final quarter. Worse yet, receiver Matt Dominguez had to be helped off the field late in the game, but indicated that his apparent knee injury did not seem to be serious.

Injuries were beginning to bite at the Riders, especially on defence. Eddie Dave had separated his shoulder and was on the nine-game injury list. Terrell Jurineack was out for the season and Lance Frazier and James Johnson missed time. It seemed as if every defensive starter was hampered by nagging pains.

The Calgary Stampeders had struggled early in the season, but had begun to turn their game around and took a giant step in that direction when they mauled the Riders 44 – 22 on September 15 in Calgary. Henry Burris threw five touchdown passes as Calgary improved to 6 – 4 – 1, hot on the heels of the 7 – 4 group from Saskatchewan. As Chris and I headed north for the September 22 game against BC, the once comfortable Rider march toward a home playoff game was dodging some land mines.

Since the game was on a Saturday, Chris and I flew up on Thursday. I hate leaving my car at the airport in Minneapolis, so Maura dropped me off at the local transit center and I rode the comfort of a city bus and then our relatively new light rail to the Minneapolis – St. Paul International airport. Arriving very early, I decided to walk around all of the various concourses to kill time and also to see the results of ongoing expansion at that facility. I finally caught up to Chris at our gate an hour and 45 minutes later, weary in the legs, but impressed by the expansive size of the terminal.

Our flight was delayed for an hour while airline personnel reshuffled the luggage. Flight delays are annoying, even when a person isn't on a tight schedule and it seemed to me this day that we may have in fact just been waiting for passengers from late connecting flights to catch up, since there was then very limited capacity on the two flights a day to Regina from Minneapolis. At any rate, with a slow customs line also hampering us in Regina, it was past mid-afternoon when we reached the Holiday Inn Express.

Grey Cup 2003 transportation heroine Laur' Lei Silzer joined us for a drink later at Bushwakker's and we enjoyed laughing about our past meetings and generally talking hopefully about the Riders' remaining games.

I had a mission to accomplish at the walkthrough on Saturday and thus we made certain to arrive in time to see the players come out of the locker room. When Joe and Nancy McNeill had visited us in August, we had attended a St. Paul Saints minor league baseball game with tickets given to us by a friend, and my mission was to repay that friend with something a bit more unique than a simple "Thank You." This friend's name is Mike McCullough and so a Rider-related gift seemed in order.

There is a contributor to Riderfans.com named Jonathan Carriere who is just one great photographer. He posts a lot of great action shots on the site and I contacted him with a special request for a Saskatchewan Roughrider #45 linebacker Mike McCullough action shot. He seemed intrigued by the request and had sent me a fine shot from the Labour Day Classic. I stopped Rider Mike briefly and asked him if he'd mind signing something at the end of his day's work and of course received an affirmative answer.

Coach Austin Addresses the Troops

The team walkthrough on this mild fall day had a noticeable sense of urgency. Coming off two consecutive lopsided losses can cause that necessary emotion in a coach, and thus the session was much longer than normal. Even I had already noticed in our July trip that the walkthroughs were much more structured and serious than in past seasons and the players seemed to respond well to this new discipline. As we waited for Mike McCullough, Coach Austin spent several minutes at the end of practice speaking to the undivided attention of the entire squad.

    Mike had remembered my request and came over. Of course, rather than just getting him to autograph the photo, I had to tell him the whole story and he and a couple of other players chuckled at the latest chapter in the tale of people with the same name. Rider Mike was even kind enough to sign his inscription "To Minnesota Mike", a touch that was much appreciated by my friend down in these parts. The Mike of Minnesota even said, "I bet he's their best player!" In the end, I continued my mission of converting Minnesotans into Rider fans, even if only one Mike at a time.

Mike McCullough

Chris and I had a nice treat in the works for Friday evening. Karen and Brent Magnus had invited us to their home, where we shared fine steaks and great companionship. Although we could have found their house on our own, Brent even came downtown to pick us up. They also presented both of us with the 2007 Pilsner flags, a very nice gesture. It was one of the best nights ever in Regina and Chris and I both deeply appreciated it.

The game on Saturday was at 5:00 PM and we thus had time to kill. Interestingly, on the previous day, the Canadian dollar had essentially reach parity with our American greenbacks for the first time since the Crusades. It was the talk of everyone we met and somewhat discouraged us from doing much shopping. I guess it's our turn after all of these years, but it was a strange feeling, after conversion and credit card fees, to pay more in USD for the weekend's expenses than our bills had totaled in CDN.

We stopped by the practice field and Hadesbeck and Poley even allowed me to whine about the exchange rate a bit more on the radio. However, we all know this was a key game after the two preceding blowouts and Joe noted it was important, win or lose, for the Riders to play better than they had in recent weeks. I had been thinking in the back of my bald little head about a home playoff game but that scenario seemed a lot more distant than it had just three weeks before.

Our tailgate, so faithfully organized and promoted by Sudsy and Nugsy, was beginning its death roll. Local law enforcement officials had also begun to drop by periodically and seemingly did not approve of the festivities. It was fun while it lasted, but we'll be seeing you on the practice field in the future, it appears. Perhaps the Riders or the city can take the lead from a new concept down here for Vikings games, where a particular parking lot is allowed for tailgate parties, with the price of a very expensive season tailgate ticket.

Tailgate Tent Team

In the game, the Riders jumped on the Lions immediately with two touchdowns in the first 11 minutes; Saskatchewan led 24 – 15 at the half and 31 – 22 at the conclusion of the third quarter. Despite multiple opportunities in the second half to tame the Lions once and for all, the Riders failed to capitalize. BC quarterback Jarious Jackson heated up, with a scoring toss to Jason Clermont early in the fourth quarter and a game winning toss to Geroy Simon with just 34 ticks left on the clock. British Columbia won 37 – 34 to sit at 8 – 3 – 1 on the season, increasing their lead on the 7 – 5 Roughriders.

Kerry Joseph had another good day, passing for 355 yards and running for two scores. Rider sophomore Andy Fantuz, plagued by drops early in the year, grabbed six passes for 90 yards and seemed to have his confidence back. Safety Tristin Clovis, in deep coverage on the game winning play, would be replaced by Scott Gordon for essentially the rest of the season.

It was an exciting game, with the wrong ending. The crowd filed out of Mosaic Stadium in near silence, collectively wondering and worrying what was happening to their Riders. Chris and I met Kelly Ramler at Tony Roma's and at least managed to end the day with a good meal.

A final trip was still on my radar with friends Tim Anderson and Harv Moen. They had picked the final regular season game, on Nov. 3 against Toronto, clearly ignoring my protestations and warnings of ugly weather that late in the season. In the interim, the sleeping giant called the Saskatchewan Roughriders jumped out of hibernation, racing to wins in the next five games, helped a bit by a pair of games against the weak Hamilton Ti-Cats, but also defeating Calgary and Edmonton on the road and Montreal at home. Receiver Matt Dominguez' knee injury was finally determined to be much worse than he had thought, and he was out for the season.

The muddled playoff picture was beginning to take shape. BC held on to their lead and kept winning, but Calgary faltered. The Stamps lost three in a row and thus the Saskatchewan Roughriders clinched their first home playoff game since 1988 when the Stamps lost on Oct. 19. The elusive quest for this game had cost people their jobs and had, as the years mounted, become a task seemingly more difficult to accomplish than the defined "finish first or second in a division of four teams."

Calgary would play at Saskatchewan on November 11. As a season ticket holder, I lined up two tickets with a simple phone call, but the difficulty and expense of transportation was proving to be a giant obstacle. Driving was possible, with the right weather, but I had an important family obligation on Saturday the 10th, so really needed to fly up to Regina on the day of the game. Hey, I love Saskatchewan football, but as the trip with Harv and Tim approached, I was seeing $800 fares for the only flight that would work and came close to just giving up.

But the gods of football work in strange ways. I have a Northwest Airlines Visa card and one day after the Riders had clinched received a mailing that simply saved the day. The mailing contained a promotion enabling use of flyer miles once per year at a discounted rate, but, importantly, with no blackout dates. In moments, I grabbed a seat on the late morning flight from Minneapolis to Regina and to this day smile at my good fortune. It was right then that I knew something out of the ordinary would be in the works for the rest of that 2007 CFL football season.

The CFL announced the Divisional All-Star teams on November 1 and initially nine Saskatchewan players were honoured. In a situation that somewhat defied belief, Rider kicker Luca Congi was named to the team, but a voting tabulation error was later discovered and Calgary's Santos DeAngelis received the actual award. However, Riders Kerry Joseph, Gene Makowsky, D.J. Flick and Jeremy O'Day were named to the offensive squad while Fred Perry, Reggie Hunt, Maurice Lloyd and Section 102 favourite James Johnson represented the defence. In addition, Kerry Joseph was chosen as the West finalist for Most Outstanding Player.

Tim, Harv and I headed out in the dark on Thursday November 1, and I sensed immediately that something was wrong. Harv was driving and it seemed to take just forever to get to Fargo, our first stop. I've made this drive more than fifty times and a person gets a sense of time and distance; I don't wear a watch, but still had a nagging sensation of an unexplained slow pace. Tim took over for the next leg to Minot and by then I knew something was amiss. A longer than normal wait at the border slowed us even more and a stop in beautiful downtown Halbrite, Saskatchewan delayed our progress even further.

When our son Carson was born in 1988, we chose his name because of its uniqueness. I think it has a nice ring to it and he's to this day a person easily remembered by those he meets, partially due to his given name. I had developed one of my Saskatchewan brainstorms a few days before, finally taking action on something I had thought of for years. Our stop in Halbrite was, in fact, at the local office of Carson Welding and Maintenance Ltd.

I'm quite pleased, that, as I've gotten older, I have lost nearly completely any fear of looking completely stupid to others. It was thus without hesitation that I had emailed Carson Welding's Halbrite area superintendent, Lionel Pouliot, a day or two before our departure. Explaining that I was most certainly the only Rider fan in Minnesota with a son named Carson, I asked if I could stop and purchase any item they might have with "Carson" on it. The answer was affirmative and I told Lionel the approximate time of day we would be in Halbrite.

Kerry On

Our slow progress was frustrating me. I try never to be late and even began to wonder if Carson Welding would even still be open when we arrived. Finally, I spotted its familiar square shape on our left and we pulled in. Lionel was out of the office, since he had better things to do than wait around for some Dumb American. However, the lady in the office was ready for me and said they all thought the idea was quite fun. She had a baseball cap and a toque all set. I tried to pay, but was rebuffed, so left a book in exchange. It was a really fun experience, my son was thrilled, and I learned once again that Saskatchewan has some of the greatest people anywhere. By the way, we proved scientifically on the way home that Harv's speedometer was off by about four miles per hour at 65 mph, explaining at least partially why this trip seemed to last forever.

We had a good dinner at Bushwakker's with Nat Hrynuik and a short casino session later, after Harv and I explained to Tim that better behavior was expected this trip. The next morning was bitterly cold and windy and the walkthrough was cancelled. The three of us spent a couple of hours wandering around at Mosaic Stadium, enjoying the hustle and bustle of a city and team awaiting the next week's playoff game with barely contained enthusiasm. Two radio stations were broadcasting live and I began what would be an unforgettable two week radio stretch by briefly being on the air with Regina radio personalities Perry Nyhus and Michael "Ballsie" Ball.

Perry Nyhus

Michael Ball

I was also able to pick up my playoff tickets in person and we eventually headed out to the Leader-Post office to deliver one to Will Chabun, who would be sitting with me the next weekend. Ironically, my wonderful bank later managed to lose Will's check after I deposited it, giving him a free ticket and me a belated credit after a brief customer service discussion. A fun lunch at Montana's followed with Bill Donison and we later had dinner at O'Hanlon's Irish Pub on Scarth Street, a great surprise of a place that I never knew existed but will surely visit again.

The Canadian dollar had hit $1.05 US on Friday and once again on Game Day radio Hadesbeck and Poley allowed me to gently mention my concern on the air. We also had a good laugh when Tom Fulton, Dave's dad and the patriarch of the Fulton Five, called in to the show just to say Hello to me. With no tailgate, Harv, Tim and I arrived early on the practice field and it was fun to watch it fill up with fans who for the most part would return the very next week for the playoff game. My cousin Doug Orth was in town and stopped by and I also met for the first time Regina area journalist and Riderfans.com contributor Stephen LaRose. Right before we went into the stadium, Jeff Banow arrived with most of his family and it was a pleasure to meet his parents and his friend Vanessa for the first time.

The Beautiful Banow Bunch

Needing a third seat this trip, I had purchased one at our family trip in July and was able to grab seat one in row five of Section 102, directly in front of Joe McNeill, who is directly in front of my normal spot. I sat there, with Tim and Harv behind the McNeill's. It was chilly, but not terrible, and Nancy McNeill brought a blanket that Tim and Harv shared.

It was a big game as a playoff tune-up for Saskatchewan, but a far larger contest for Toronto. The Argos had come from nowhere in the Eastern Division with six consecutive victories and could gain the East title with a win on this day. Toronto began the game with the ball and the wind and it was over quickly. Michael Bishop led a scoring drive to open the game and the Riders trailed 17 – 0 by the end of the first quarter. It was 24 – 12 Argos at the half but the Riders managed only a single point in the entire second half and fell to the newly crowned Eastern Division champions by a final of 41 – 13.

Harv, Tim, and I did the unthinkable – we left the game early, with a bit over five minutes to play. One of my pet peeves on some internet chat sites are the folks who think they have the right to decide what makes a great Rider fan – many of them argue that a REAL fan never leaves any game early. Well, I plead guilty, but when and why people leave is their own concern and doesn't by itself define anything. I'd guess Mr. Austin would have left this one early if he been able to.

Since the game had begun at 1:00, we had some driving time and drove through to Kenmare, North Dakota to shorten our final leg home the next day. As we listened to the post-game show, Joe Hadesbeck made a statement that made just tons of sense to me. Noting that Toronto took the ball at the start of the game, scored, and deflated the crowd, Joe mentioned he hoped the Riders would take the ball at the start of next week's playoff game. I made a mental note to follow that comment through later.

The outcome of this final regular season game was basically unsatisfactory, but we had seen the Riders bounce back before in this 2007 campaign. I also knew I had a long week ahead back in Minnesota waiting for the start of a trip I had nearly given up hope of ever making.

Chapter 20

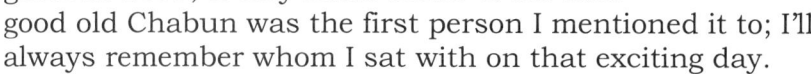

West Division All-Stars

Near the conclusion of each Canadian Football League regular season, all-star teams from each division are announced. It is thus only fitting that we recognize in this chapter the very special people who have made sizable contributions to the McEvoy treasure chest of Saskatchewan memories.

Many people have made us feel good about our attachment to the Riders and their fans. Some names are forgotten, lost in the passage of time; some names were never known, but played some small part in our enjoyment of these many holidays. A group whose number increases annually stands out for all of us. These all-stars are the people who helped us learn the importance of the Saskatchewan Roughrider mystique, the people whose friendship is of great importance to us, the people whose kindnesses and good will are important factors in our annual trek.

Alphabetically, the first all-star to be introduced is **Will Chabun**, the man who became our first non-Rider contact when he led us on a tour of the *Leader-Post* in 2000. Will is clearly a Renaissance man, with varying interests ranging from planes to punts. His wide breadth of experience always makes for interesting discussions and his semi-dignified manner hides one very faithful and energetic Rider fan. When I was deciding what to do with my extra ticket for the historic home playoff game in 2007, it only made sense to me that good old Chabun was the first person I mentioned it to; I'll always remember whom I sat with on that exciting day.

One of my favourite stories to recount is the web of circumstances leading up to the discovery in 2003 of Regina's legendary Elk Man, **Bill Donison**. Since he came into our lives,  Bill has become a good friend and a person we usually hook up with on our various trips to Regina. A man full of great stories of days past, he always entertains us with a string of tales ranging from his Regina Pats tryout during the last Ice Age to driving adventures in his cherished Caddy. It was a great experience to be a part of hooking up Bill and his wife Kathy with the Australian McEvoy's in 2005. In a way, Bill is something of a role model to me, since I certainly hope I'm able to be in the shape he's in when I get to be his age

Grey Cup in 1998 was a pivotal celebration in my life as a CFL fan. As I recounted earlier, my first sojourn to a Grey Cup party came within minutes of being a classic meltdown. Had Chris Melin, Corey Edmondson and I failed to make a connection when we did, it is highly likely that any desire to continue travels to the CFL championship game would have been squashed permanently. Eskimo fans **Bambi and Arnie Fearon**, the leaders of the group who befriended us on that November day, remain good friends whom we see much too seldom. It's always a pleasure to meet up with them and the rest of their Edmonton crew, with the locale at recent Grey Cups usually being the Rendezvous Saskatchewan party. Maura had heard about them for years and it was fun that she could finally meet these fine folks in 2005 in Vancouver. As the first people we ever met at Grey Cup, Bambi and Arnie have a real special place in the old Gopher heart.

One of the greatest feelings about attending a Grey Cup is the warmth of seeing good friends in a familiar setting. Since 2000, Chris Melin and I have annually made the rounds with one or more of the **Grey Cup Guys**. These five characters have all become close friends of both Chris and I; since our November meeting is often the only time we see some of them, we all try to make the most of our time together. Their unconditional acceptance of us, especially of the Old Guy, always makes me feel like everything is right with the world.

Rider Pride on the American Side

Govind Achyuthan is certainly the spiritual leader of the Grey Cup Guys. This man's Rider allegiance is second to none and his absolute knowledge of the history of the team is really downright scary. Gov is perpetually upbeat and has the elfish gleam in his eye that makes one wonder what he is up to next. From India by way of Holdfast, Saskatchewan, Govind now lives in Calgary. However, he's not a guy to let a few hundred miles stay in the way of attending a Rider game and can always be found in Regina on game days. Govind is the type of fan many of us could only hope to be.

Jeff Banow is perhaps the Grey Cup Guy I see most often, since we generally meet up for at least a few minutes on the practices field before Rider games. A native of Esterhazy, Jeff now lives in Saskatoon and works in several locations around Canada. He has the ability to be serious and hilarious in the same sentence, knows more about music than anyone I know and is a Rider fan to the core. His lasagna experience in Ottawa in 2004 is the stuff of which legends are made and served to solidify the bond of our group, let alone be the source of great one-liners time and time again.

I first met **Dave Fulton** at a Grey Cup party in 2000. In a way, he may be the most serious of the Grey Cup Guys but he finds that cloak easy to toss aside when our party circumstances dictate. A native of Regina, Dave's family have also become friends, and I'm always excited to see dad Tom and brothers Warren and Kevin also. Dave works in Toronto, where he spends a decent amount of time trying to keep his son from becoming an Argos' fan. It's been a great time to get together with Dave here in the Twin Cities when he's been working locally, since he one of the group we virtually never see in Regina. I consider him a very good man and a special friend.

One of the most interesting people I've met in my Saskatchewan travels is another Grey Cup Guy, **Jason Isaac.** Also a Regina native, Jason is both a man I'd hate to cross and

West Division All-Stars

a man I know I could always depend on. He's irreverent, occasionally cranky and has a soft side that has just amazed me on several occasions. We see Jason occasionally on the Labour Day weekend, but some years only at Grey Cup. He has a talent for making me feel especially welcome and is my favourite guy to catch up with after a long absence. Like Gov, Jason lives in Calgary and the two of them are close friends. Jason can also text message faster than anyone I've ever seen.

The final Grey Cup guy, **Marty Neumeier**, is also from Esterhazy, where he and Jeff Banow were childhood friends.

Marty has more than a bit of mischief in him and his Grey Cup Saturday antics have entertained friends and strangers alike. Marty now lives in Coleman, Alberta, near Crow's Nest Pass, and works in Yemen with a traveling schedule that makes Ferdinand Magellan seem like a stay-at-home. As fate would have it, Marty was in Yemen in November of 2007 and missed the excitement that the rest of us experienced. A sensational fan, he noted to me that it was more important that the Riders win than that he personally be present, but I truly wished he would have been able to be there. Marty and his wife Melissa stayed with us in Minnesota in 2006 and it was fun to get to know this unique guy just a little bit better.

Those readers who were part of the glory days of the fan website Total-cfl.com will easily understand why **Brad Lawryk** was named to this all-star roster. Brad, a Regina native who now lives in Williams Lake, British Columbia, was the driving force behind a tool that brought hundreds of CFL fans together. The friendships that resulted from Brad's dedication are important to hundreds of people and his role as webmaster cannot be understated in my personal fan history. Sitting with Brad at Dave Ridgway's 2003 Canadian Football Hall of Fame induction was a proud moment for me and I think the two of us did a good job at that event symbolically representing Rider fans everywhere.

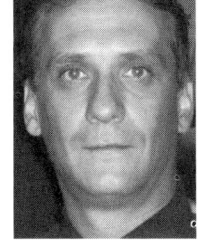

Rider Pride on the American Side

Like any CFL all-star team, this one has some import players. This trio of rascals are not Canadians, but somehow were able to slip into this prestigious group. I refer of course to my traveling companions from here in Minnesota, Tim Anderson, Harv Moen and Chris Melin, the guys who make the extra trips I make each season both possible and extremely enjoyable.

Chris Melin has made well over a dozen Regina and  Grey Cup trips with me and has become, as you might expect, an accomplished fan of the Canadian Football League and the Saskatchewan Roughriders. His companionship, wit and youthful perspective add a tremendous amount to our travels. Chris is an avid fan of many sports and we've spend several afternoons in Regina visiting shops looking for hockey cards. My friends have become his and Chris' passion for the Riders does not take a back seat to very many fans in our group. I was especially pleased when Chris made a last minute decision to head to Toronto for the 2007 Grey Cup, since it would not have felt quite right to have been there without him.

Tim Anderson has been part of my late-season travel entourage for the past five years. He's an accomplished amateur golfer and, like me, was fortunate to be able to manage an early retirement. He enjoys sports, especially hockey, and rapidly adapted to the speed and excitement of the CFL. The third member of our autumn group is the only one of us who continues to make the daily trek to the salt mines. **Harv Moen** is originally from Madison,  Minnesota, where he went to high school long ago with former Rider lineman Tim Roth. Like Tim, Harv is a huge hockey fan – his son Jeff  was an excellent goaltender for the University of Minnesota in the mid-1990's. For me, the annual trip with Harv and Tim is enjoyable for a multitude of reasons, the primary one being that it enables a third seasonal jaunt for me. These fellows are fantastic travel companions since they share the "let's just get there quickly" mentality needed for a long drive. It's also fun for me to be the *youngest* member of our little group.

We are guaranteed to see two members of this all-star squad on every trip to Regina. **Joe and Nancy McNeill** sit in Row 6 of Section 102, directly in front of us. They have proven countless times that being neighbourly can certainly extend to Mosaic Stadium also. Besides bringing blankets for us on cold football days, Joe and Nancy have done a wide range of nice things to benefit the McEvoy family, including getting a photo of the  first edition of this book with the Grey Cup itself. We see them often in Regina and it was exciting to have them as guests here in Minnesota in 2007. The McNeill's are huge fans of both Jimmy Buffet and amusement parks, but are also very knowledgeable, dedicated football fans. For me, it was great to spend time with them at the Grey Cup in 2007 and I'll never forget sitting with them at the home playoff game, since the Rider win that day clearly meant the world to them.

One of the nicest ladies I've ever met is **Liz Measner**. During the formative McEvoy trips to Taylor Field, Liz became one of the first people we knew, before we ever attended any practices or knew anyone else in Regina. Her greeting was always friendly and she and the Rider Store staff came to very positively represent the entire Rider organization to us. Liz has done many favours for us, not the least being a great customer for the first edition of this enterprise, and I'll never forget the day she led Chris Melin and I on a merry tour of the depths of the stadium to meet Art McAvoy.

A fellow who has become a great friend is **Kelly Ramler** of Regina. He's a man with a quick wit and a very likable, no nonsense attitude about life in general and the Saskatchewan Roughriders in particular. Kelly is originally from Annaheim, Saskatchewan, and several times has had me roaring with

Rider Pride on the American Side

laughter with his succinct comparisons of that metropolis and its inhabitants to the population of the similar burg of Dog River, the *Corner Gas* locale. Over the years, Kelly has provided transportation, rescued forgotten items, and been a great man to share some of Tony Roma's ribs with a cold Pilsner. His lone fault may be his penchant for sitting on the East side, but he's seen the good life on the West side with us on occasion. If the day would ever come, Lord forbid, that there were no Riders in Regina, we'd still come up to visit with this good friend.

In the early years of traveling to Regina, never in my wildest dreams did I imagine becoming friends with Rider legendary kicker **Dave Ridgway**. This is Dave's eighth West All-Star selection and his choice here was a virtual no-brainer. From our accidental meeting in 1998, Dave became a good friend of our family, and helped us understand both the game and the fan possibilities that existed for the Rider faithful. We were pleased to be invited to his Hall of Fame induction in 2003 and gladly participated as both fans and friends. Knowing Dave is a good thing in itself, but his friendship has also paved the way to meeting many new acquaintances and expanding our Regina experiences. Dave and I talk regularly and it's always extremely easy to pick up just where we had left off.

From the first time we met, **Roy Shivers** and I seemed to hit it off. Our common love of baseball was a factor, but for some reason the former Rider GM always found a few minutes to see how the McEvoy family was doing and it was a gesture we appreciated. As years passed and times changed, Roy still managed to check with us and he and I enjoyed a few good conversations back in his office. Maura and I certainly enjoyed getting together with Roy in 2007 Las Vegas and we await with interest the impact of his new position as the Director of Player Personnel for the BC Lions.

Any Saskatchewan fan present at the Rogers Centre on November 25, 2007 will remember many things about that great day for the rest of their life. I'll always remember being with the greatest Rider fan I know, **Troy Souster.** Originally from Delisle, Saskatchewan, Troy now lives in Saskatoon. As co-organizer of a successful tailgate and fellow Section 102 resident, he's a guy easy to find on game day. It was exciting fun to plan our 2007 Grey Cup weekend together and the actual weekend made me glad that this was the guy I was able to spend time with. Troy's Rider attitude is both perpetually optimistic and necessarily realistic and I find those attributes perfect for extended conversations about our favourite team and its players. If there's ever a movie made about the Perfect Fan, Troy gets my vote for the lead male role.

Chapter 21

One Fine Day

One of my emotions in the long week before November 11 was just a bit of guilt. The demand for playoff game tickets had been tremendous and some disappointed people failed to secure admission to the game. For me, it had been almost too easy – a few phone calls and a couple of clicks on the computer gave me an airline ticket using flyer miles, my game ticket, and bargain priced motel and car rentals. But I had made it possible for the ticket-less Chabun to attend and at least felt decent about that.

Early in the week I received a phone call from a writer named Mark Spector of the *National Post*. Mark is the lead sport columnist in the sports section of that newspaper and had been given my name by Rob Vanstone. Mark was putting together an article about Rider fans' reactions and plans for this long awaited game and included me among those people he interviewed. It was an easy and fun conversation with a man who knew how to put his subjects at ease and of course I'd be lying if I said it was not fun to see my name in the newspaper. This story provided a pretty good laugh also. I had mentioned to Mark about my great aunts moving to Canada in 1905 but it came out in the article that this move had occurred when I was young. Several of my eagle-eyed Canadian friends pointed out that it was not a real stretch to imagine the old Minnesotan as a youngster in 1905!

When traveling, I generally pack very late in the process because the task of packing isn't a favourite way to spend time. I constantly worry about forgetting something important, but of course never have. For reasons unknown, I decided to start packing very early in this week. Perhaps I thought it would make the time go faster, or perhaps I wanted extra moments to remember everything. Whatever the reason, I packed, unpacked and repacked several times as the weather forecast jumped round like a golf ball on concrete. I did not want to

One Fine Day

check luggage and really didn't have to since I would be gone for just one day, but I also wanted to be certain that my game day experience would be a warm one.

By Friday I was pretty set, but still had two days to wait. My nerves were a bit on edge, since I seldom travel by air alone and the nagging concern about getting to the game on time was always present in my thoughts. The league had thoughtfully moved back the starting time of the game to 4:00; my flight was due to arrive at 1:55, and I would be fine so long as there were no delays. However, it was easy to think back to my last flight with Chris Melin in September and realize the type of delays we experienced that day would have made me late for this playoff game.

Since I had no control over the flight itself, it was easy to attempt to influence those variables I could have impact on. I managed to move my seat up to the second row during on-line check-in and packed only a small carry-on to minimize my waiting time once we arrived in Regina. I felt confident nothing could fluster me for the next 48 hours.

It's amazing how often things happen to mess up my mental plans. Mid-morning Friday brought an email from Sharon Gerein, the producer of CBC Saskatchewan's *Afternoon Edition.* She had seen the Spector article and asked me to be on the radio show that afternoon with host Colin Grewar. It would be fun, but scary at the same time and it was one of those things that I wished I could do right then, rather than wait for a few hours until air time.

Colin Grewar

Rider Pride on the American Side

As usual, there was no reason for concern. Colin has had this show since 1990 and he's smoother than silk. It was like sitting down with a cup of coffee and a friend and easy to forget that it was actually on the air.

Saturday went quickly, since it was Parents' Weekend at Hamline University and full of events and concerts at Carson's new school. I woke very early on Sunday, went to Mass, and headed to the airport.

The flights to places like Regina originate here in the Twin Cities at airport gates well off the beaten path. It took me quite a while after I checked in to reach my gate, but I still had plenty of time. As soon as I turned into the gate area, I spotted a Rider jersey and knew my wait time would pass quickly. Meeting Rider fan Andrew Sedley of Yorkton, who had been at a business function in Rochester, Minnesota, the two of us had a good Rider conversation until it was time to board. The flight left just about on time and I was feeling home free. Since the seat beside me in the second row was empty, I passed that information on to Andrew and my new friend slid up from his seat further back. I discovered I was not alone in worrying about getting to the game on time.

The two fans were the first off the plane and first in the customs queue. When I told the agent I was in town for the Rider game, he grinned and sent me through with no other questions. Andrew had offered me a ride, but I had a car lined up and we both finally realized as we parted company that we had in fact made it to this elusive playoff game.

Andrew Sedley

One Fine Day

When I saw no line at the rental car counter, I knew I was in for a great trip. Our flight had touched down at 1:55 PM and I actually reached the Sherwood House before 2:20, checked in, and was on my way to Mosaic Stadium before 2:30. The practice field was alive with fans, as I knew it would be. With the mass of moving humanity, it was nearly impossible to attempt to find anyone, so I decided to go into the stadium.

It's easy to admit that the excitement was getting to me. A week's worth of worrying about getting to Mosaic Stadium had just washed away in a flood of perfect connections and short lines and I needed to calm down. A dog and a beer sounded wonderful and I savored them slowly by myself sitting outside of Section 102 and immediately felt relieved.

Joe and Nancy McNeill arrived shortly afterward and we chatted in our seats with the anticipation of fans eager for the game to start. The weather was very similar to the previous week and I knew immediately it would not be an issue. Fans were filing in quickly, many armed with the noise-producing Thundersticks passed out for the occasion. As we neared game time, the stadium announcer advised the crowd of Winnipeg's 24 – 22 Eastern Semi-final win over Montreal and I was happy for Chris Cvetkovic, recovered from his injury and back as the Bombers' long snapper. It was fun to spot him on the Maxtron later as that game's highlights were shown.

Well before kickoff, the noise was pleasantly deafening. A crowd of enthusiastic Rider fans can make a lot of noise and the addition of the poignant *"Poing"* of the Thundersticks added to the decibels. Will Chabun wandered in and we were ready to go.

My friend Joe Hadesbeck knows a lot of football and his hope that Saskatchewan would take the ball was quickly realized. Scrimmaging from their own 48 yard line following the kickoff, Kerry Joseph, on a play that appeared to be a run, pulled up and threw ahead to receiver D. J. Flick. With just one man to beat, Flick made a neat move and raced in for a 62 yard score with only 30 seconds gone in the first quarter. The crowd understandably, justifiably and completely went just crazy.

Joseph continued to move the Riders and Luca Congi added two field goals in the first period as Saskatchewan moved to a 13 – 0 lead. Calgary scored a touchdown in the second quarter on a wild 111 yard interception/lateral play, but Congi hit two more field goals late in the half for a 19 – 7 Rider lead.

A Thicket of Thundersticks

Henry Burris had a quiet first half and was clearly impacted by the crowd noise. He got untracked a bit in the third quarter with an early touchdown pass to Ken-Yon Rambo. Luca Congi and Sandro DeAngelis traded field goals later in the quarter and Calgary closed the gap to 22 – 17 by the end of the third quarter.

The CFL and the Riders did a great job in presenting this game. The game experience had a Grey Cup feel and even the interludes seemed to be fan-based rather than having the more typical advertising orientation. I'm one of the few Minnesotans who has *The Last Saskatchewan Pirate* in his iPod and so the inclusion of Captain Tractor live at the third quarter break was just a stroke of genius in my opinion.

Fifteen minutes to go; the wind had died down to a breeze that barely fluttered the flags, making me thankful again that Saskatchewan had not tried to depend on having it in the fourth quarter. The Rider defence had been tough all day, limited Stamps running back Joffrey Reynolds to only 11 yards in the five carries he had in Calgary's abbreviated running game. Reggie Hunt was all over the field, leading Saskatchewan in tackles and also being credited with a sack and a forced fumble. The Riders were also able to grind out some hard fought ground yardage, as Joseph gained over 100 yards to help pick up the slack for the missing Wes Cates, out with a foot injury.

Hank Prepares to Fumble

Congi added four more points, on a single and his sixth field goal, giving the home team a 26 – 16 lead with about 5 minutes left. Henry Burris wasn't quite finished, tossing a second TD to Rambo with 53 seconds left. Even I knew an onside kick was coming and the crowd was silent for possibly the only time all day when Calgary appeared to have recovered. But the CFL's most penalized team came through for the Riders as the Stamps were called for being offside on the play and Saskatchewan recovered the second attempt and ran out the clock for the 26 – 24 historic win.

Kerry Joseph had come up huge again, adding 395 passing yards to his impressive rushing total. Flick and Andy Fantuz each had over 100 receiving yards and Corey Grant added 83 more. It was a true team victory in a pressure cooker situation.

The emotion at the game's end was simply staggering. Years of fan frustration melted away in the smoke of fireworks and the whirl of confetti. As I looked around, I spotted many fans unable to even stand, virtually knocked down by the realization that a monkey the size of King Kong was no longer on the back of their green jersey. Tears of joy were commonplace and put the significance of this day in proper perspective for a visitor from Minnesota. I was in the middle of something very special, something impossible to adequately describe, but something every one of you who were at Mosaic Stadium on that day will easily understand.

Will and I filed out slowly with the exhausted crowd and

Rider Pride on the American Side

I was glad that I'd shared this moment with both he and the McNeill's, all three being important people in my Regina life. I later met a large group for dinner in an atmosphere of good times amid much optimistic talk of the games to come. To be with passionate Rider fans in the hours after this victory was by itself more than worth the trip.

My sleep was fitful and spotty, probably due to the excitement of a long, satisfying day. Awake for long stretches, I reflected on the great triumph and felt good for the Rider team and organization. As I left the parking ramp at the Minneapolis airport exactly 23 hours and 58 minutes after I had entered, the realization hit me that what had really mattered most was seeing long-suffering Saskatchewan Roughrider fans getting the satisfaction they so richly deserved from this fantastic experience. As a 24-hour period I'll never forget came to a close, I was thankful to have been a part of it.

Still fired up on Monday evening, I called in to CKRM's *Sportsline* program on Monday evening. Perry Nyhus answered the phone, remembered me, and put me on right away. As I chuckled at my good fortune, I was able to ask the Rider guest, D.J. Flick, a semi-intelligent question, but also tell him about Maura's observation of his skills earlier in the season. But the excitement of the previous day caused the real reason for my call. As the risk of sounding stupid, but with the need the express a thought, I ended my call by stating how much it meant to me to see the Saskatchewan Roughriders and their incredible fans able to experience the joy of the previous day. Joe Hadesbeck nicely added as I finished, "That didn't sound stupid at all."

The Slingbox and I watched the Western final against the British Columbia Lions with multiple levels of anticipation and apprehension on November 18. Winnipeg had defeated Toronto for the first berth in the Grey Cup game, but starting quarterback Kevin Glenn suffered a broken arm and was done for the year. This revelation obviously made the West champion an immediate favourite.

Saskatchewan's defensive players were a ferocious bunch on this day. The Riders scored 18 points off of four BC turnovers on this day and added seven sacks. Utah State rookie John Chick, steadily improving all season, played his best game to date, registering two of the sacks and applying constant pressure from his defensive end position.

One Fine Day

The score at the end of the third quarter was Riders 26, Lions 17; a tally that would also be the final tally. As the minutes ticked away in the final stanza, the realization set in that another football trip would be in the works at the end of this magical 2007 season.

I like surprises, but generally try to avoid unpleasant ones by thinking ahead. It seemed logical that a bit of advanced planning could put the wheels in motion to be able to make final arrangements as soon as the game had ended.

My partner in the escapade was good old Sudsy, Troy Souster of Saskatoon. Chris Melin had decided to pass, so Troy and I teamed up during the week to scout out our possibilities. A hotel room was easy to nab, since Jeff Banow had multiple rooms lined up and turned one over to us. Fellow Grey Cup guy Dave Fulton also offered a spot; it ended up his dad Tom and his brother Warren used Dave's room and stayed right down the hall from us.

Despite the short notice and the upcoming American Thanksgiving weekend, I found a very affordable flight. The game was being played in Toronto, a destination with ample flights from the Twin Cities; had it been anywhere else, I doubt I could have snagged a seat at any decent price.

Game tickets were a quandary – there were seats still available on Ticketmaster, but they were of borderline quality and we debated taking a chance and waiting to buy them on the street in Toronto. Troy and I finally decided we would not take the chance, since we could never forgive ourselves if we were forced to pay through the nose in Toronto, or, even worse, not even get into the game.

I spent most of the fourth quarter with the Slingbox minimized in one browser window while I scouted out tickets and airfare in others. When the final gun sounded in the Rider victory, I called an excited household in Saskatoon and the new Souster/McEvoy team collectively decided to go on a wild spending spree. Within seconds, I purchased two game tickets and a plane ticket and Troy worked with Jeff to switch the room to Troy's name.

Just as I finished, the phone rang, as I suspected it might. Chris Melin, my faithful traveling companion, could not bear the thought of missing this upcoming milestone and had jumped on board. He was able to get a flight and would be arriving in Toronto on Friday evening. It was too late to get a

Rider Pride on the American Side

seat at the game with us, but with our extended group of Canadian acquaintances to draw on, Chris was not too concerned about getting a game ticket.

It would be my third CFL trip in four weekends, but my very understanding daughter Meredith said it best when she told me, "You'd be @#%#& at yourself forever if you didn't go." Better yet, Meredith's mom felt the same way.

Chapter 22

"Is It Irish Day?"

The next three days were a madhouse. I spent most of Monday morning reading up on the Rider victory including seeing internet videos of the celebration at the Regina Airport when the team returned from Vancouver in the wee hours. Emails flew back and forth from a number of friends and acquaintances who, like me, loved to share the great news that we Riders fans had received. It was clear that getting to Toronto from Saskatchewan was not as easy for everyone as my effortless arrangements had been and I felt the pain of several friends who just could not work out the trip. Kelly Ramler was one, slated to work Grey Cup weekend and unable to rearrange his schedule. Brent and Karen Magnus could not swing it either, and Rosetown friend Marilyn McIntyre was struggling to make arrangements for her group of seven.

But other friends would be joining the celebration. Joe and Nancy McNeill had made reservations a few weeks before based on their faith in the team's 2007 turnaround. My cousin Ross Orth and his wife Dianne Miller would be coming from Swift Current, all five of the Grey Cup guys were on board and literally dozens of website acquaintances would be heading east. Troy would be arriving on Thursday, while my flight would get me to our hotel in mid-afternoon on Friday. Chris would follow later Friday and we made arrangements to be at the hotel for his late arrival.

Maura was also going to be on the move, heading to Germany for a quick visit to experience the traditional German Christmas markets. She'd be leaving just a couple of days after I returned, so our life was a happy scramble for several days.

Full of American Thanksgiving turkey, I headed to the airport on Friday morning, November 23. My flight's gate was again back in the far reaches and a long walk brought me to it in plenty of time. As I wandered and waited, I spotted two

Rider Pride on the American Side

Bomber fans in an airport bar, having a 9 AM beer. They had driven to Minneapolis from Winnipeg the day before, finding the extra mileage less expensive than other options. My seat partner was a fellow named Michael Prount of Winnipeg, headed to Toronto with the double pleasure of seeing the University of Manitoba Bison in the Vanier Cup and his Bombers in the Grey Cup.

The flight was on time, and Michael and I decided to team up to get downtown. The other Bomber guys had offered us a ride, but it would be coming later and we felt we could get a jump start by heading out on our own. Part of my time earlier in the week had been spent deciphering Toronto's mass transit system and I was armed with maps and instructions sure to help us make the trip successful. We took a bus to the end of the subway line and settled in for a long ride toward the inner city.

After a brief moment of panic because my maps were not to scale, we reached our transfer point and moved to the platform to catch a train to the hotel. As we waited in the subterranean depths, a grizzled older fellow was giving me the eye. As he approached us, I could not imagine what had caught his attention.

Rider attire had been the subject of much soul searching as I packed for this trip. Like Cinderella at the ball, it would be important to be well dressed and thus I had devoted at least a couple of minutes to wardrobe selection. One item was pulled from the very bottom of a drawer. It was a 1989 Grey Cup shirt, last worn at Rendezvous Regina in 1998. Autographed by Dave Ridgway on the day we first met, it was a treasured collectible brought out now only because of the historic weekend.

Unshaven and with teeth needing more than a bit of dental work, this man was staring at my chest as he neared our position. "In town for the game?' he asked, in a tone that comforted me. When I replied in the affirmative, he squinted ever harder at my shirt. "Is that Ridgway's signature?" was the next query, as a wobbly finger pointed at an aging Sharpie inscription. When I again replied positively and briefly explained the significance, he nodded and said, "Ridgway. Best there ever was." Dave had just called a day before, certain I would be going to Toronto, wishing me a good trip, and hoping I could snag him a souvenir game ticket and a program. I

"Is It Irish Day?"

smiled at the encounter and told the old fellow he was right on.

Michael and I reached my hotel, close to where he was to meet his friends, and parted ways. I went up to our room, where Troy was waiting to admit me and immediately launched in a retelling of his first day ever at a Grey Cup weekend. He'd been able to score free tickets to the Rogers CFL Player Awards the previous evening and excitedly recapped the happenings while I unpacked. We wasted little time in heading down to the South Building of the Metro Toronto Convention Centre where most of the major parties, including Riderville, were taking place.

I amuse easily and love things like subways. We figured out the route and easily and quickly made it to our destination. This convention centre is huge, one of the largest complexes I have ever seen. Snaking through the hallways and skywalks, it was clear that the Grey Cup was not the only show in town, as several other conventions and gatherings filled much of the facility.

My first stop at Riderville would be brief. Sharon Gerein from CBC Saskatchewan had called on Thursday, asking if I would appear again on Colin's show, this week broadcasting live from the Riders' team hotel. Troy and I were scheduled to be on at 6 PM and Mitchell Blair had also asked us to come to his program, being broadcast from the Renaissance Hotel at the Rogers Centre.

Even in mid-afternoon, Riderville was packed. Troy had been there Thursday and knew the drill, so he led the way. Just a few steps into the room, I spotted Joe and Nancy McNeill and as they turned, saw they were talking to Regina mayor Pat Fiacco. As a lover of coincidence, I was amused that this was the fourth consecutive year I'd seen the Mayor almost immediately upon Grey Cup party arrival. To see the McNeill's right away was a bonus also, and I encountered them at random more times than I could count as the weekend progressed.

The beverage lines were long and excruciatingly slow. Forced to wait in line first to buy drink tickets and then again to actually get a beverage was very frustrating to me, a guy who detests waiting in line anyway. It was really the only clunker of the weekend, as the convention centre staff running the show just never got it working smoothly. We all longed for the days when the fine Riderville volunteers kept the lines moving smoothly and quickly.

The first few minutes of each year's first Grey Cup party are always worth the wait. Friendships are renewed, backs are slapped, and handshakes are warmly given to both old friends and new. Troy and I, after our slow movement through the queues, had just a few minutes to socialize before we needed to head off to *The Afternoon Edition.* No worries, since we knew we would be back, so we headed together toward the maze of hallways to find our way to the Westin Harbour Castle Hotel

My partner thought he could find the way once we were outside, but we had no idea how to exit the huge building in the direction we needed to go. As we headed down the hall, Troy recognized the man directly in front of us. He whispered that we were following Keith Pelley, the outgoing president of the Toronto Argonauts. Keith had been on the radio on the practice field in Regina with Jim Hopson and I'd seen him there on my weekend with Harv and Tim. Hailing him, I explained our directional dilemma and he very obligingly led the two hayseeds to the proper exit.

It was chilly and we moved quickly. Several Rider Pep Band members were moving in the same direction and we determined that their destination was the same as ours. As we reached the entrance of the hotel, Eddie Davis and his wife were getting into a cab, but he stopped to say Hello and introduce us and we wished him well on Sunday.

We sailed through the revolving doors into a sea of bodies, but my gaze was in the distance, trying to spot the CBC Radio setup. A body bumped me hard, and I turned to the laughing face of Dustin Cherniawski. After we explained our presence, he noted that the entire team and staff were on their way to dinner. Kent Austin was walking past and I was able to pass on to him Dave Ridgway's best wishes from earlier in the week. Spotting D. J. Flick, I introduced myself and explained that I was the fellow on the radio with him the previous week. As the team filed out, I was also able to say Hi to trainer Ivan Gutfriend, whom I had met a couple of times before.

Troy and I laughed at our good fortune in being there right then, another coincidence enabling us to have a Regina-like experience right there in the big city. We ambled over to the radio spot, met Colin Grewar and the crew, and, since we were a bit early, went to the bar to have a beer until they were ready for us.

"Is It Irish Day?"

    Our wait was short and we headed over to the makeshift studio. Colin was warm and friendly and asked us a few background questions. Troy hadn't planned on being on, but there was no reason for him not to be, and we both enjoyed a several minute session with a very easy man to talk with. I would have enjoyed meeting Sharon Gerein also, but she was back in Regina holding down the fort. We're forever thankful to her for supplying us with CD's of our appearances as great keepsakes.

       D. J. Flick   **Ivan Gutfriend**

Troy and I hung around to finish our beers and were both given *CFL on CBC* Grey Cup hats, saving me the expense of buying my annual souvenir. The Toronto Grey Cup items were expensive, but I later grabbed Carson and Connor their traditional shirts in a convenience store at a fraction of the convention centre price.

    We headed to our next gig to find a flustered Mitchell Blair, who was having technical difficulties with his hookup back to Saskatchewan. He apologized time and again, but it really didn't matter to us. The temporary patch they had worked out repeated my voice back in the headset a few seconds after I said something and it was hard to keep a flow going. However, Troy got to say Hello to his family back in Saskatoon and we appreciated Mitchell thinking of us. I still get a smile whenever I recall the thrill of being on Saskatchewan radio so many times in such a short period. Sitting with Troy and a beer talking with Colin Grewar was especially one of those experiences a person never expects to happen in their lifetime.

We wisely decided to have some dinner and headed to a lively, noisy place called the Loose Moose. Returning to Riderville, we avoided the line due to our previous admission and joined the fun once more. I happened to be wearing my Rider jersey with "Minnesota" on the back and struck up several interesting conversations due to it. One was with Doug McConachie, the sports editor of the *Saskatoon Star-Phoenix*, who told me a fun tale about a 1990's Rider team photo where Ridgway and Glen Suitor had jokingly put their hands on each other's knee in what ended up to be the photo the team unknowingly chose to use to create a few tens of thousands of copies for fan distribution. I asked Dave about it later and he laughed heartily, even saying he and Glen were in danger of having their salaried docked to pay for a new print run. Doug even insisted that he and I pose for a shot of the two of us groping each other to commemorate the Suitor/Ridgway photo!

Doug McConachie

Riderville was loud and fun, despite the long lines and we continued to meet old friends and new. Troy and I had planned to be back at the hotel to meet Chris at about 11 PM, so left with the Banow clan to head back, with a stop at the Spirit of Edmonton party planned en route. We met Sheldon Banow, Jeff's brother who lives in Toronto for the first time, and he led us on a merry jaunt beneath the Toronto streets to the Edmonton party. This party was a bit tame compared to years past suffering perhaps from the virtual absence of Rider

"Is It Irish Day?"

fans, who were busy at their own place. Seeing no one we knew, we headed to our hotel in time to greet Chris, catch up a bit and turn in after a long, fun, busy day.

Troy was off to the Spirit of Edmonton Breakfast on Saturday morning and Chris and I slept in a bit. Our room was driving me crazy – it was drafty and something in it caused me to constantly feel like I was getting a cold, although I never did and was better immediately every time we left the room. After a typically long search, we found a breakfast spot and soon headed back to the convention centre. We probably made our appearance at Riderville too early to have any staying power, arriving before 1 PM. I was meeting my cousin Doug Orth and his wife Dianne Miller, plus their friends Frankie Jordan and Ray Finlay, and also immediately ran into Joe and Nancy McNeill once more. The McNeill's had a great story – returning to their hotel on Friday, they decided to eat dinner in the restaurant there, amid a sea of green clad Rider fans. Their server was a bit perplexed by the crowd, quizzing the McNeill's by asking "What's with the green - is it Irish Day?"

Doug Orth, Gainer the Gopher, Ray Finlay

One of the great things about Grey Cup is reuniting with friends. I had seen some of the boys at the home playoff game, but several notables were missing then and I was able to catch up with them in Toronto. Brothers Warren and Kevin Fulton were two of these; I'd not seen them since at least 2005 and it was fun to catch up with them. Warren lives on Vancouver

Island, recently retired from the Canadian Navy and now works as a scuba diving inspector for the British Columbia government. Kevin mentioned the first time we'd met, in Calgary in 2000, when I was searching for leads to discover Elk Man Bill Donison. The Head Fulton, Dad Tom, was also in the house and is truly a good guy; it's not hard to see why his sons are all good guys also.

After a round or two of "Paint the Whole World Green", there was a general commotion near the stage. Rider quarterback Kerry Joseph, just two days removed from being named the CFL Most Outstanding Player for 2007, was up on stage. He gave a brief speech, thanked the crowd for their support and by his very appearance showed why most CFL players are so well liked by the league's fans. I'd love to say I was able to get a decent photo in the melee because of my extreme agility, but in fact was just lucky.

Kerry Joseph at Riderville

The place was by now jammed, with a long line stretching down the hall. Chris and I still hadn't caught up with Troy and decided to get some food. The Banow Bunch had concert plans, so we left fairly early with them to have some dinner. As we left, it was clear that getting back in would be a tough proposition. The line stretched for hundreds of people and was moving slowly. Troy was well back in the crowded line, still flushed from his Spirit of Edmonton Breakfast debut, but willing to wait to get in.

We briefly toured the rest of the Grey Cup portion of the

"Is It Irish Day?"

building, seeing lots of neat displays and picking up some World Poker Tour toques. I ran into Edmonton friends and great fans Brian and Linda Edward and was happy to chat for just a short while. As we meandered out to the street level, a realization finally hit me. Jeff Banow said once that every Grey Cup is different – some are more raucous than others, some have better parties, some offer the opportunity to see more friends, but each is different and good in its own way. These were again wise words from the youngster, and very true. For me, this Toronto Grey Cup was different. I seemed much less interested in partying, for a couple of reasons. First, the lines drive me crazy, partially because I'm certain the organizers could have done better, but partially because I just don't like lines. But, more importantly, this year I was here primarily for the football game, not the parties, and wanted to be rested and ready for Sunday. It was my eighth Grey Cup and there would certainly still be parties at the ninth.

Saturday Afternoon Riderville Lineup

So, we found a decent restaurant and ate a leisurely dinner. As expected, the Riderville line was impossible so Chris and I decided just to wander back in the general vicinity of the subway. We were a bit fascinated by underground Toronto, with its many nooks and crannies and shops of all types seemingly open all hours. As we passed a small pub, I heard my name called and was surprised, not expecting anyone I knew in such a locale.

The beckoner was Jason Isaac, who, with his cousin Rob King, had also tired of the crowds. The two were shooting a game of chalk-less pool in the calm, friendly hotel bar. They invited us in and it was nice to relax in relative quiet and have a conversation without shouting. I much enjoy Jason – he's gruff and gentle at the same time and always fun to be around. We'd met Rob before also and shared some good thoughts before heading back to our hotel to rest up for the largest football day of our Canadian football lives.

Chapter 23

The Joy of Troy

Troy Souster has a Rider pre-game ritual of sorts. He returned to our hotel on Saturday night full of enthusiasm and informed us that he needed to work on his hair. Now, Troy rivals me for being coiffurely-challenged, so we wondered what he was thinking about. He dug in his luggage for a trimmer and emerged with a new and shorter dew a few minutes later. Just like stepping on third base or forever wearing the same socks, this was Troy's little superstition and something he needed to do. Our friend from Saskatoon then proceeded to tell of his evening, including a wait beyond my personal temperament to get into Riderville. However, his eyes gleamed as he broke the big news that we had been invited to the Rider's team Victory Party after the Grey Cup game.

With that great thought rolling in our sleepy heads, we turned in to prepare for Sunday. As dawn broke on Game Day, we rose early and eventually headed out for breakfast. The first several spots were jammed and our eventual destination was a quaint place called the Senator Restaurant where we enjoyed a breakfast in the smallest booth in all of Canada. As usual on Grey Cup Sunday, we then had time to kill since the pre-game festivities were still a few hours away.

Dave Ridgway had asked me to get him a program and a game ticket for his collection of Grey Cup artifacts. The program seemed like a piece of cake and I headed to the vicinity of the convention centre quite sure I could grab one and then bring it back to the hotel for safe keeping. Getting a ticket might be another matter, but I'd worry about that later. I jumped on the subway and made the long, climate-sheltered walk from Toronto's Union Station. It was still before noon, but there was already a long line to buy Grey Cup souvenirs and I joined it. After a short wait, I discovered that the inventory did not include game programs and was told with certainty that they were not for sale anywhere in the building. I checked around a bit outside, but it was obviously much too early for the stadium vendors to be out in force with their wares. Resigning myself to the terrible fate of being forced to carry a program around later, I began to head back to the hotel. Of course, I immediately ran into Joe and Nancy McNeill, my perpetual rescuers, who had a backpack and cheerfully agreed to purchase and store a program and also ask around in their group for a spare game ticket.

The semi-obsessive Minnesotan, relieved that he would not be burdened protecting a program, headed back to meet Chris and Troy. As I meandered back toward the route to Union Station, I became confused in the cavernous depths of the Metro Toronto Convention Centre and asked a security person for directions. Many times in conversations with Canadian friends, I was heard disparaging remarks about the supposed smugness of Toronto's population, but had not experienced such self-importance personally. However, when I approached the security lady, I received a small dose.

Here in Minneapolis/St. Paul, we have a huge layout of elevated walkways between buildings and refer to them as "skyways." It was thus pretty natural for me to ask how to find the "skyway" back in the direction I needed to go. With a look of absolute disdain at my hillbilly stupidity, I was patronizingly informed that the correct term here in the world's most important place was "skywalk." A really small thing, but her pickiness just hit me completely wrong. I said my confession, accepted my penance and was on my way.

Two separate free tailgates were part of the festival, one on Front Street and one on Bremner Street, basically on opposite sides of the convention centre. I scurried back to the hotel, caught up with Troy and Chris, and we decided to head for the area at about 2:00. Chris was not sitting with us and had purchased a ticket via Jeff Banow after Jeff had vouched for his character. I was hoping to meet some folks, so we split up after deciding Troy and I would rendezvous at our seats an hour before kickoff.

My hope was to catch up with my cousin Ross, but I'd not heard back from them after leaving a message earlier. A similar call to Jack Bedell did not generate a contact, but I had another group of folks well worth meeting up with.

The Joy of Troy

In the first part of the week following the Western Final, there were dozens of newspaper and internet stories detailing the efforts of serious Rider fans to get to Toronto for this important game. Some were heartwarming, some were heartbreaking, but all showed the resolve of the Saskatchewan spirit. I was aware of a particularly complex tale of a family who refused to give up their quest to attend the game and had planned to meet up with them.

My only in-person meeting with Marilyn McIntyre of Rosetown, Saskatchewan had been at the Labour Day Classic in 2006. I had really appreciated her efforts in hooking me up with my Orth cousins in 2005 and had heard from her several times in the days preceding my trip to Toronto. No doubt there are other stories from that week showing Rider fan determination, but to fail to tell the McIntyre story here would be to ignore the impressive efforts of a passionate group of fans.

Marilyn's traveling troupe included seven people, an uneven number destined to cause some difficulties. Along with her husband Randy were two sons, a daughter, one of the sons' fiancée, and a Slovakian exchange student. Marilyn experienced on-the-job travel agent training in the early days of the week before the game. Their eventual itinerary was staggering – a drive on Friday from Rosetown to Calgary to catch a late night flight to Montreal, since they could not successfully reach Toronto directly. The group arrived in Montreal at daybreak on Saturday, staying there until Sunday morning, when they flew into Toronto. On Monday morning, after a night in a Toronto hotel, the group would begin the reversal of their inward journey by heading back to Montreal. To complicate matters, daughter Natashia, a student at the University of Saskatchewan, needed to be back in Saskatoon bright and early Monday morning, so a red-eye flight from Toronto Sunday night was booked for her. With this daunting plan in place, the search for seven game tickets began and you'll need to trust me that it was just as complicated, but eventually successful.

As I tried to contact Marilyn, I just wandered around on my own. Despite the crowd, I ran into several folks I know, including Brad Ruston and Brad Maurer, a new acquaintance from Melville whom I'd just met earlier in the month at Mosaic stadium. The Melville lad had to reintroduce himself, since the face-paint and bandana he wore at our first meeting were absent on this Grey Cup Sunday and I did not immediately recognize him. I soon heard from the McIntyre group and we determined a place to meet.

Mounting excitement, just as had happened at the West semi-final, was beginning to make me a bit shaky. I spotted a street vendor and, as before, calmed myself down with a good dog and a soda; however, I almost was compelled to report this merchant to the High Price Police, since the reasonable price of $4.00 for both items did not fit in well with the Toronto cost structure.

Finally the phone rang and Marilyn explained they were at the assigned spot, but did not see me. I'd been looking for them, but missed seeing Marilyn, who's a bit vertically challenged, because she was behind the rest of the group. They had just picked up the last of their game tickets and had seats for all, even though not together. It was a lot of fun to meet the entire family and to congratulate them on their fortitude and dedication in making it to the very gates of the Rogers Centre. In the photo below, Marilyn and Natashia are in the front, with Lucas Gallo, Evan McIntyre, Lisa Watson, Sean McIntyre and Randy McIntyre in the rear.

The Magnificent McIntyre Family

After a short, but well worthwhile visit, it was almost time to head into the stadium. The gates were open and I waited just a bit to let the initial crush of eager humanity break up the lines a bit. It seemed like every fan was showing colours of either Saskatchewan or Winnipeg, with the Rider fans seemingly outnumbering those of the Bombers. I laughed when I spotted a Manitoba group who somehow knew that they would be on the "shorts" end of the final score.

Prognosticating Bomber Fans

    Heading to my gate, I entered with Dave Fulton and his son Scott, who made certain to show me the Argo shirt under his Rider outer layer. Dave's undoubtedly a great parent and hopefully will keep working on this misguided lad.

    My assumption had been that the general "feel" of the Rogers Centre would be similar to our Metrodome, but I was mistaken. I found a much more open layout, since in the Dome here a person cannot view the action at all from the concourse. Troy was easily found and we scoped out our seats, finding immediately that we would not be able to see the video board. We were just about exactly on the goal line on the hotel end of the building, with our seats on the same side as the Rider bench. Our spot in Section 137 would have been right in left field home run territory for baseball, but this day was back a bit from the field, but in decent position nonetheless.

    Troy and I made our way right down to field level. It was still well before kickoff and there was plenty of room to watch the Riders warm up and grab some photos. I continually am amazed when I see someone I know on the field at a time like that and was initially surprised to see Rider Director of

Communications Ryan Whippler walking around until I realized that he was, in fact, supposed to be there. We stayed for quite a while, enjoying the view, and realized on the way back that Joe and Nancy McNeill, along with Nancy's brother Dennis Anderson, were seated basically directly in front of us. Joe and Nancy has purchased extra tickets from some British Columbia fans earlier in the week and were obviously mixing in well with their Lion fan counterparts.

Andy Fantuz, Nathan Hoffart, D. J. Flick

Kickoff neared and the seats around us began to fill up. There were plenty of Bomber fans, but the fans clad in green outnumbered them by at least a three to one margin. Our section was a bit like a cave, and the seats a few rows in front of us and to our right were empty, since their field view was blocked by the football-only seats in the baseball left field area. A boisterous group of about a dozen college-age Bomber fans made a noisy entrance and I just knew they would do something completely stupid. Sometimes I hate it when I'm right; in the moment of silence for Canadian troops serving overseas, one of them was compelled to shatter the reverent moment by shouting "Go Bombers!", a gesture that to me was tasteless beyond comprehension and brought further angry shouts from green and blue fans alike.

Finally, after a week that seemed eternal, the game began. On paper, Winnipeg seemed no match for Saskatchewan, since the broken arm suffered in the East Final by Bomber quarterback Kerry Glenn forced the Manitobans to start untested Ryan Dinwiddie at quarterback. Dinwiddie is from Elk Grove, California and set several school records in his college career at Boise State. However, he had never started a game in the CFL and in most Rider minds his presence made the Bombers a long shot underdog.

The Winnipeg defence, however, had not been informed of this fact and played ferociously all day. Luca Congi missed a 42 yard field goal attempt in the first quarter and the Bombers put points on the board first with a Troy Westwood field goal following a Kerry Joseph interception by Winnipeg's Greg Moss. Dinwiddie looked flustered at times but did complete a key pass of 42 yards to Milt Stegall in the field goal drive.

The Riders struggled offensively early in the game, with Kerry Joseph misfiring on several passes and with receivers failing to make the play on a few others. Two conceded safeties in the early stages of the second quarter gave the Bombers a lead of 7 – 0 and the green and white clad sections were desperate for something to get excited about. However, a decent Rider drive resulted in a Wes Cates' fumble into the end zone and the Bombers recovered to quash the Saskatchewan threat.

A break came two plays later. Dinwiddie was looking for veteran receiver Milt Stegall all day and the Rider secondary did not take long to figure out that preference. James Johnson intercepted a pass thrown to Milt and with a nifty return, took it to the house to tie the score at seven apiece. Johnson also nearly made a second steal and looked like he had the Bomber's plan pretty well figured out.

Luca Congi hit from 45 yards out just as the clock ran out in the first half and Saskatchewan led 10 – 7 in a game that clearly had lots more action to come. A Rider fan had to be concerned about the dearth of effective offence, but the Saskatchewan defence was largely continuing their solid play from the preceding week's game at BC Place. They had kept the explosive Bomber running back Charles Roberts in check; he would gain only 47 yards on the day. Troy and I had watched most of the first half in an earnest silence and I for one was glad to see Johnson's big play since it put Saskatchewan back in the game. The interception also provided the additional benefit of temporarily silencing the large Bomber group in front of us from their constant insulting catcalls.

The halftime was long, filled with the tunes of Lenny

Kravitz. I walked around for a bit, just to unwind and people watch. The restroom was another Canadian revelation – the very small size and capacity were surprising, since it made the rooms at Mosaic Stadium seem enormous. We finally settled back into our seats, knowing that in this game a three point lead was tenuous at best and that there were 30 more hard fought minutes to be played.

Official View of a Congi Field Goal

The spectator portion of the game had some interesting moments also. Early in the second half, a fellow walked to his seat carrying a beer keg and was promptly asked to go for a long walk with the stadium security personnel. A young, attractive Winnipeg fan also caused a stir near us when she paraded through the area wearing fan attire consisting of body paint and a completely transparent top.

The Riders forced a break early in the third quarter. John Chick, the rookie defensive end from Utah State, was having a sensational game and forced a Dinwiddie fumble. Scott Schultz recovered at the Winnipeg 10, but the Bomber defence limited the damage to another Congi field goal. Momentum seemed to move a bit as Dinwiddie hooked up long for a 50 yard touchdown to former Rider Derick Armstrong, right down in front of Troy and I. Winnipeg had taken the lead again at 14 – 13, but James Johnson's second interception led to a very key series. On third down from the Bomber 10, Kerry Joseph kept the ball but the official's initial spot placed the ball short of a first down, handing the ball back to Dinwiddie on downs.

Although we could not see the scoreboard, our section did have monitors in the rafters above us. Troy and I both thought the spot of the ball was short of Joseph's progress; a well-chosen Saskatchewan challenge reversed the original spot and gave the Riders a first down, much to the consternation of the Bombers. In his evident frustration, Winnipeg head coach Doug Berry challenged the challenge, a disallowed tactic that resulted in a delay of game penalty. The defense stiffened, but Congo hit another field goal and the Riders again grabbed the lead at 16 – 14 when the third quarter ended.

Receiver Andy Fantuz, in the final game of a breakout season, finally teamed with Joseph to give Saskatchewan an offensive touchdown. The man who would earn top Canadian honours for the game on the strength of four grabs for ninety yards took in a pass over the middle and literally went through three defenders in a 20 yard sprawl for a score. The Riders led 23 – 14, but the crowd, including Troy and I, were none too comfortable. The Bombers scratched back, netting another safety and then a Westwood field goal with just less than four minutes remaining. The sometimes beleaguered Winnipeg kicker had a strong game, punting 11 times for a 46 yard average and giving the Riders generally mediocre field position. Of course, the perfect snaps from Chris Cvetkovic made Westwood's job a lot easier.

Joseph and the Riders needed a couple of first downs to get things done. On a running play, for a frightening instant, it appeared he had fumbled, but the play was reviewed and the final say was "down by contact" with no fumble. Saskatchewan did get a first down with 2:11 left, but faltered and were forced to punt. Ryan Dinwiddie, the self-proclaimed "California Gunslinger" had 1:21 to become a legend.

He completed two passes and then, in fact, a legend *was* born. Looking again for Milt Stegall, Dinwiddie was picked off for the third time by James Johnson, who with that play forever etched his name in Rider lore. One could only feel good for this player, whose road to Riderville had a number of bumps along the way in a football career that had only begun in junior college. I knew Joe McNeill, a Johnson fan from the very first, was smiling in his seat several rows ahead of us.

The realization of the moment had not even set in when the final gun sounded. As the confetti began to shoot toward the roof and the players began to celebrate, I turned to my companion. Troy Souster, just one great Rider fan, was pretty close to being overwhelmed. Like many of you, he had waited seemingly forever for this day and this moment. For once in my life, I think I did just the right thing. Grabbing Troy's shoulder in a hug, I yelled, "Man, I'm glad to be here right now with you!" I'll be very honest – this Rider victory and Troy's reaction to it is one great memory that I'll have forever.

The lady behind us took a photo of Troy and I that I now have framed in my living room. In the shot, a grey haired guy smiling broadly is posed with a young man whose look might be best described as a bit dazed. It is a lasting recollection of a very special time and place and I'm guessing many of you have your own version of it.

Game over, Grey Cup awarded, and still we stayed, along with many other Saskatchewan football fans. I convinced the young man sitting next to us to part with his ticket, promising him a Ridgway autograph for his troubles. Joe McNeill wandered up, also a bit in the Troy dazed state, and he had come up with a ticket also. We left our seats and celebrated with Dave Fulton, who had been seated in our vicinity. Finally, we followed the Rider Pep Band out into the Toronto streets.

Pep Band Procession

The area in front of the Rogers Centre was a madhouse. Since many non-Riders fans had already departed, the crowd was nearly all Saskatchewan fans, full of shouts, back-slapping and cheers of the Rider victory. We had a post-game plan to meet Chris for dinner back up by our hotel, and then would head to the team party with our certain invitation.

I really love traditions, but the post-game Grey Cup eating tradition is beginning to wear on me. The recent roster included no food at all in 2004 due to the Lasagna Crisis, a terribly expensive meal in Vancouver in 2005, and excruciatingly slow service in Winnipeg in 2006. Hoping for a better fate here in 2007, Troy and I headed for our previously identified rendezvous with Chris Melin.

Bad fortune again awaited us. The original spot was long since closed on this Sunday night. Chris was at another spot, and we joined him there only to find that the kitchen was closed and last call was being announced. We did grab a beverage and had a toast while we debated our nutritional fate.

A Toast to the Winning Riders

As we pondered, Troy clicked through his cell phone to locate the magic number to call for party admittance. Perplexed immediately, he scrolled through and through his phone book to no avail. The eventual determination was that he had keyed in the number but had failed to save it. Disappointed, but still famished, we headed around the corner to the bartender's suggested alternative locale.

Stymied there by a long, long line for a table, we bravely

headed to the pub across the street from the hotel. The place was friendly looking and crowded. We noticed immediately that the patrons outnumbered the help by a troubling ratio and sensed the continuation of our fine tradition. No food was to ever appear, despite apologies from the server; the reason wasn't clear and just didn't much matter.

Troy left well before Chris and I and he enjoyed the company of the entire Rider team later that day in the Calgary airport. Chris and I had an easy flight home, buoyed by the spirits of the Grey Cup win and thankful for both our Saskatchewan friends and ourselves that we had all been part of something truly bigger than the typical football fan would ever experience.

Chapter 24

The Cup Runneth Around

Good stories came out of Saskatchewan in abundance in the days following the Grey Cup win. The players were clearly incredibly fired up and full of great quotes. Of the many I heard and read, my favourite was good old Scott Schultz, who stated the very obvious to a reporter when he said, "It's kind of a big deal."

A big deal it was in Regina when the team returned home. Despite completely miserable weather, several thousands fans came to Mosaic Stadium to greet the Riders on Monday. On Tuesday, the planned parade was interrupted by even more frigidity and moved inside the Legislative Building at the invitation of Premier Brad Wall. The *Leader-Post* overflowed with good stories and I had dozens of emails from both fellow Rider fans and friends down here who saw the result somewhere in the meager American media coverage. I did think for a bit about how exciting it would be to be present for some of the Regina festivities but realized I had in fact experienced quite a bit anyway.

The Grey Cup itself was in Saskatchewan and soon began making the rounds. For anyone who may have disagreed that this was a "big deal", the fan reaction to the opportunity to be with the cherished treasure clearly would have proven those doubters wrong. As players and team officials made the rounds to nearly every nook and cranny of the province, the fans responded as only the Rider football faithful can. I received at least 20 emails from friends and acquaintances showing their personal moment with the trophy and saw dozens more on the internet. In one of the nicest gestures of all time, I too, despite the miles between us, had a rendezvous of sorts with the Earl himself.

Joe and Nancy McNeill had been invited to see the Grey

Cup one Sunday morning at Mayor Pat Fiacco's place. Nancy, ever the thoughtful sweetheart, thought of her Mosaic Stadium neighbour. Bringing along a copy of the first edition of this book, Joe and Nancy sent me a treasured photo proving that, along with its other qualities, the Grey Cup knows its literature.

Rider Pride on the Grey Cup Side

Another item floating around in cyberspace was a revised map of Canada, with the province of Saskatchewan amazingly taking on a new shape, distinctively similar to that of the Grey Cup. Items like this are always good for a quick smile when received for the first time in an email, but tend to lose their steam when received it for the 27th time. But it was certainly fun to read about the jubilation present in Riderville and I think I enjoyed it nearly as much as if I had been there.

It took me a while, but I was eventually able to get the souvenir tickets and program for Dave Ridgway sent to him in Indiana and then send up photos that he'd autographed to those who had helped out. I'm sure the young fellow sitting next to me, Chris Coben of Saskatoon, had figured that old guy had scammed him out of his ticket by the time his reward finally arrived, but hopefully it was worth the wait.

As the holiday season approached, good news on the roster front emerged. Wes Cates, Marcus Adams and Wayne Smith all re-signed with Saskatchewan, keeping three good

The Cup Runneth Over

players in the fold. But as the holiday season began to wind down, news of a different nature developed. Kent Austin, the first man in history to quarterback and coach the same team to a Grey Cup win, interviewed for, was offered, and then accepted a position as quarterbacks coach and offensive coordinator at the University of Mississippi, his alma mater. With the permission of the Saskatchewan franchise, the Austin era ended sooner than the Saskatchewan faithful desired or expected.

Reaction, as you might have expected, displayed a wide range of thoughts and emotions. A common theme could be described as "disappointed understanding." Disappointed because of what Kent had accomplished and might still in the future, but a realistic understanding of the lure of returning home to a dream job. A minor theme, as we have come to expect from those internet misfits down in their parental basements, was a nasty dose of bitterness. For me, it was a perfectly reasonable decision for the Austin family. My perspective would be that the success Kent enjoyed in 2007 was a pleasure unlikely to be duplicated. Many people in the organization share in the credit for the Rider success but in my viewpoint, his contribution was the key ingredient. In a way, the pinnacle had been reached, incredibly quickly, and the further challenges for Kent may well be in a place other than Saskatchewan.

Eric Tillman very publicly commenced a search for a new coach and on February 6 Rider offensive coordinator Ken Miller was announced as Saskatchewan's new head coach. Tillman made a series of other moves during the frigid times of the 2008 winter to keep his team in the news. The popular Corey Holmes was released in a salary cap move in late January amidst a series of announcements of signings of potentially significant yet untested free agents. I was happy to hear from Dustin Cherniawski that he had signed and look forward to seeing him again in 2008 and beyond.

In early February, Tillman announced the trade of defensive end Fred Perry, a fan favourite, to the Edmonton Eskimos for quarterback Steven Jyles and a swap of the teams' 2008 second round picks. Agree or disagree, this move had the Rider faithful hopping. Nearly 400 comments on the trade were posted on the Riderville website immediately after the trade, along with a whopping 1,100 on the larger Riderfans forum. It seemed like a controversial blockbuster at the time, but was soon to fade away in the wake of bigger moves.

As the free agent signing date of February 15 drew near, the news was mostly good for the Rider Nation. Receiver Matt Dominguez stayed in green and white and hopefully can return to form and stay healthy. My guy Eddie Davis is back in 2008, along with fan favourite Chris Szarka and receivers Corey Grant and Chris Getzlaf. Saskatchewan did lose linebacker Reggie Hunt to Montreal and offensive lineman Jermese Jones to Calgary.

On March 5, Will Chabun alerted me to breaking news on the *Leader-Post* website. In a salary-cap prompted trade, Most Outstanding Player Kerry Joseph was dealt to the Toronto Argonauts. A complete chapter could be written about the motives and the reactions to this move, but it may be safe to say that Eric Tillman's longevity in Saskatchewan could be directly tied to the accuracy of his firmly stated assessment of this entire situation. The media and fans can agree, grumble, and dissect this one until Saskatchewan approves Daylight Savings Time, but in reality the won-loss record will be the final judge.

For some, I'm sure that these off-season developments, more than one surprising in nature, may have added just a smidge of tarnish to the finish on the Grey Cup. I just cannot look at things that way; for me, 2007 was just a fantastic year to be a Saskatchewan Roughrider fan. The experiences I had, the friends I made, the memories I hold and the excitement I shared will be part of me with or without new coaches, quarterbacks and middle linebackers. It was a time of celebration for an entire province, a time that dwarfed a mere football game and I will always be able to say, in my Dumb American way, "I was there."

It's a great statement to be able to make.